AF690101

LEGISLATED RIGHTS

The important aspects of human wellbeing outlined in human rights instruments and constitutional bills of rights can only be adequately secured as and when they are rendered the object of specific rights and corresponding duties. It is often assumed that the main responsibility for specifying the content of such genuine rights lies with courts. *Legislated Rights: Securing Human Rights through Legislation* argues against this assumption, by showing how legislatures can and should be at the centre of the practice of human rights. This jointly authored book explores how and why legislatures, being strategically placed within a system of positive law, can help realise human rights through modes of protection that courts cannot provide by way of judicial review.

Grégoire Webber is Canada Research Chair in Public Law and Philosophy of Law at Queen's University and Visiting Senior Fellow at the London School of Economics.

Paul Yowell is the Benn Fellow in Law at Oriel College, University of Oxford.

Richard Ekins is Tutorial Fellow in Law at St John's College, University of Oxford.

Maris Köpcke is Lecturer in Law at the University of Barcelona.

Bradley W. Miller is Justice of the Court of Appeal for Ontario, Canada.

Francisco J. Urbina is Assistant Professor of Law at the Pontifical Catholic University of Chile.

Legislated Rights

SECURING HUMAN RIGHTS THROUGH LEGISLATION

GRÉGOIRE WEBBER
Queen's University, Canada

PAUL YOWELL
Oriel College, University of Oxford

RICHARD EKINS
St John's College, University of Oxford

MARIS KÖPCKE
University of Barcelona

BRADLEY W. MILLER
Court of Appeal for Ontario

FRANCISCO J. URBINA
Pontifical Catholic University of Chile

CAMBRIDGE
UNIVERSITY PRESS

CAMBRIDGE
UNIVERSITY PRESS

University Printing House, Cambridge CB2 8BS, United Kingdom

One Liberty Plaza, 20th Floor, New York, NY 10006, USA

477 Williamstown Road, Port Melbourne, VIC 3207, Australia

314-321, 3rd Floor, Plot 3, Splendor Forum, Jasola District Centre, New Delhi - 110025, India

79 Anson Road, #06-04/06, Singapore 079906

Cambridge University Press is part of the University of Cambridge.

It furthers the University's mission by disseminating knowledge in the pursuit of education, learning and research at the highest international levels of excellence.

www.cambridge.org
Information on this title: www.cambridge.org/9781108426572
DOI: 10.1017/9781108551069

© Grégoire Webber, Paul Yowell, Richard Ekins, Maris Köpcke, Bradley W. Miller and Francisco J. Urbina 2018

This publication is in copyright. Subject to statutory exception and to the provisions of relevant collective licensing agreements, no reproduction of any part may take place without the written permission of Cambridge University Press.

First published 2018

A catalogue record for this publication is available from the British Library

Library of Congress Cataloging in Publication data
Names: Webber, Grégoire C. N. (Grégoire Charles N.), author.
Title: Legislated rights : securing human rights through legislation / Grégoire Webber [and 5 others].
Description: New York : Cambridge University Press, 2018. | Includes bibliographical references and index.
Identifiers: LCCN 2017058819 | ISBN 9781108426572 (hardback)
Subjects: LCSH: Human rights. | Legislation.
Classification: LCC K3240 .L4455 2018 | DDC 342.08/5—dc23 LC record available at https://lccn.loc.gov/2017058819

ISBN 978-1-108-42657-2 Hardback
ISBN 978-1-108-44523-8 Paperback

Cambridge University Press has no responsibility for the persistence or accuracy of URLs for external or third-party internet websites referred to in this publication, and does not guarantee that any content on such websites is, or will remain, accurate or appropriate.

Contents

Preface

This book explores the moral value of legislation and its capacity to realise human rights. It articulates the special role and responsibility of the legislature in securing human rights in positive law. Our title, *Legislated Rights*, signals a contrast to the theory and practice of much contemporary human rights law, which privileges the judiciary as the principal defender of human rights. We aim to shift the key premises of debate in human rights law, where it is regularly assumed that human rights are the special province of the courts and that legislation represents a threat rather than a means of protecting them.

The chief value of the Universal Declaration of Human Rights, the European Convention on Human Rights, and similar treaties and domestic bills of rights lies not in providing standards for courts to enforce against political authorities, but rather in articulating the aspects of human wellbeing that should be actively pursued and promoted by *all* authorities responsible for a community. Among those authorities, we contend, legislatures have the central and strategic role in realising human rights. Many aspects of human wellbeing identified in rights instruments can be adequately advanced only through general measures adopted through legislative action. Law's point, we argue, is to bring human rights into being in a political community.

Our argument aims to make a contribution to the fields of jurisprudence, constitutional theory, and human rights law. It does so with special attention to institutions. We argue that much human rights law and theory proceeds without a sound account of right ordering between institutions and their proper functioning. We seek to recover the insight of Hersch Lauterpacht, who drafted the International Bill of the Rights of Man (a forerunner to the Universal Declaration) from a viewpoint that embraced the legislative specification of rights, arguing that the details of the substantive law that safeguards rights, such as liberty of the person, equality before the law, and freedom of association, are regularly found in ordinary legislation.

In seeking to recover such an approach, this book offers a theoretical understanding of human rights law, understood as human rights in the legal practice of the European and Commonwealth courts. This area of legal practice is wider than philosophical accounts that focus on the idea of human rights as those possessed 'simply in virtue of being human' or on a minimal core the violation of which could justify intervention by other states in the affairs of the infringing state. The Universal Declaration, European Convention, and similar instruments cover an extensive, ambitious range of issues going well beyond such a narrow core. Our aim is to counter widespread misunderstandings about the nature of rights and to describe a method for providing more secure legal protection for human rights.

This book consists of six chapters and an introduction. Although each substantive chapter has a different author, the chapters individually and collectively pursue the book's central argument. They are intended to stand together, not like the chapters of an edited collection united by a set of related themes, but like the chapters of a single-authored monograph. For this reason, while each chapter specifies an author, the book as a whole is jointly authored.

Grégoire Webber and Paul Yowell

Acknowledgements

This book grew out of two workshops held in Oxford on the theme of how legislation secures human rights. Following the first, in which original drafts were discussed, we sought to bring the contributions into a single argument, as a jointly authored book, and tested that proposal at the second workshop. The process of revising chapter drafts benefited from the careful study and incisive commentary of several workshop participants and other colleagues; at the risk of omission, we signal our special thanks to Nick Barber, Paul Brady, Graham Buitenhuis, Dominic Burbidge, Denis Chang, Fernando Contreras, Grant Huscroft, Sulman Iqbal, Jeff King, Randy Kozel, Martin Luteràn, Adam MacLeod, Jeff Pojanowski, Gil-Ad Schwartz, Jan van zyl Smit, Leah Trueblood, Charlie Webb, Jacob Weinrib, and Angela Wu.

Finola O'Sullivan and John Berger at Cambridge University Press set a high standard for professionalism and we signal our gratitude to them and their colleagues. We also acknowledge the financial support of the Canada Research Chair program, the Conicyt Fondecyt Iniciacion N° 11150872 grant of the Chilean Ministry of Education, and the Programme for the Foundations of Law and Constitutional Government in the University of Oxford.

Bradley W. Miller's contribution was completed prior to his judicial appointment and he wishes to thank Grégoire Webber and Paul Yowell for subsequent minor editorial changes to his chapter prior to publication.

A copy of Thomas Somerscales' *Antiguo Muelle de Valparaíso* (1882) was provided for the book's cover image by the Museo de Bellas Artes de Valparaíso, Palacio Baburizza. We acknowledge and thank them for this courtesy.

We reserve a special note of acknowledgement for John Finnis. He has helped shape the ideas in this book in many ways: first, as the supervisor of each of our doctoral theses, from which emerged many of the main claims in the book; second, as an active participant in each of the two workshops that gave direction to this project; and third, as a ready voice of encouragement throughout this project's development. We dedicate this book to him.

Note on the Cover Image

Thomas Somerscales' *Antiguo Muelle de Valparaíso* (1882) depicts a moment when Valparaiso, Chile, was the leading sea port in South America and one of the continent's wealthiest cities. The artist's vision of the harmony of civilisation and nature, and of the varied but organised human activity that creates prosperity and beauty, represents a condition that is not realistically possible to achieve without the order that can be brought about by the Rule of Law and in particular *legislated rights*. No human project is immune to the ruptures of nature, however, and in 1906 an earthquake destroyed the buildings in the painting and much of the infrastructure of Valparaiso, resulting in the deaths of around 4,000 inhabitants. The combined effects of the quake and the opening of the Panama Canal in 1914 meant that Valparaiso never regained its turn-of-the-century prominence, and much activity and commerce was transferred inland to Santiago. But Valparaiso was rebuilt and remains a vibrant city, and its historic quarter is a UNESCO world heritage site.

In 2015, a public presentation of chapters in this book took place in Chile, at the Pontifical Catholic University in Santiago. While later touring Valparaiso, we experienced an 8.3-magnitude earthquake that struck the region. Tsunami warnings resulted in the precautionary evacuation of roughly one million people. The lives of many, including those in or in proximity to high-rises, were saved by legislated measures imposing strict building code standards and a coordinated emergency response strategy. It is tragic that fifteen people are reported to have lost their lives as a result of the earthquake – one in Valparaiso and most others in locations where it seems that modern codes have not been implemented. It is a testament to the relationship between the right to life and positive, legislated measures that the number of casualties was no higher.

Grégoire Webber and Paul Yowell

1

Introduction: Securing Human Rights through Legislation

Grégoire Webber and Paul Yowell

1.1 THESES AND COUNTER-THESES

The legislature is well placed to secure and promote human rights. That is this book's central thesis. It may seem an obvious proposition, but its truth and importance have been obscured in modern, court-centred modes of human rights discourse. The Universal Declaration of Human Rights, the European Convention on Human Rights, and similar instruments outline aspects of human wellbeing in need of respect, protection, and promotion, but they neither exhaust nor perfectly express the content of human rights. We argue that the legislature is under an obligation to give the broad, goal-oriented standards included in these instruments a specified, relatively precise legal form. That obligation is often fulfilled through legislation, and we explore how and why legislatures are able to secure human rights through modes of protection that courts cannot provide by way of judicial review. This book contends that legislatures should be, and in well-functioning democracies commonly are, at the centre of human rights practice. One of our purposes is to illuminate the moral value of positive law and our title, *Legislated Rights*, refers specifically to the value of law as enacted by legislatures – statutory law – which in its central case is made for the common good and exhibits the virtues of generality, clarity, and other desiderata of the Rule of Law.

This approach to human rights is new in comparison to prevailing approaches that focus on the role of courts, but it is not novel. Many figures in the tradition of Western legal and political thought – figures as various as Aristotle and Blackstone, Aquinas and Bentham – have emphasised the central, strategic responsibility of legislative assemblies. That responsibility includes securing the rights of persons, a responsibility that is prior to and reaffirmed in human rights instruments like the Universal Declaration and the European Convention. It is sometimes claimed that the decades leading up to and including World War II shattered confidence in democratically elected legislatures, specifically in their willingness and ability to respect the rights of persons. And yet, at the post-war beginnings of the modern human rights project, the legislature's role continued to be recognised as central. The Universal Declaration, drafted as a non-legal, non-justiciable document setting common standards for all nations and all governing institutions to achieve, includes calls for legislation to be enacted across a range of human rights, needs, and goods. Many of the broad aims of the Declaration can be realised only through a detailed legislative programme.

This vital legislative role has been obscured by developments in theory and judicial practice regarding rights. It is telling, for example, that the UK Supreme Court's President, Lord Neuberger, has said that before the United Kingdom ratified the European Convention in 1951, 'the UK simply did not recognise human rights other than through the common law'.[1] Absent from his account is any mention of pre-1951 legislation that protects and promotes rights later identified in the European Convention, such as the Representation Acts, the Habeas Corpus Acts, the Education Acts, industrial labour legislation, and the National Health Service Act 1946, to name but a few examples. One implication of Lord Neuberger's claim is that the UK did not recognise the right against slavery until the adoption of the Convention's Article 4, notwithstanding the Slavery Abolition Act 1833. This implication is reaffirmed in his invitation to contrast the pre-1951 'dark ages' with the 'age of enlightenment' brought about by the Human Rights Act 1998, which gave the Convention effect in domestic British law. One can avoid such a truncation of vision by recognising legislatures as part of the human rights story.

In modern human rights discourse, however, it has become axiomatic that the legislature is to be expected to act contrary to human rights and that only a judicially enforced bill of rights will secure a commitment to rights. That axiom animates human rights in legal practice and the theoretical scholarship engaging with that practice.[2] The general view that the legislature is a chief threat to rights and courts the main or the only forum where human rights are vindicated, typically by correcting the abuses of the legislature, has taken hold in much theory and judicial practice regarding rights. That theory and practice are settled in the view that a bill of rights guarantees human rights and legislation is a standing threat to that guarantee. This discourse is grounded on a number of distinctive theses about the nature of legislatures, courts, rights, and the common good. Too often these theses are simply assumed or implied

1 Lord Neuberger, 'The role of judges in human rights jurisprudence: a comparison of the Australian and UK experience' (Address at the Supreme Court of Victoria, Melbourne, Australia, 8 August 2014) para 1, www.supremecourt.uk/docs/speech-140808.pdf, accessed 23 May 2017.

2 Although the main legal instruments and treaties we engage with – the Universal Declaration of Human Rights, the European Convention on Human Rights, the UK Human Rights Act – all appeal, as we do, to the expression 'human rights', we could employ the expressions 'fundamental rights' and, where fitting, 'constitutional rights', which are used more or less synonymously in much constitutional theory and human rights law.

in human rights discourse, without analysis or defence. This book spells out these theses, criticises them, and proposes counter-theses to replace them.

In developing our critique, we identify a *central case of the legislature and legislation.*[3] The idea of a 'central case' is appealed to by a range of legal philosophers,[4] not to deny the reality of non-central cases of legal order, legislation, legislatures, constitutions, etc., but rather to give explanatory priority in philosophical argument to those cases that are fully responsive to the reasons that favour introducing legal order, legislation, legislatures, constitutions, etc. What are the reasons that would lead one to favour introducing the legislature and legislation in the governance of a political community? Doubtless they include the reasons referred to by constitutional drafters when they confer authority on legislatures 'to make laws for the peace, order, and good government of the Commonwealth'.[5] More generally, we say the legislature is 'established to act deliberately in response to reasons to change the law'.[6] It is the business of the legislature to understand a need for the law to be changed in some way, to form and revise reasoned proposals to change it, to debate, and then to choose a proposal to bring about a change to the law through the act of legislation. A sound understanding of those reasons awards the legislature with authority to secure human rights as an integral part of promoting the common good of the political community in all of its complexity. The common good of the community is that set of conditions that enable each and every member of the community to realise his or her development and wellbeing. Those conditions need to be secured through collaborative efforts, which include law-making and the coordination of action through legal order. The common good is the proper end of legislation and human rights are integral to the community's common good.

Our central case account is about the relative *practical capacities* of legislatures and the special suitability and responsibility of legislation in securing human rights.

3 Our conception of the legislature and legislation is influenced by Jeremy Waldron's scholarship: see esp. *Law and Disagreement* (Oxford, Oxford University Press 1999) and *The Dignity of Legislation* (Cambridge, Cambridge University Press 1999). Our grounding for legislative authority includes, but extends beyond, Waldron's appeal to democracy and reasonable disagreement.

4 See HLA Hart, *The Concept of Law* (3rd edn, Oxford, Oxford University Press 2012) 123, 81; Joseph Raz, 'About Morality and the Nature of Law' (2003) 48 *American Journal of Jurisprudence* 1, 5; John Gardner, 'Nearly Natural Law' (2007) 52 *American Journal of Jurisprudence* 1, 3; John Gardner, 'Hart on Legality, Justice, and Morality' in *Law as a Leap of Faith* (Oxford, Oxford University Press 2012) 228; NW Barber, *The Constitutional State* (Oxford, Oxford University Press 2010) c 1; John Tasioulas, 'On the Nature of Human Rights' in H Ernst and JC Heilinger (eds.), *The Philosophy of Human Rights* (Berlin, Walter de Gruyter 2012) 17; and, with qualification, Jeremy Waldron, 'The Core of the Case Against Judicial Review' (2006) 115 *Yale Law Journal* 1346. The central case method is interrogated most patiently by John Finnis: see, inter alia, *Natural Law and Natural Rights* (2nd edn, Oxford, Oxford University Press 2011) ch 1, *Aquinas: Moral, Political, and Legal Theory* (Oxford, Oxford University Press 1998) ch II, and 'Law and What I Truly Should Decide' (2003) 48 *American Journal of Jurisprudence* 107.

5 See e.g. Commonwealth of Australia Constitution Act, s 51; Constitution Act, 1867 (Canada), s 91.

6 Richard Ekins, *The Nature of Legislative Intent* (Oxford, Oxford University Press 2012) 127.

Due to its important focus on *institutions* and their capacities, constitutional theory occupies a methodological middle ground between philosophy and empirical analysis. Our appeal to central case analysis navigates this middle ground. It is informed by the fact that many legislatures in different times and places have failed to be fully responsive to the reasons that favour introducing a legislature and legislation in a constitutional system, reasons that situate responsibility for human rights and common good at the centre of legislative responsibility. The appeal to those reasons, however, allows the central case analysis of the legislature to show *how* legislatures in different times and places have failed to be what they *ought* to be. No amount of comparative empirical analysis can provide this philosophical argument, which is informed by and not blind to empirical realities. Thus, our central case account of the legislature and legislation is not 'about ideal cases, still less about ideal worlds untroubled by wrongdoing, scarcity, misunderstanding, and fear'.[7] It is important to emphasise, in turn, that claims about the central case are not claims about what is normal or usual in the sense of empirically regular or statistically likely. The study of central cases in legal theory does not deny the existence of defective instances of law or legal institutions. Rather, it is precisely by understanding central cases that we understand what is flawed or lacking in such deviant (and so non-central) cases. The study of medicine proceeds on the basis of ideas about the healthy functioning of the body, and that is what enables doctors and researchers to identify pathologies. So it should be in the philosophy of law and human affairs. But as we will see in the theses below, influential theorists have characterised as paradigmatic what ought to be understood as legislative pathologies. This contributes to lowering expectations about what legislatures can achieve.

One thesis inhibiting an understanding of the legislative role is the claim that the legislature's main function is to promote the general welfare by aggregating preferences or maximising overall utility (Thesis 1). Scepticism about the legislature's capacity to protect human rights sometimes focuses on the legislature's susceptibility to demagoguery, temporary passions, and corruption, but there are other kinds of scepticism that run deeper.[8] Some theorists hold that even when the legislature is free of such contingent faults, its role does not embrace reasoned deliberation about human rights or the moral principles that inform them. Rather, the legislature is conceived as promoting social welfare in an aggregative sense, and this is said to be

[7] Finnis, *Aquinas* 47.

[8] Ronald Den Otter, for example, states that 'the most honest rationale for the practice of judicial review is rooted in pessimism about the likelihood that ordinary citizens or their elected representatives could decide important constitutional cases competently'. *Judicial Review in an Age of Moral Pluralism* (Cambridge, Cambridge University Press 2009) 19. See also WJ Waluchow, *A Common Law Theory of Judicial Review: The Living Tree* (Cambridge, Cambridge University Press 2007) 265 ('[L]egislators are often prepared not only to compromise or deny constitutionally protected rights for the sake of placating a potentially resistant or even hostile electorate; they may opt not even to address the relevant issues of constitutional right').

its essential function.[9] Dworkin goes so far as to call the political process a 'machine' or 'computer' that counts and registers all preferences in society in order to 'translate' them into law.[10] This conception of legislating leads some theorists to accept or treat utilitarianism as the principle upon which legislative institutions are expected to deliberate, even if the utilitarian calculus is not the final measure of political justification.[11] The aggregation of preferences becomes a substitute for reasoned deliberation. Other theorists, while accepting that individual legislators may and should engage in reasoned deliberation, contend that those legislators together – and so the legislature – cannot be understood to be collectively engaging in the type of reasoning that characterises human agency.[12] Representatives within legislatures, on this account, engage in debates, and the legislative processes can in some machine-like fashion produce authoritative texts, but those texts are not the product of reasoned deliberation; the legislature is institutionally incapable of reasoning as an agent.

From this viewpoint, it is hard to ground an account of legislation as central to the protection and promotion of human rights. Those influential voices whose views are captured by Thesis 1 do not purport to formulate either (a) a sheer normative claim – e.g., the legislature *ought* to maximise utility, and it would be *good* all things considered if it did – or (b) a mere empirical observation – e.g., the legislature *always* and *everywhere* does maximise utility. Rather, they express a view about what the legislature is especially *suited* to do, distinctly *capable* of doing, given the kind of institution it is. A legislature, on this view, is better than any other government institution at aggregating preferences or maximising utility. Correspondingly and importantly, it is *worse* than other government institutions (most notably worse than courts) at taking responsibility for rights. It is worse because it is not fit for that purpose. And because it is worse, not fit for purpose, it matters little whether the legislature endeavours to protect rights. The legislature can legitimately limit itself primarily to that which it is able to do – aggregate preferences – within the framework of a constitutional system that duly reins in legislative power by subordinating it where needed to the courts as

9 See for instance: William H Riker, *Liberalism Against Populism* (Prospect Heights, IL, Waveland Press 1982); *Axa General Insurance Limited* v. *The Lord Advocate* [2011] UKSC 46 [49] (Lord Hope); Johan Steyn, *Democracy through Law* (Aldershot, Ashgate 2004); Christopher Eisgruber, *Constitutional Self-Government* (Cambridge, MA, Harvard University Press 2001); Owen Fiss, 'Between Supremacy and Exclusivity' in Richard W Bauman and Tsvi Kahana (eds.), *The Least Examined Branch* (Cambridge, Cambridge University Press 2006).

10 Ronald Dworkin, 'Social Sciences and Constitutional Rights – the Consequences of Uncertainty' (1977) 6 *Journal of Law and Education* 1, 10; *A Matter of Principle* (Cambridge, MA, Harvard University Press 1985) 366.

11 Ronald Dworkin, *Taking Rights Seriously* (Cambridge, MA, Harvard University Press 1977) 22, 90. For critical discussion, see Paul Yowell, 'A Critical Examination of Dworkin's Theory of Rights' (2007) 52 *American Journal of Jurisprudence* 93.

12 See John Gardner, 'Some Types of Law' in Douglas E Edlin (ed.), *Common Law Theory* (Cambridge, Cambridge University Press 2007) 59; Joseph Raz, *Between Authority and Interpretation* (Oxford, Oxford University Press 2009) ch 11; Waldron, *Law and Disagreement* ch 6. For critical discussion, see Ekins, *The Nature of Legislative Intent* ch 4.

chief guarantors of moral correction and respect for rights. As a view about the legislature's *relative capacity*, Thesis 1 thus combines normative and empirical elements. Once this view is properly unpacked, we contend that it does not withstand scrutiny and deserves to be abandoned in favour of a very different and more positive view about a legislature's *relative capacity* to protect rights.

Thus, in opposition to Thesis 1, we argue that the legislature is capable of principled, reasoned deliberation, and the central case of legislative action consists in reasoned deliberation to promote the common good, which has as its concern the wellbeing and rights of all persons in community (Counter-thesis 1). The lists of rights and principles in human rights instruments sketch an outline of the common good across a range of human values, goods, and needs, including: life, liberty, security, equality, privacy, family life, property, religion, expression, association, and assembly. In legislating for the common good, the legislature should not be willing to ignore the interests of some persons or to sacrifice their vital needs and goods. The common good is that set of conditions that enable each and every member of the community to realise his or her wellbeing, both individually and cooperatively with others. Such an understanding rejects aggregative conceptions of the 'greater good', whereby the rights, needs, or goods of some persons can be outweighed by the interests of the rights, needs, or goods of some greater number of persons. Theories – like classical utilitarianism – that adopt an aggregative conception of the general welfare and that downplay or ignore the importance of rights should be rejected even as a provisional guide for legislative deliberation.

The legislature is capable of genuine, principled reasoning and its deliberations can and should be grounded in the most fundamental principles of practical reasoning. Counter-thesis 1 articulates a claim about legislative capacity, which methodologically is related to legislative *action*, all with a view to formulating the *nature* of the legislature, a nature articulated by reference to the *reasons favouring* legislatures in constitutional systems. We defend the claim that legislators are capable of joint, reasoned action. The rules that govern the law-making process are not designed to aggregate preferences, but to enable the legislature to deliberate and change the law for reasons. Theoretical accounts of the legislature and its role in relation to human rights misfire in assuming the sceptical thesis expressed in Thesis 1 rather than attending to the reasons for legislative action. Without holding in view an understanding of the legislature as capable of securing human rights, whole lines of constitutional inquiry are closed off from pursuit. Thesis 1 denies that the legislature can defend human rights. If, however, both courts and legislatures are in principle tasked with promoting rights, and in principle both have the institutional capacity to do so, then new philosophical questions take centre stage and new empirical studies present themselves. That is what we aim to establish in proposing and defending Counter-thesis 1.

A second thesis holds that the legislature, unlike the court, is institutionally biased towards majority interests and against minorities and is thus unfit to engage in principled decision-making about human rights (Thesis 2). According to this thesis, the legislature functions well with regard to aggregating preferences (the task assigned to it by Thesis 1) and thus can be entrusted with certain decisions about expenditures, taxation, allocation of resources, and other broad matters of public policy. Basic features of its institutional structure, however, make the legislature systematically biased against minorities. Majority voting within the legislature, together with majority or plurality voting to elect representatives to the legislative chamber, condition law-making to attend to the interests of the majority of the electorate. Legislation can be presumptively justified on the grounds that it is an act of the majority; consequently, a judicially enforced bill of rights is needed to protect the rights and interests of minorities against legislative majorities that are actively prejudiced against them or that neglect their rights or interests because of a predisposition towards majority concerns.[13] Courts are well placed to protect minorities and their rights, in part because of their independence and counter-majoritarian role and in part because of the standing of even a single litigant to challenge decisions made by or with the approval of the majority. One strand of this approach locates the fundamental problem not in the legislature itself but in the democratic process that elects it and the public this empowers; for Den Otter, to take an example, judicial review is justified because we live in a world 'where the vast majority of citizens are either incapable of making informed, reflective decisions on basic questions of public morality or unwilling to make the effort to do so'.[14]

The most concentrated and influential expression of this theoretical approach is Dworkin's *dual-forum thesis* and his theory of rights as trump cards against the general welfare. In Dworkin's account, Thesis 2 (the legislature is biased towards majorities) is a necessary consequence of his stark version of Thesis 1 (the legislature aggregates individual preferences). The combination of these two theses requires that principled reasoning takes place in an institution outside the legislature. The division of labour between the two forums (court and legislature) corresponds to a distinction between the reasons and justification employed by each institution. Rights are a matter of principle – 'a requirement of justice or fairness or some other dimension of morality'[15] – and the special responsibility of courts; policies are goals to be reached – 'generally an improvement in some economic, political, or social feature of the community'[16] – and are the responsibility of the legislature. The legislative pursuit of policies is presumptively justified, subject to the power of courts to

[13] David Faigman, *Constitutional Fictions: A Unified Theory of Constitutional Facts* (New York, NY: Oxford University Press, 2008) 175 captures this 'classical' thought this way: 'Legislatures, of course, are the quintessential voice of the majority and thus, speaking classically, it is their tyranny that the Bill of Rights was intended to block.'

[14] R Den Otter, *Judicial Review in an Age of Moral Pluralism* (Cambridge, Cambridge University Press 2012) 19.

[15] Dworkin, *Taking Rights Seriously* 22.

[16] Ibid.

trump such pursuits with the rights of individuals. Rights, on this view, are vindicated when courts uphold a claim of right against legislation pursuing the general welfare.

We reject this majoritarian conception of the legislature and argue that the legislature is not inherently biased against minorities and is fit to engage in principled decision-making about human rights (Counter-thesis 2). In any given vote, the majority of ayes or nays will win, but it is a conceptual mistake to think that this entails the existence of a 'majority' as a stable, unified, collective group that acts through time and transmits its preferences through the political process.[17] The mistake arises in part from misunderstanding the dynamics of a series of votes[18] and in part from overlooking the complexity of the voting public and the reasons for voting.[19] More fundamentally, however, this mode of analysis is not well suited to explain the way in which the legislature acts. That action is best understood by attending to the reasons of those who act, as they conceive them. From this internal point of view,[20] focusing on 'the majority' is a distraction. Legislators do not cast their votes because they count the 'majority's moral convictions about how others should live' as the ground for political decision.[21] The individual legislators whose votes, taken together, constitute the majority in favour of a legislative proposal support it because they reason that some matter requires legislative action. Reliance on majority voting procedures does not entail, as Dworkin suggests in his account of 'statistical democracy', 'that anything a majority or plurality wants is legitimate for that reason'.[22] Still less does it entail that each one of the members whose votes constitute the majority considers the fact that being in a majority is itself a legitimate, or even a relevant, reason for casting a vote to approve the proposed legislative measure. Understood from the point of view of legislators and their reasons for supporting or opposing a proposal, 'the majority' is not an unprincipled, unreasoning collective

[17] See John Finnis 'Human Rights and Their Enforcement' in *Human Rights and Common Good: Collected Essays, volume III* (Oxford, Oxford University Press 2011) 24–26. See also Jeremy Waldron's helpful distinction between the 'decisional' majority and minority (the ayes and nays) and the 'topical' majority and minority ('the majority and minority groups whose rights are at stake in the decision'): 'The Core of the Case Against Judicial Review' 1397.

[18] See GEM Anscombe, 'On Frustration of the Majority by Fulfilment of the Majority's Will' (1976) 36 *Analysis* 161.

[19] As Richard Bellamy observes, 'most legislation is not the product of a homogeneous majority imposing its will upon a constituent minority, but of a series of compromises brokered by winning coalitions of different minorities': *Political Constitutionalism* (Cambridge, Cambridge University Press 2007) 241.

[20] In *The Concept of Law*, HLA Hart showed that a full understanding of a legal system requires a theorist to give a central place to the internal point of view, this is, to the point of view of the person who sees law as a reason for action – not simply a brute command issued by an authority powerful enough to sanction noncompliance. Hart extended this internal focus in his notion of the 'conscientious legislator', who deliberates on the basis of his 'beliefs and values' and a 'sense of what is best' in lawmaking decisions. See *The Concept of Law* 273, 275.

[21] As is argued by Dworkin, *A Matter of Principle* 68.

[22] Dworkin, *Freedom's Law* (Cambridge, MA, Harvard University Press 1977) 364. See also Den Otter, *Judicial Review* 252.

and the fact that 'the majority' (of electors or of legislators) wants something is, we argue, itself no reason to favour it.

It is true and important that democratically elected legislative majorities sometimes fail to protect the rights of minorities and sometimes oppress them. It is also true and important that certain minorities (whether tribe, caste, aristocracy, oligarchy, prince, or other) have sometimes oppressed majorities or other minorities. Nothing in our argument denies that those with power will sometimes yield to the temptation to abuse it. Nor does anything in our argument require heroic assumptions that legislators always form their own view of the merits of a legislative proposal, and never favour a proposal for partisan advantage rather than for the common good. There are a number of ways in which legislatures and individual legislators can deviate from the central case and a great number of examples when they have done so. Lacking in historical support, however, is the broad claim that democratic legislatures are intrinsically biased against minorities. That claim, sometimes expressed, other times assumed, has been taken to justify an expansive supervisory role for courts. Debate over the institutional roles of legislatures and courts requires a sound understanding of the practices of both, with such understanding informed but not exhausted by a careful account of history. Such an account includes attention to how legislatures, governed by majority voting procedures, extend the positive law to protect the human rights of minority groups. Among some of the better-known examples are the abolition of first of the slave trade and later of slavery by the Westminster Parliament,[23] the prohibition of racial discrimination in employment in the US Civil Rights Act 1964 and the later extension of this to other groups (for example, with the US Americans with Disabilities Act 1991), and the US Voting Rights Act 1965.[24] Chapter 5 provides a detailed account of legislative and judicial involvement in the long campaign for racial equality. More fundamentally, the claim that democratic legislatures are inherently biased against minority interests mistakes an aberration for the central case, failing to understand that when the legislature commits injustice and violates human rights, it is departing from, *not fulfilling*, its responsibility to legislate for the common good. We do not deny the reality of past instances of legislation violating human rights, or of legislatures past and present whose members act not for sound reasons but as tools of a state or party politburo. But we deny that such legislation was or is a central case of legislative action. Misunderstandings of the legislature that begin with the sceptical views of Theses 1 and 2 culminate in Theses 3 and 4, which have, as we will see, the surprising upshot of conceiving of the legislature as an institution that fulfils its proper function precisely by *infringing* human rights.

23 Slave Trade Act 1807 and Slavery Abolition Act 1833.

24 For elaboration on this theme, see JD Heydon, 'Are Bills of Rights Necessary in Common Law Systems?' (2014) 130 *Law Quarterly Review* 392, esp 394–5.

The third thesis holds that the legislature regularly and permissibly acts in opposition to human rights, since it must infringe rights to achieve other aims for the sake of the public interest (Thesis 3). This thesis has taken hold in the jurisprudence of the European Court of Human Rights and the jurisprudence of many other European and Commonwealth courts.[25] It is a widely held assumption that human rights instruments not only set out to guarantee rights, but also authorise their infringement, subject to conditions. When confronted with a rights claim, the European Court typically begins its judgment by first determining whether a legislative measure has infringed a human right. If so, the Court proceeds to determine, at a second stage, whether there is a justification for the infringement. The second stage consists in the application of a proportionality analysis, which weighs the value of the aim and effects of the legislative measure against the burdens imposed on the rights claimant in order to evaluate whether the infringement is justified. The point of this exercise, with few exceptions, is not to interpret and to vindicate the priority of the right, or even to set defined limits, applicable in future cases, to how far the right can be infringed. Rather, the point of the exercise is to decide whether, in the immediate case, the public interest in the legislative measure outweighs the burden imposed on individual interests. European and Commonwealth jurisprudence regularly concludes that the public interest outweighs individual interests and therefore prevails over declared rights, with the consequence that the legally justified infringement of legally guaranteed rights is common. The presupposition of this judicial reasoning is that the legislature, perhaps very often, has a duty to infringe rights because not to infringe a right would be without justification: such infringement is 'necessary in a democratic community'.[26]

We reject the claim that the scope of the legislature's authority involves or extends to acting in opposition to human rights and argue to the contrary that sound legislation does not oppose human rights, but rather affirms the requirements of human rights, including by specifying the broad, goal-oriented standards included in human rights instruments into relatively precise legal form (Counter-thesis 3). The reasonable legislature does not set out to secure some public benefit either by deliberately infringing human rights or even by accepting such infringements as a side-effect. Legislation, in its central case, does not oppose rights; it is made for the community's

[25] For an overview of the case law approach of the European Court of Human Rights, see Grégoire Webber, *The Negotiable Constitution: On the limitation of rights* (Cambridge, Cambridge University Press 2009) ch 2 and Kai Möller, *The Global Model of Constitutional Rights* (Oxford, Oxford University Press 2012); for an overview of the case law approach of the Supreme Court of Canada, see Bradley W Miller, 'Justification and rights limitations' in Grant Huscroft (ed.), *Expounding the Constitution* (Cambridge, Cambridge University Press 2008). More generally, see Aharon Barak, *Proportionality: Constitutional Rights and their Limitations* (Cambridge, Cambridge University Press 2012).

[26] This is the expression employed in the 'limitation clauses' of the European Convention, arts 8(2), 9(2), 10(2), 11(2). Similar expressions are to be found in other limitation clauses. See Webber, *Negotiable Constitution* 59–65.

common good and for the rights of persons that are an integral part thereof.[27] Because the open-ended human rights standards of the Universal Declaration and the European Convention are in need of specification, they leave open answers to the questions: What do my rights entitle me to do (or be free from)? Who is to do (or forbear from) what in satisfaction of my rights? To answer these questions, a series of legislative measures must be selected from among reasonable and morally underdetermined alternatives, and they must be authoritatively established. The human right to freedom of expression, for example, must be specified in relation to intellectual property and copyright, commercial advertisement, perjury, seditious libel, and official state secrets. Such specification is not fully settled by reason. Within a zone demarcated, on one side, by what reason requires and, on the other, by what reason prohibits, the legislature must make choices in settling which relationships between persons will realise the commitment to freedom of expression in the community. Such choices are informed by local factual circumstances and predictions about causes and effects. The legislature must attend to all of these in detail and stand ready to adjust the law as circumstances change (for example, as online communication displaces print and other traditional media, and new phenomena like digital piracy and cyber-bullying arise). In determining that libel and sedition are to be prohibited, and copyright is to be protected, the legislature is not best understood as infringing freedom of expression; rather, the legislature is seeking to specify the scope and content of the right to freedom of expression in pursuit of the community's common good, which includes not only freedom of expression, but also the reputation of persons and the progress of arts and sciences. In arriving at a series of specifications of prohibited, permitted, and supported relationships between persons, the legislature deliberates about what rights persons have prior to any legal specification and how best to instantiate and realise all rights in legal form. This deliberation is moral reasoning informed and framed by empirical and technical reasoning, developing into legal concepts, principles, doctrines, and rules.

A fourth thesis claims that, with few exceptions, human rights are defeasible, because they are conditional on the weight of individual interests which of necessity must be balanced against other interests (Thesis 4). This general conception of human rights grounds rights in (and sometimes equates them with) individual interests and accepts that these interests will be in competition with other interests and with the public interest.[28] Reasoning about human rights generally takes the

[27] Defenders of the view that rights are an integral component of the common good include Joseph Raz and John Finnis: see Joseph Raz, 'Rights and Individual WellBeing' in *Ethics in the Public Domain* (revd edn, Oxford, Oxford University Press 1994) and Finnis, *Natural Law and Natural Rights* 210–18.

[28] A sample of scholarly accounts that adopt this approach includes: Robert Alexy, *A Theory of Constitutional Rights* (Oxford, Oxford University Press 2002); Möller, *Global Model*; Mattias Kumm, 'Institutionalising Socratic Contestation: The Rationalist Human Rights Paradigm, Legitimate Authority and the Point of Judicial Review' (2007) 1 *European Journal of Legal Studies* 1. In addition,

form of evaluating whether infringements of rights are justified, by appealing to proportionality analysis and its requirement that one balances individual interests and the competing public interest. It bears noting that there is an important difference between the philosophical debate on whether some rights are sometimes defeasible and the human rights law debate on whether all rights can be anything other than defeasible. In much case law, reasoning about justifying the infringements of rights regularly overpowers thinking about rights themselves, with the consequence that proportionality and balancing have become the central judicial inquiries. Scholars tracking and rationalising the jurisprudence of the European Court of Human Rights conclude that rights have neither 'special importance' nor 'special normative force'[29] and that 'comparatively little is decided by acknowledging that a measure infringes a right'.[30] One influential set of these scholars identifies the autonomy interest as the fundamental moral value at stake in human rights cases generally and treats lists of distinct human rights like rebranded versions of the same generic product; liberty, association, expression, family life, and so forth are different ways of expressing the autonomy interest, which is said to be the foundational value for human rights.[31] That framing allows rights to be defined without reference to the interests of persons other than the individual right-holder and views with suspicion any restriction on the putative right-holder's ambitiously defined 'interests'. This individualistic bias is overcome at the cost of endorsing the thesis that rights must sometimes be infringed. This distorts the judicial analysis of the rights claim, making it harder to perceive or articulate the relationships between persons and moral evaluations in question. Here, the proportionality analysis is used to assess whether legislation sufficiently respects the claimant's interest, given the other interests in play. In opposition to the idea that human rights are inviolable, the thesis that rights may be infringed is held forth as a virtue because it allows for an expansive reading of human rights and the concomitant expansive jurisdiction of courts to adjudicate across a wide range of issues.

We argue that these supposed benefits are illusory or weak and are accompanied by significant costs and we defend the counter-thesis that the legislature is capable of securing human rights by specifying them in a form so that rights are not defeasible against countervailing interests or the general welfare (Counter-thesis 4). The

---

this account is developed in the case law of the European Court of Human Rights and a number of European and Commonwealth courts.

[29] Kai Möller, 'Proportionality and Rights Inflation' in Grant Huscroft, Bradley W Miller, and Grégoire Webber (eds.), *Proportionality and the Rule of Law* (Cambridge, Cambridge University Press 2012) 156, 172. Along similar lines, see Alexy, *Theory of Constitutional Rights* 48–49, 57, 74; Barak, *Proportionality* 40.

[30] Kumm, 'Institutionalising Socratic Contestation' 11.

[31] See Möller, *Global Model* ch 2–5. Möller goes as far as claiming (88) that '[f]or framers of new constitutions the idea of a comprehensive right to personal autonomy calls into question the necessity of a set of distinct constitutional rights. Nothing would be lost in theory by simply acknowledging one comprehensive right to personal autonomy instead'.

account of rights reviewed above in Thesis 4 results in the loss of rights: rights lose their intelligibility and integrity because they collapse into a single interest (autonomy) or a family of interests, all of which focus exclusively on the putative right-holder. Lest anarchy prevail, these interests are subjected to constraints to preserve the same and other interests of other persons and their communities. On this view, rights are not conclusive or even suggestive of right action and instead serve, once infringed, as gateways to evaluations of proportionality and balancing, where other persons and their rights and interests are acknowledged.

The Universal Declaration of Human Rights reflects a better view of rights as distinct, integral, constitutive parts of the common good and propounds human rights in ways that require implementation through extensive and detailed activity by the legislature. Reasoning about human rights should generally take the form of determining what specific standards and rules are required to secure rights, and it should centrally include deliberation about how such standards and rules should be expressed in the community's positive law. This does not mean that legislated rights are more important than the human rights standards they specify. Ours is not Bentham's view that rights are 'the child of law' with the law being the sole parent of rights, because 'from "laws of nature" [can come only] "imaginary rights"'.[32] Rather, with HLA Hart we understand that human rights are grounds of legal rights.[33] That relationship of grounding is complex, for the legislature's task is not simply to replicate human rights in positive law. We argue that most human rights standards, as formulated in the Universal Declaration and similar instruments, are incompletely specified and that the values and principles reflected in the formulations of rights require further detailed work by legislatures and others responsible for the community in order to be realised. Unlike the under-specified, defeasible human rights articulated in the case law of the European Court, the account of legislated rights that we defend challenges the idea that rights should be justifiably infringed by appeals to the public interest in evaluations of proportionality and balance. In one sense, the legislature does engage in balancing and proportionality reasoning in deliberating about and deciding upon the content of legislation, in the way that any reasonable agent must, in practical reasoning, take account of conflicting reasons for action, trade-offs, and side effects. But it is unhelpful and distorting to conceive of such reasoning as a contest between the 'individual interest' and the 'state interest',[34] or as reasoning about how far the legislature can interfere with or infringe human rights, which is the view of legislative action entailed by the approach to

[32] Jeremy Bentham, 'Anarchical Fallacies' in Jeremy Waldron (ed.), *Nonsense Upon Stilts: Bentham, Burke and Marx on the Rights of Man* (London, Methuen 1987) 46.

[33] HLA Hart, 'Are There Any Natural Rights?' in Jeremy Waldron (ed.), *Theories of Rights* (Oxford, Oxford University Press 1984) 79. For the purposes of this claim, we take human rights to be synonymous with natural rights, as does Hart in this essay.

[34] For an explanation of how this two-part framework fails to capture relevant considerations, see T Alexander Aleinikoff, 'Constitutional Law in the Age of Balancing' (1987) 96 *Yale Law Journal* 943.

rights in Thesis 4. Taken to its logical conclusion, this approach entails that all legislative activity is rights-infringing and that the question that lies before the legislature is not how it can promote and protect human rights, but rather how to limit its infringement of rights as it pursues other aims.

Contrary to this view, we argue that insofar as the human rights outlined in the Universal Declaration and European Convention are incompletely specified (that is, too open-ended to be non-defeasible), they should be understood to invite further specification. That specification needs to be made, in the first instance, through legislation. Human rights need positive law not only to add security for the respect of the rights of persons, but also to realise – by specifying in law – the requirements of human rights. Legislatures should be understood as full partners in this enterprise of promoting and protecting human rights, and not as a standing threat to rights against which courts must serve as guardians.[35]

* * *

We anticipate that some of our counter-theses will have struck some readers as implausible, or unduly optimistic. The critical view of legislatures is widespread, frequently as a reaction to the irresponsibility, self-interest, malfeasance, partisanship – or indeed simple incompetence – of some elected politicians. Such a reaction is understandable and often justified, and it would be naïve to pretend otherwise. We contend, however, that the pervasiveness of the critical view makes the need for a central case account of legislatures all the more urgent.

As noted above, claims about the central case build on the good reasons why one would favour introducing, maintaining, and complying with the legislature and its legislation, reasons articulated in the real-world circumstances of human experience and not in ideal circumstances that wish away human imperfections. On no sound understanding of those reasons, we contend, are legislatures vested with a mandate to infringe rights.[36] Rather, the understanding of those reasons and so of the central case of the legislature and legislation is sharpened by situating them both in relation to the vast number of examples of non-central cases. Those cases are non-central because they betray the reasons favouring the legislature and legislation, including where legislatures act irresponsibly or with animus towards persons, where legislation is designed to secure private advantage rather than common good, or where legislators vote without caring to turn their attention to the legislative proposal

[35] That partnership does not subordinate legislatures to courts, but rather highlights how, true to each of their roles in the separation of powers, both institutions are necessary to realise human rights in the community. Centrally, courts are needed to apply the legislated rights in the course of adjudication, with such legislated rights having been crafted with a view to judicial enforcement.

[36] Compare Peter Hogg's extraordinary claim that the Canadian Charter of Rights and Freedoms 'authorized Parliament and the Legislatures *to enact laws that infringed the Charter*, provided that the law was a "reasonable" limit': Peter W Hogg, 'Canada: From Privy Council to Supreme Court' in Jeffrey Goldsworthy (ed.), *Interpreting Constitutions: A Comparative Study* (Oxford, Oxford University Press 2007) 103 (emphasis added).

before them. By identifying where and why particular truths about legislatures and legislation of a time and a place fail to earn their place as general truths about legislatures and legislation (central cases), our understanding of the promise and failings of legislatures and legislation is strengthened.[37] Scholarly analysis goes astray if it grounds a theory of the legislature and legislating on what are in truth failures to exercise responsibly the distinctive capacities of the legislature; that is, failures to legislate well. To rehabilitate the role of the legislature with respect to human rights, we focus on rehabilitating a philosophical understanding of the legislature's capacities and nature. Our central case account of the legislature does not, so far forth, respond to empirical research that depicts a legislature of a given time and place as subject to corruption, special interests, self-interest, irresponsibility, cynical partisan manoeuvring, and other deficiencies. Our undertaking is nonetheless vital, for – as the discussion above makes clear – many scholars making claims about legislative irresponsibility do so *not* on the basis of a sociological-empirical foundation, *but rather* on the basis of a philosophical understanding of the point of legislatures and legislation. Some of their arguments close off – conceptually rule out – the possibility that legislatures have a responsibility to secure and promote human rights. Our philosophical approach does not define away the problem of legislative failures, but it maintains that one best understands and appreciates those failures for what they are: *failures to be what the legislature and legislation are supposed to be*. Our aim is to demonstrate that a sound conception of legislative activity includes the responsibility of legislatures to secure and promote human rights.

1.2 HUMAN RIGHTS LAW

This book offers a new philosophical understanding of human rights law, understood as human rights in the *legal* practice of the European and Commonwealth courts.[38] Our new philosophical understanding situates legislation, rather than litigation and adjudication, at the centre of jurisprudential and legal thinking on human rights. Among the benefits of this new philosophical understanding are that it counters widespread misunderstandings about the nature of rights and describes a method

[37] See Grégoire Webber, 'Asking Why in the Study of Human Affairs' (2015) 60 *American Journal of Jurisprudence* 51.

[38] It is worth noting a distinction between, on the one hand, the philosophy of human rights in its most general sense, and, on the other hand, theoretical inquiries into human rights law. These branches of inquiry only partially overlap in their understanding of 'human rights'. Our engagement is with debates surrounding instruments like the Universal Declaration and the European Convention. The understanding of human rights in both instruments goes well beyond an understanding of human rights as rights possessed by all human beings 'simply in virtue of being human' (see, e.g., J Griffin, 'Discrepancies between the Best Philosophical Account of Human Rights and the International Law of Human Rights' (2001) 101 *Proceedings of the Aristotelian Society* 1) or an account that a human rights violation could justify intervention by other states in the affairs of the infringing state (see, e.g., John Rawls, *The Law of Peoples* (Cambridge, MA, Harvard University Press 1999).

for providing more secure legal protection for human rights. The counter-theses we defend in Section 1.1 are philosophical and not theses regarding the concrete workings of institutions in particular legal systems. That is not to say, however, that our counter-theses are empirically uninformed. They draw on the study of the European Court of Human Rights and human (and constitutional) rights law in the United Kingdom, United States, and other common law and European jurisdictions. Like the theses that we challenge, our approach is directed by an understanding of rights, institutions, and the common good – and how these concepts link together. Our arguments aim to recall the unique capacity of positive law to solve coordination problems, to promote important aspects of individual wellbeing, and to prevent or minimise injustice. Those ends served by positive law relate, sometimes directly and sometimes indirectly, to the various goods and values sketched in the Universal Declaration and European Convention in the name of human rights. In its most complete sense, the category of human rights law is not restricted to bills of rights and instruments like the Universal Declaration and the European Convention and to case law interpreting and applying them. By reserving the label 'human rights law' for a distinct, quasi-constitutional legal category used by courts to evaluate and transform the rest of the law, scholars and lawyers misdirect their understanding of the relationships between positive law and human rights. On the argument defended in this book, human rights law is not primarily a *specialised* branch of legal learning but is rather the object of *every* branch of legal learning.

To illustrate this conception of human rights law, consider the Universal Declaration's affirmation, in Article 3, that 'Everyone has the right to life', recalled in Article 2 of the European Convention with specific reference to the need for positive law: 'Everyone's right to life shall be protected by law.' The positive law's special responsibility to protect everyone's right to life is pursued in a variety of ways, sometimes directly by prohibiting actions inimical to life and sometimes less directly by regulating activities that pose significant risks to human life. The criminal law of murder, the tort of wrongful death, occupational safety regulations, and traffic rules all realise and specify the right to life.[39] That realisation and specification confronts great complexity. For example, in communities confronting grave risk to life due to earthquakes, the legislature secures the right to life by building codes that implement the lessons of earthquake engineering and seismic design. These codes set out different building requirements depending on the underlying soil, the height and weight of the proposed construction, and the risk category of the proposed construction (e.g., agricultural storage buildings, office or residential buildings), among other considerations. They outline strict compliance and enforcement requirements for reinforced concrete walls, structural steel, and related technical matters.

[39] For a similar understanding of the relationship between positive law and the right to health, see Joint Committee on Human Rights, 27th Report of 2005/06, *Legislative Scrutiny: Corporate Manslaughter and Corporate Homicide Bill* (2005–06, HL 246 HC 1625) 7.

Although not commonly considered to be a human rights instrument, the Chilean building code prompted the following news headlines following recent earthquakes in 2014: 'Experts: strict building codes saved lives in powerful Chile earthquake';[40] 'Earthquake and Tsunami in Chile: massive evacuation and building codes help to reduce loss of life'.[41] In Haiti, which lacks such codes, 230,000 deaths were caused by a 2010 earthquake far less powerful than the one that struck Chile the same year.[42] The basic idea is this: the right to life is secured in part by the enactment and enforcement of earthquake building codes.[43]

Aspects of human wellbeing captured by reference to the right to life are also captured by the Universal Declaration's Article 25, which provides that 'Everyone has the right to a standard of living adequate for the health and wellbeing of himself and of his family.' The responsible legislature sets out to protect the health and wellbeing of persons against general threats and specific dangers, all the while acknowledging that its authority is not like that of a parent, who can require a child to observe healthy eating habits, to exercise, and to sleep reasonable hours. The legislature acts to realise the right to health and wellbeing by many direct and indirect measures, including: requiring testing and approval for new drugs; regulating the medical profession; categorising medication as available 'over-the-counter' or only by prescription; licensing commercial food preparation and imposing hygienic standards; mandating disclosure of contents of food products, nutritional information, and negative health effects; authorising and funding various educational programmes on healthy lifestyles and vaccination; and in some jurisdictions by directly providing medical care or insurance through public funds. Less directly but not less importantly, the right to health is secured and promoted by laws on pollution and clean air and water, and in establishing public works like sewer systems and waste removal. The proper scope of such laws and public programmes is a matter of debate. But the reasonableness and grounds of law-making in this area derive from the principle that the legislature should secure the conditions that promote human health and wellbeing for everyone in the community. That principle includes a wide scope for persons to make free choices in matters that relate to their health and wellbeing.

The point here is that detailed positive law is necessary for realising many human rights. Legislation is central in the production of the necessary, detailed positive law

40 Ray Sanchez, 'Experts: Strict building codes saved lives in powerful Chile earthquake' (CNN 3 April 2014) www.cnn.com/2014/04/02/world/americas/chile-earthquake/, accessed 8 October 2015.

41 UNESCO Media Services, 'Earthquake and Tsunami in Chile: Massive Evacuation and Building Codes Help to Reduce the Loss of Life' (17 September 2015), http://en.unesco.org/news/earthquake-and-tsunami-chile-massive-evacuation-and-building-codes-reduce-loss-life, accessed 23 May 2017.

42 The Week, 'Quake comparison: Chile vs. Haiti' (28 February 2010) http://theweek.com/articles/496367/quake-comparison-chile-vs-haiti, accessed 23 May 2017.

43 For discussion, see *Özel and Others* v. *Turkey* (2015) (applications nos. 14350/05, 15245/05 and 16051/05) (European Court of Human Rights).

provisions and of the general legal framework in which other bodies can also create positive law.[44] Though legislatures are central in this task, they often work in conjunction with other bodies. Consider the Criminal Procedure Rules in England and Wales, which have as their stated 'overriding objective' that 'criminal cases be dealt with justly', which includes the subsidiary objectives of acquitting the innocent and convicting the guilty, dealing with the prosecution and the defence fairly, respecting the interests of witnesses, victims, and jurors, and dealing with a case efficiently and expeditiously.[45] To achieve these objectives and so to specify the right to a fair criminal trial, the rules outline the rights and duties of various participants at various stages of the trial, including custody and bail, disclosure of evidence, introduction of witness statements, summoning witnesses, cross-examination, evidence of bad character, evidence of a complainant's previous sexual behaviour, and additional measures on the conduct of the trial and sentencing. Some of the rules go into considerable detail. For example, a party wishing to introduce in evidence a witness's written statement must, before the hearing, serve a copy on the court officer and the other parties and, at or before that hearing, serve on the court officer the statement or an authenticated copy.[46] If the party seeking to introduce a witness statement is the prosecution, it must also serve on the defendant a notice of his or her right within seven days of service to object to the introduction of the statement in evidence on the grounds that the witness should give the evidence in person. The technicality of much of the rules is at some distance from the European Convention's affirmation in Article 6(2) that 'Everyone charged with a criminal offence shall be presumed innocent until proved guilty according to law', but that should not obstruct from view the reality that the rules seek precisely to design a legal procedure for criminal prosecution that respects and indeed realises the presumption of innocence, as well as the other rights listed in Article 6(3).[47] Reason alone cannot design a fair trial without recourse to choices from among reasonable alternatives; there is, for example, no magic in the number seven for the number of days available to a criminal defendant to object to the introduction of a witness statement by the prosecution. But without some limit in the number of days, the defendant would be without the right to object to a last-minute submission, save perhaps by discretion of the court. The rules represent those choices made by the law-maker to realise the right to a fair trial, in part by reaffirming and in greater part by specifying the requirements

[44] This point is well brought out by Jeff King, *Judging Social Rights* (Cambridge, Cambridge University Press 2012). A careful discussion at pp. 41–57 begins with the statement: 'The main engine for protecting social rights is and always will be primary legislation adopted by a representative legislature, and so any good-faith commitment begins here.'

[45] Rule 1.1.

[46] Rule 27.4.

[47] Compare how the relationship between the positive law, including the common law, specifying the right to a fair trial and Article 6 of the European Convention is explored in *Al-Khawaja and Tahery* v. *United Kingdom* (2009) 49 EHRR 1 and *R* v. *Horncastle* [2009] UKSC 14.

of that right. Similar examples could be given for the 'immensely complex' and 'intricate regimes' that characterise social security legislation ('the range of benefits is mind-boggling'), health care and education legislation ('arguably [even] more complicated'), and so forth.[48]

Without positive action by legislation, and positive law more generally, many human rights would fail to be realised. That is true not only for what some refer to as 'positive' rights (such as the right to state provision of primary and secondary education), but also of the more classical, 'negative' rights. As intimated above, the right of persons to freedom of expression is in need of specification in positive law in order to demarcate the boundaries of that freedom. It will be accepted that no person may, in the name of freedom of expression, 'advocate some public policy ... by interrupting a church service, or a classroom, or a sickroom, or a session of Congress or of the Supreme Court, or by ringing a doorbell and demanding to be heard'.[49] The positive law's regulation of libel, defamation, intellectual property, contempt of court, incitement to religious hatred, publication of confidential documents, disclosure of the criminal record of a minor, and so forth express judgements on what is needed to protect various human goods (among them truth) and to realise right relations. An overarching argument of this book is that well-formed and soundly reasoned positive law contributes greatly, and in many cases indispensably, to securing right relations between persons. In maintaining the need for positive law to realise human rights, no part of our argument denies the possibility that the legislature (just as the court) will err, and fail to realise rights in a given community. The legislature will err straightforwardly in acting contrary to a determinate human right, for example by authorising torture or slavery.[50] Errors are less straightforward but no less real in areas where, because reason underdetermines what is required to realise a human right in community, the legislature must choose from among a range of reasonable alternatives; here, the legislature errs in selecting from outside this range, for example by failing to attend to all participants in determining a fair trial process or by failing to review a previously enacted reasonable scheme now that circumstances have changed.

On the prevailing conception of 'human rights law', many aspects of positive law just reviewed fall outside the special concern of human rights law. Insofar as the specification that a defendant has 7 rather than 8 or 30 days to object to a witness statement would relate to human rights law, it might be by way of a

48 King, *Judging Social Rights* 42–3.

49 Alexander Meiklejohn, 'The First Amendment is an Absolute' [1961] Supreme Court Review 245, 261.

50 Aspects of the rights to be free from torture or slavery are in need of specification. Consider the Convention right to be free from torture as engaged in deportation proceedings (e.g. *ex p* EW [2009] EWHC 2957), in the context of interrogation (e.g. *Ireland* v. *UK* (1978) 2 EHRR 25), and in state-sanctioned incarceration (e.g. *ex p B* [2005] 2 AC 270). Specification by positive law is required in each case.

challenge to the positive law for failing to respect 'the right to a fair trial'. In this challenge, the case would typically be framed by claiming that positive law infringes the rights of persons, using rhetoric that at times rises to the level of accusing the legislature of having acted with animus towards the claimant. What this strategy obscures is that the reasonable legislature will have had these very rights consciously in view when adopting the positive law. (This is not to say that the word 'right' needs to have been mentioned in legislative debate.[51] Legislators can engage with human rights without appealing explicitly to the vocabulary of rights.)

For example, in providing that a 'person who aids, abets, counsels or procures the suicide of another, or an attempt by another to commit suicide' shall be criminally liable,[52] the Westminster Parliament is not best understood to have intended to infringe a person's 'right to decide how and when to die, and in particular the right to avoid a distressing and undignified end to life', even if such infringement is justified.[53] Parliament is better understood to have reasoned about how to affirm and protect human life in the special context of the criminal law, with a view that the intentional taking of life is to be avoided, and to have considered (alongside compassion for the would-be suicide-seeker and his or her family) the rights of other persons who, but for the criminal prohibition of this and other forms of participation in intentional killing, would be at increased risk of oppression and death.[54] Parliament's legislative scheme may be unreasonable, but an honest demonstration of its failings is not best approached by postulating that it ignored the rights of persons or set out to infringe them.

The true scope of human rights law is captured by understanding the multiplicity of ways in which positive law relates to human rights. The criminal and tort laws on assault and rape, in addition to the wide range of health regulations reviewed, realise and specify the right to security of the person. Compulsory school attendance measures, the provision of a publicly funded school system, and the availability of government bursaries and loans realise and specify the right to education. Freedom of information laws, privacy legislation, and competition laws in relation to ownership and control of the media realise and specify the right to freedom of expression. The law of contract, the provision for limited liability corporations and partnerships, the regulation of publicly traded companies, the regulation of collective bargaining,

51 For discussion, see *Wilson* v. *First County Trust (No 2)* [2003] UKHL 40 and compare *Hirst* v. *UK* [2006] 42 EHRR 41, esp [79]. See generally Aileen Kavanagh, 'Proportionality and Parliamentary Debates: Exploring Some Forbidden Territory' (2014) 34 *Oxford Journal of Legal Studies* 443.

52 Suicide Act 1961, s 2(1), repealed and re-enacted in modified form in Coroners and Justice Act 2009, ss 59–61.

53 *R (Nicklinson)* v. *Ministry of Justice* [2014] UKSC 38 [29], summarising the judgments of the European Court of Human Rights in *Pretty* v. *United Kingdom* (2002) 35 EHRR 1 [67]; *Haas* v. *Switzerland* (2011) 53 EHRR 33, [51]; *Koch* v. *Germany* (2013) 56 EHRR 6 [46] and [51]; and *Gross* v. *Switzerland* (2014) 58 EHRR 7 [60]. See also [79], where this summary account is endorsed.

54 Some of these themes were explored in the Second Reading debate in the House of Commons on the Assisted Dying (No 2) Bill 2015–16 (11 September 2015).

limitations on working hours, the law of unfair dismissal, and provision for overtime pay all realise and specify the right to work and the right to fair and just working conditions. Without the clarity and direction provided by positive law in these and other ways, the human rights to health, life, security of the person, education, speech, and work would be under-realised in political communities. The expression 'human rights law' should not be taken primarily to denote a specialised subset of legal materials; properly understood, it expresses the specific role of positive law – and centrally legislation – in securing right relations between persons.

1.3 SYNOPSIS OF THE ARGUMENT

This book consists of six chapters in addition to this introduction. Although each chapter has a different author, the chapters individually and collectively pursue the central argument of this book and defend the four counter-theses summarily articulated above. They are intended to stand together not like the chapters of an edited collection united by a single (or set of related) theme(s), but like the chapters of a single-authored monograph pursuing an argument. Chapters 2 to 5 build a positive case for the argument that the legislature is well placed to secure and promote human rights, providing specified legal form to the broad, goal-oriented standards of instruments such as the Universal Declaration and the European Convention. These chapters set out an account of rights and the common good, the need for positive law in political community, the central place of legislation as reasoned action as part of that positive law, and – on the strength of these accounts – the relationship of human rights to legislated rights. Building on this positive case, Chapters 6 and 7 provide an exposition of the judicial role under this theory of legislated rights and an associated critique of certain features of, and arguments for, the existing practice of judicial review of legislation.

Chapter 2 defends an account of rights as right relations between persons. The standard form of rights-talk takes its cue from the wording of rights in the Universal Declaration and European Convention, which, with few exceptions, employs the formulation 'P has the right to *x*'. This two-term structure of rights signifies the importance of the subject matters *x* (life, liberty, security, privacy, etc.) that persons (P) have by right, but does not identify which measures will realise everyone's rights by identifying duty-holders and the content of their duties that correlate to the right(s) in question. Absent such specification, rights are only incipiently directive of right action. Despite this, the European Court of Human Rights and other European and Commonwealth courts award practical meaning to two-term rights, albeit a meaning that renders inevitable the infringement of rights. The intellectual commitments of that understanding of rights reveal an absence of concern for the relationships between persons necessary to realise the rights of each and every member of the community, relationships that are defined not only by rights held but also by duties owed, powers conferred, immunities enjoyed, and so on. Concern for these relationships, and for the reasons for action that both rights and law establish, frames a sound understanding of rights as a three-term relationship between two persons and an action. This account of rights invites one to be concerned with the justice of a claim of right made on or against another, requiring one to situate a claim of right in relation to another person in recognition of the relationships between persons it seeks to establish or to change. The justice of a claim of right invites evaluation whether the claim is, as a colloquial idiom puts it, *in the right* (is just, is in accordance with justice). This evaluation like any other is to be directed by reason, but reason will often fail to provide a single best conclusion: one confronts true, genuine choice in selecting from among reasonable alternatives, choice that gives shape to a community beyond what conformity to reason prohibits and requires.

The facilitative role of positive law in making that choice is the subject of Chapter 3. In many ways, realising human rights by specifying them into concrete and actionable demands of justice requires a broad framework for cooperation of the kind that only a legal system can supply. Critical aspects of human wellbeing can only be adequately protected and fostered in and through complex collective endeavours involving miscellaneous kinds of conduct (including mutual restraint) by large numbers of persons. Individual contributions to such collective schemes are often specific enough that they could reasonably have been otherwise, but in their actual convergent implementation they can severally become apt and proportionate, indeed necessary, means to realise justice, and therefore be due by right to those whose wellbeing is at stake. Positive law is ideally suited to help communities set up and sustain salient, dynamic, and systemically coherent schemes of specific convergence. Law's central technique of legal validity makes it possible to mark specific courses of conduct in a widely salient way, in the face of both moral under-determination and moral controversy. By virtue of empowerments and associated criteria of validity, moreover, the responsibility to choose and mark can be allocated to those who, in justice, ought to bear it, whether on grounds of expertise, proximity, or the inherent value of their self-directing choice. Law therefore enables communities to specify rights dynamically, that is, in the course of a process, involving the decisions of different persons and institutions at different times. Sound limits on their respective scope of empowerment, in turn, will secure a needed degree of coherence among these manifold and changing initiatives, so as to weave them into a genuine *system*.

Which legal institution ought to undertake the task of law-making to achieve coordination in community in the service of rights? That question is taken up in Chapter 4, which defends an account of legislative reasoning, the kind of reasoning that fulfils the legislature's responsibility to the community to craft the complex means-ends measures needed to change the law so as to secure human rights. The widely assumed disjunction between judicial *reason* and legislative *will* is challenged as misleading, for it fails to perceive that reasonable action involves the exercise of will in response to reasons. It also fails to perceive that the value of law in general and legislation in particular lies in their centrality to the stable, reasonable form of order that is necessary for people to secure their common good. Also challenged is the understanding of legislating as the aggregation of preferences or reason-based votes. To exercise legislative power is to respond intelligently to the reasons for changing the law. This response is not wholly settled by reason, such that legislating merely declares what the law should have been already, but is the exercise of will in settling which, among reasonable possible courses of action, is to be the community's choice. Conceiving of legislation in this way grounds a better understanding of the relationship between rights and legislation: open-ended human rights instruments inform legislative deliberation with a view to adopting specified human rights that are the object of legislative choice. The central case of legislation is reasoned action and the legislative will of the legislator is a response to reasons that gives effect as fully as possible to rights rather than constituting a standing threat of tyranny to which rights-as-trumps are a partial response.

The discussion in Chapters 2 to 4 is united in Chapter 5 around the central theme of the relationship of human rights to legislated rights, with a special focus on the institutional dimensions of that relationship. The account of legislated rights is explored, first, by contrasting it with the account of 'human rights' in the received approach of European and Commonwealth courts and in Dworkin's account of rights as trumps. Unlike the account of legislated rights defended in this book, both of these accounts allow rights to be defeasible by arguments about the general welfare. Rights so conceived fail to share in the characteristic force of law and legal rights: the force of being obligatory and directive of right action, and excluding from play countervailing arguments about the general welfare. The account of legislated rights is explored, second, by reviewing how the Universal Declaration of Human Rights calls for action by legislatures. Because human rights declarations are incompletely specified, such that the values and principles reflected in the formulations of rights require further, detailed work by legislatures in order to be realised, legislated rights stand to human rights as specifications of the latter, sharing in by realising the moral force of human rights. Legislated rights can achieve the very aims of human wellbeing imperfectly articulated in human rights instruments. This chapter also considers the claim that legislatures are ill-suited for protecting the rights of minorities because of the majoritarian character of elections, and argues, by way of a comparative analysis of judicial and legislative involvement in the movement towards racial equality over the last two centuries, that legislatures have been at least as effective as courts, and perhaps more so, in achieving that goal.

The two final chapters of the book examine the question of judicial review under a bill of rights. They draw on Chapters 2 to 5 to consider how the account of legislated rights bears on the theory and practice of judicial review. These are questions that ought to be of concern to all who study existing practices of judicial review of legislation on human rights grounds. Chapter 6 extends the central claim that legislation secures and promotes human rights to the domain of legal adjudication. In the adjudication of human rights claims, legislation is sometimes conceived as an obstacle to sound decision-making, imposing legal constraints on the ability of judges to reason morally. Against this view, it is argued that legislation is in principle an aid, not an obstacle, to sound judicial decision-making. Adjudication in the absence of direction by positive law risks undermining the adjudicative function of courts, including by frustrating Rule of Law commitments to be governed by laws rather than persons, by placing undue weight on the ability of non-Herculean judges to determine (without the aid of law) what justice requires, and by undermining certainty and predictability in the governance of human affairs. Many of the commonly understood institutional advantages of courts are derived precisely from their commitment to decide cases *according to law*. The legal practice of constraining and so directing legal adjudication by faithful application of technical legal categories increases the likelihood that justice and other values at stake in adjudication will be realised. When the adjudication of human rights claims proceeds – as the doctrines of proportionality and balancing have it proceed – independently of the direction offered by law, and appeals without mediation to foundational moral principles, these advantages are lost. The point of this chapter is not directly to question the capacity of courts to challenge legislation for violating human rights, but to draw attention to how legislation assists human rights adjudication by providing legal direction to judges in compliance with and furtherance of the Rule of Law.

Chapter 7 examines a question left open in the preceding chapters: is the practice of judicial review under a bill of rights inconsistent with the theory of legislated rights here defended, including the account of legislation as reasoned activity and the claim that legislatures have a primary responsibility for the specification of human rights? It is acknowledged that not all legislative activity conforms to the central case of legislation that is awarded explanatory priority throughout the book. The question then arises whether, given the potential pathologies of legislatures and legislation, judicial review of legislation under a bill of rights is a sound addition in a community's commitment to human rights. Against the tide of opinion that judicial review is an unqualified good given the standing risk of such pathologies, the answer defended is cautious: judicial review is not *necessarily* a sound response to the risk of non-central cases of legislating. Two premises in the common assumption that judicial review is necessarily to be favoured are in need of further reflection. First, the spectre of majoritarian abuse – particularly the tyranny of the majority – is analysed with regard to the dockets of human rights courts. The evidence suggests that contemporary human rights litigation in select jurisdictions is increasingly a second forum for law-making (or law-changing) proposals that have failed legislatively, and failed for reasons other than contempt or disregard for any person or group. Second, the assumption, at times articulated, at other times not, that the practice of judicial review introduces only one risk – the failure to intervene – is challenged against some pathologies of human rights adjudication, including the potential for judges' reasoning to be distorted by demands of concreteness (which creates a bias in favour of the complainant before the court and against other persons affected by the claim but not represented as a party before the court), the problem of uncertainty (which grants judges wide discretion over what sort of proof is required to justify legislation), the infringement/justification division explored in Thesis 3 (which tends to obscure and distort a sound understanding of the common good), and the doctrine of proportionality (examined in the preceding chapter). These pathologies are liable to frustrate attempts by the legislature to realise rights in positive law. It is not claimed that the balance sheet of risks of pathologies with one or the other institution favours or opposes judicial review of legislation *per se*. The aim is rather more modest: to highlight how an account of legislated rights provides additional resources for evaluating whether to introduce judicial review where it is absent, and for assessing the scope of practices of judicial review where it is present.

* * *

One aim of this book is to reorient general thinking about the nature of rights, legislatures, and courts, and legal and judicial reasoning. We propose a new account in which legislatures are not defined in opposition to human rights but are recognised to be capable of serving as full, priority partners in the project of protecting and promoting them. Indeed, we argue that positive law, and legislation especially, is central and indispensable to the human rights project. A sound theory of human rights must be aware of the unique capacities that legislatures have for realising rights in community. Such a theory stands in opposition to the theses challenged above and, we argue, embraces the following counter-theses: (1) the legislature is capable of principled, reasoned deliberation, and the central case of legislative action consists in reasoned deliberation to promote the common good, which has as its concern the wellbeing and rights of all persons in community; (2) the legislature is not inherently biased against minorities and is fit to engage in principled decision-making about human rights; (3) sound legislation does not oppose human rights, but rather affirms the requirements of human rights, including by specifying the broad, goal-oriented standards included in human rights instruments into relatively precise legal form; and (4) the legislature is capable of securing human rights by specifying them in a form so that rights are not defeasible against countervailing interests or the general welfare.

As Waldron has observed, 'legislation and legislatures have a bad name in legal and political philosophy'.[55] Part of the burden of this book is to develop a philosophical account of legislation and legislatures by articulating how human rights are secured not only or even especially by courts, but by the painstaking, everyday work of legislatures seeking to craft laws to promote and protect human rights.

[55] Jeremy Waldron, *The Dignity of Legislation* (Cambridge, Cambridge University Press 1999) 1.

Our argument is not contingent on whether human rights courts have a general tendency to make morally correct judgments regarding human rights problems. We contend that many such judgments – whether correct or incorrect – rest on unarticulated premises that, upon investigation, are shown to be unsound. Our goal is to recalibrate the premises of debate, such that the project of securing human rights is grounded on stronger philosophical and jurisprudential foundations.

2

Rights and Persons

Grégoire Webber

2.1 INTRODUCTION

Philosophical thinking on rights progresses and regresses. It is a mark of regression that human rights jurisprudence and scholarship (a) assume that rights and law generally oppose each other, (b) conceive of rights in a way that omits the relationships between persons necessary for the respect of the rights of each and all, and (c) rob rights of their priority and conclusiveness by relegating all but select rights to defeasible status, as captured by the now common currency of justified infringements of rights. None of this is as it should be.

This chapter examines how human rights jurisprudence and scholarship reached these positions and demonstrates how a study of the relationships between rights and law and justice chart a path to correcting these errors. The relationship of rights to positive law is suggested by civilian traditions tracking the meanings of the Latin *ius* (*jus*). Where English employs the single term 'law', other languages use two: (i) *lex, loi, ley, legge, Gesetz* for 'a law', 'a statute'; and (ii) *jus, droit, derecho, diritto, Recht* for 'law' (or a 'legal state of affairs') and for 'in the right', 'just'. The pairings of 'law' and 'in the right' in civilian traditions invite one to see as law's concern the pursuit of that which is right and, as suggested by the academic career of the term *ius*, what is right is giving to each and all their rights (see Section 2.6). The relationship of rights to 'the right' (justice) is suggested not only by their common Latin root, but also by a conceptual relationship affirmed by different persons in different places and times, including the drafters of the Universal Declaration on Human Rights.[1] A conclusion wherein acts, arrangements, and states of affairs just can be equivalently expressed as an affirmation that each person's rights are respected and complied

[1] Universal Declaration of Human Rights, preamble: 'Whereas recognition of the inherent dignity and of *the equal and inalienable rights of all members of the human family is the foundation of* freedom, *justice* and peace in the world' (emphasis added).

with by such acts, arrangements, and affairs. Thus understood, rights, like justice, enter the stage in a community of persons; like justice, rights are concerned with the interpersonal relationships set out in various acts and arrangements established in political communities. In other words, rights and law do not oppose each other, because it is the responsibility of law to realise rights in community.

In an effort to develop an understanding of rights as right relations between persons, this chapter begins by exploring how human rights law-in-action has moved some distance from the inter-definability of rights and justice and from an understanding of law as regulating right relations between persons (Sections 2.2–2.4). The intellectual commitments of that approach reveal an absence of concern for the relationships between persons necessary to realise the rights of each and every member of the community, relationships defined not only by rights held but also by duties owed, among other incidents of relationships between persons. Concern for these relationships, and for the reasons for action that both rights and law establish, frames a sound understanding of rights as three-term relations between two persons and an act or forbearance (Section 2.5–2.6). On this understanding, the justice of a claim of right made on or against another invites evaluation of whether the claim is in the right (is just, is in accordance with justice). This evaluation is directed by reason, but reason will often not provide a single best conclusion: one confronts true, genuine choice in selecting among reasonable alternatives, choice that gives shape to a community beyond what conformity to reason prohibits and requires (Section 2.7). This chapter's orienting argument is that the received meaning of the expression 'human rights law' misleads in its near exclusive focus on bills of rights and case law interpreting and applying such instruments. On a sound understanding of rights and their relationship to law, human rights law is to be found in all areas of positive law. The law of tort, of contract, of property, of crime ... all seek to respect and to specify the human rights of each and all in community (Section 2.8). The point of a community's positive regulation is to realise *justice according to law*, an expression that can be reformulated, without loss of meaning, as: to realise *rights according to law*.

2.2 TWO-TERM RIGHTS

The Universal Declaration of Human Rights sought to affirm, so far as a situated human undertaking would allow, the universal reach and force of human rights against the particularities of history and geography. The success of this undertaking, upon the final vote before the UN General Assembly in December 1948, rested on the various levels of abstraction with which the instrument was drafted, such that each one of the declared rights could be realised in law in a variety of different ways. The drafters sought to affirm rights without specifying in every respect the interpersonal relationships that constitute rights in community.

The wording of the Declaration was initiated by a draft prepared by the first director of the UN Secretariat's Human Rights Division, John Humphrey, who instructed his staff 'to study all the world's existing constitutions and rights instruments'.[2] The making of the Declaration proceeded from the local as it aspired to the universal: national and regional attempts to set out rights and freedoms for select communities informed the grander appeal to universality for all communities.

As the Human Rights Committee set to work on Humphrey's draft, René Cassin, French delegate to the committee and important member of the drafting subcommittee, was mindful 'to find a formula that did not require the Commission to take sides on the nature of man and society, or to become immured in metaphysical controversies'.[3] The challenge was to affirm rights common to humankind, to affirm that each right was to be read in relation to every other, and to do so in a manner that would be acceptable to the world's many political communities.[4]

How did the Universal Declaration achieve this? In surveying the Declaration's thirty articles, one observes two different sets of formulations employed by the drafters: 'Everyone has the right to ...' and 'No one shall be ...'.[5] The Human Rights Committee might have used the same formulation throughout, such that 'Everyone has the right to life' could have been expressed as 'No one may be deprived of life' just as 'No one shall be held in slavery or servitude' could have been expressed more generally as 'Everyone has the right to freedom of labour'. And yet, the two formulations are more than different stylistic modes of expressing the same commitment. The first formulation identifies some abstract *subject matter* (thing, general act-description) that all have a right to: liberty, life, equality, freedom of religion, freedom of association, etc. The second formulation differs by identifying some *action* that is prohibited: an injunction against a deed, a duty not to perform a given act. The difference is significant.

The Universal Declaration's list of duties not to perform a given action includes: *holding* another in slavery or servitude; *performing* torture, cruel, and inhuman or degrading treatment or punishment with respect to another; arbitrarily *arresting*, *detaining*, or *exiling* another; *finding* another guilty of a retroactive criminal offence or *imposing* a retroactive criminal penalty on another; arbitrarily *interfering* with another's privacy, family, home, correspondence, or *attacking* another's honour

[2] Mary Ann Glendon, *A World Made New: Eleanor Roosevelt and the Universal Declaration of Human Rights* (New York, Random House 2002) 56.

[3] Glendon, *A World Made New* 68.

[4] Jacques Maritain, 'Introduction' in UNESCO *Human Rights: Comments and Interpretations* (UNESCO/PHS/3 (rev.), Paris, 25 July 1948) i: 'It is related that at one of the meetings of a Unesco National Commission where Human Rights were being discussed, someone expressed astonishment that certain champions of violently opposed ideologies had agreed on a list of those rights. "Yes", they said, "we agree about the rights but on condition that no one asks us why"'.

[5] Variations of one or the other formulation are also found in the Declaration, including 'All are ...', 'Everyone is entitled to ...', and 'No one may be ...'. In addition, some Articles employ formulae that could have been, but were not, re-worked in keeping with the rest of the Declaration, e.g. Art. 16(3): 'The family is the natural and fundamental group unit of society' and Art. 21(3): 'The will of the people shall be the basis of the authority of government'.

and reputation; arbitrarily *depriving* another of his or her nationality or *denying* him or her the right to change nationality; arbitrarily *depriving* another of his or her property; and *compelling* another to belong to an association.[6] By contrast, the provisions of the Universal Declaration that employ the formulation 'Everyone has the right to ...' contain no verb other than 'to have'. No action or inaction by anyone or any group of persons is highlighted as giving content to the rights that each and everyone *has*. A review of human rights instruments inspired by the Universal Declaration, including the European Convention on Human Rights, discloses that both sets of formulations continue to be used, with preference for the first and its key words: 'has the right to'.

This same preference is manifested in modern rights-talk, which standardly employs the form 'P has the right to *x*'. This two-term grammar of rights – one class of persons P ('Everyone', 'Every citizen', 'Every accused person'), one subject matter, thing, or general act-description *x* ('life', 'liberty', 'expression') – signifies the importance of the 'subject matters' ('things', 'general acts') that persons 'have' by right. The Universal Declaration and the human rights instruments it has inspired single out life, liberty, security, equality, conscience, religion, expression, work, education, and culture as subject matters of special concern. But what is it to have a right *to life*, or *to liberty*, or *to culture*? The standard grammar of modern rights-talk does not answer the question and, as we will see, does not facilitate the evaluations and judgments necessary to do so.

The open-ended feature of the formulation 'Everyone has the right to ...' was well known to the drafters of the Universal Declaration, who sought, as stated in the Declaration's preamble, 'a common understanding of these rights and freedoms', but not one that would require the same relationships between persons to be established in all of the world's communities. For this reason, the formulation in Article 3 that 'Everyone has the right to life' was favoured over attempts 'to reach agreement on specific issues such as euthanasia, abortion, or the death penalty';[7] so, too, was there no attempt to settle debates surrounding hate propaganda and libellous speech in Article 19's declaration that 'Everyone has the right to freedom of opinion and expression'.[8] The examples can be multiplied. Notwithstanding the absence of agreement on specific issues in the Declaration, the settling of such issues is central to understanding the rights declared. Under the generality of *one* 'subject matter' that 'everyone' is declared 'to have' a 'right to' lies a *multiplicity* of possible acts, arrangements, and states of affairs that, if just, will respect, promote, protect, and comply with everyone's rights. The range of reasonable acts, arrangements, and

[6] Arts. 4, 5, 9, 11(2), 12, 15(2), 17(2), 20(2).

[7] Glendon, *A World Made New* 92. See further ibid. 152, 155.

[8] Art. 19 does specify that the right '*includes* freedom to hold opinions without interference and to seek, receive and impart information and ideas through any media and regardless of frontiers' (emphasis added).

states of affairs was contemplated by the drafters of the Universal Declaration who preferred not to stipulate which among them was to be selected for each and every community, a selection that each and every community must nonetheless make so as to provide 'everyone' and 'all' with the 'right to' the enumerated subject matters.

This lack of specificity within the Universal Declaration was reasonable, for reasons to be returned to in Section 2.7. For now, note two important features of acts, arrangements, and states of affairs that are absent from the understanding of rights disclosed by the favoured expression 'Everyone has a right to ...'. The first absent feature is *another* who stands in a relationship to the person who has the right to a given 'subject matter'. Compare this with the relationships implied in the injunctions 'No one shall be ... held in slavery or servitude; subjected to torture or to cruel, inhuman or degrading treatment or punishment; subjected to arbitrary interference with his privacy, family, home or correspondence'. *No one* shall perform these acts against *anyone*. The class of right-holder and the class of duty-holder are both universal. In turn, when the formulation is of the more familiar '... has a right to ...', different acts and arrangements will contemplate different relationships between persons in relation to the actions and activities more or less captured by the umbrella terms 'life', 'equality', 'expression', etc. The complex matrix of relationships between persons necessary to respect and comply with everyone's rights is illustrated by the range of legal rights, liberties, powers, immunities, and so forth that give shape to a modern legal system, a theme returned to in Section 2.8.

The second absent feature from the favoured understanding of rights: relationships between persons centred on *acting* and *doing*. The intelligible sense according to which justice requires *giving* to persons what is theirs by right highlights how all acts, arrangements, and states of affairs realising rights in community must set out what is required, forbidden, and permitted between persons. So: a judicial official is required *to sentence* a convicted criminal to a penitentiary term (or is forbidden from doing so due to the age of the convict); a university admissions officer is required *to apply* affirmative action selection criteria to applicants (or is forbidden from doing so); a neo-Nazi is at liberty *to utter* hate speech against a targeted group of persons (or is forbidden from doing so); and new employees are at liberty *to join* the workplace union (or are required to do so). In concluding that the prison sentence should (or, not) be given, that hate speech should (or, not) be prohibited, and so on, the familiar subject matters – liberty, equality, expression, association, etc. – are realised in a community of persons. Without such measures, these 'subject matters' would not be fully realised in the life of the community.

The specification of such measures requires far more than the resolution of the grand moral-political questions surrounding which practices and activities may be undertaken in the name of the enumerated 'subject matters' (incarceration and *liberty*, hate speech and *expression*, affirmative action and *equality*). Critically, such specification also requires the identification of such persons who will stand in a relationship to the right-holder. Here again, a multiplicity of possible relationships manifests itself. For who must act (or forbear from acting) by virtue of *my* rights? And how should *I* act (or forbear from acting) so as to respect and protect *your* rights? With their special emphasis on the two-term grammar 'Everyone has the right to *x*', the Universal Declaration, European Convention, and other bills of rights do not have direct answers to these questions. Despite signalling in Article 29(1) that everyone has not only rights but also 'duties to the community in which alone the free and full development of [one's] personality is possible', the Universal Declaration does not explicitly draw attention to the fundamental point that the duties one owes are not quite to 'the community' but to each and every *member* of that community, duties without which the all-important subject matters enumerated in the Declaration cannot be translated into rights.[9] The Declaration maintains a firm focus on duties only when it forgoes the language of rights, as with the less common formulation 'No one shall ...'. Here, the negative duties are on everyone and are owed to everyone: each and every member of the human family stands in a relationship to all others not to enslave, to hold in servitude, to torture, to subject to cruel, inhuman, or degrading treatment or punishment, and so forth. The all too common assumption that human rights are held only 'against the state', save for the limited doctrine of 'horizontal effect', fails to capture the promise of the Universal Declaration and its affirmation that human rights require each and everyone to acknowledge and act on their duties *to each other*.[10] Present-day campaigns against 'modern slavery' in agricultural labour, sexual exploitation and trafficking, and domestic servitude do not target 'state action'; they target violations of human rights by non-state actors. Critically for the argument of this chapter, these campaigns call for *the need for positive law* to secure right relations between persons.[11]

2.3 RECEIVED APPROACH TO HUMAN RIGHTS LAW

When employing the standard two-term grammar of rights, the Universal Declaration and European Convention do not identify which acts, arrangements, and states of affairs will realise everyone's rights. Thus, the standard declaration of human rights in these and other instruments is only incipiently directive of right action: it orients choice in the exercise of practical judgment, but does not provide sufficient guidance for action. A conscientious reading of the Declaration and Convention is of course alive to the need – present in the mind of the drafters – to complete the specification of these rights, and yet a rather undisciplined and, as I aim to show,

[9] The European Convention makes only one explicit reference to duty, at Art. 10(2): 'The exercise of these freedoms, since it carries with it duties and responsibilities ...'.

[10] See the International Covenant on Economic, Social and Cultural Rights, preamble: 'the individual, having duties to other individuals and to the community to which he belongs, is under a responsibility to strive for the promotion and observance of the rights recognized in the present Covenant'.

[11] See the report of the UK Joint Committee on the Draft Modern Slavery Bill, *Draft Modern Slavery Bill* (2013–14, HL 166, HC 1019) and the Modern Slavery Act 2015 (UK).

hazardous reading has taken hold. Re-directing our attention from the Declaration and Convention to human rights law-in-action in the courts of European and Commonwealth jurisdictions, one observes that the unspecified two-term grammar of rights is awarded *practical* meaning in the case law and by many who study it. What is incipiently directive of right action becomes practically directive by treating the two-term 'Everyone has the right to *x*' as a legally cognisable right.

Yet, the open-ended affirmation that 'Everyone has a right to *x*' fails to provide answers to the questions: 'How should I act?', 'What am I to do to respect your rights?', 'What may I do in the name of my rights?' Despite this, the two-term grammar of rights favoured by bills of rights is held out by the received approach to human rights law as providing an answer to a preliminary question. When faced with the queries – 'Do I have the right ... to criticise my government's health care policy, to engage in a seminar room debate over some controversial moral-political question, to publish information contrary to a court-ordered publicity ban?' – judicial and academic proponents of the received approach direct one *to interpret* the bill of rights' declaration that 'Everyone has the right to freedom of expression'. The instruction is coupled with the directive to give a broad and comprehensive construction so as to favour the radiating effect of the right.[12] Thus, 'expression' is taken to *include nearly all* expressive activity, 'free' is taken to *exclude nearly all* restrictions on expressive activity, and 'everyone' is taken to mean each and every one without exception. Armed with the lawyer's interpretive craft, one concludes that 'Everyone has the right to free expression' stands for the legally cognisable claim that I have the right to say anything to anyone at any time without interference.[13] With this conclusion, one returns to the queries put forward and replies: 'Yes, I can ... criticise my government, engage in debate, violate a publicity ban ... all in the name of my *right* to free expression.'

The same interpretive approach holds for other rights common to bills of rights. To the queries – 'Do I have the right to a ballot ... at age fifteen, while lawfully imprisoned, despite being a lifetime non-resident of my country of citizenship?' – the

[12] See Aharon Barak, *Proportionality: Constitutional Rights and their Limitations* (New York, Cambridge University Press 2012) 71 ('interpretation should reflect the spectrum of reasons underlying the right's creation'); Robert Alexy, 'Constitutional Rights, Balancing, and Rationality' (2003) 16 *Ratio Juris* 131–2 (advocating a 'broad and comprehensive' reading of rights); Kai Möller, *The Global Model of Constitutional Rights* (Oxford, Oxford University Press 2012) 76 ('the scope of freedom protected by rights must extend to everything which is in the interest of a person's autonomy'); Mattias Kumm, 'Who is Afraid of the Total Constitution?' (2006) 7 *German Law Journal* 341 (the 'right to liberty' is to be interpreted as the 'freedom to do whatever one pleases to do').

[13] Students of human rights law will be aware that some courts have sometimes refused to follow this interpretive approach in every respect, excluding certain instances of expression (e.g. violence) and allowing certain regulations (e.g. 'time, place, and manner' restrictions). In so doing, these courts sometimes break rank with what others label the new 'global model' of human rights law: see Möller, *The Global Model*; Mattias Kumm, 'The Idea of Socratic Contestation and the Right to Justification: The Point of Rights-Based Proportionality Review' (2010) 4 *Law & Ethics of Human Rights* 140. See also the less strident, but similar arguments in Barak, *Proportionality*.

reply is: 'Yes: every citizen has the right to vote *without qualification*', for no qualifications (save citizenship) are discoverable, via the employed techniques of legal interpretation, when reading the declaration: 'Every citizen has the right to vote'.[14] The examples can be multiplied in relation to the other subject matters included in bills of rights and the answers provided will, almost invariably, be: 'Yes: your desired action can be pursued in the name of your rights'. In this way and notwithstanding the juridically primitive formulation 'P has the right to ...', proponents of the received approach to human rights law purport to give legal-practical meaning to two-term rights.

However, it would be mistaken to conclude that this interpretive approach assists one in answering the only truly practical question: 'How should I act?' For under the received approach to two-term rights, it is only a partial exaggeration to conclude that each and everyone has the right to do whatever each and everyone wishes to do, including – as we will come to see – a right to be free of duties to respect the rights of others. This recalls Hobbes' account of natural rights, according to which 'every man has a right to everything', a right that translates into the denial of any duties to respect the *rights* of others, a consequence made especially clear in Hobbes' statement that every man has a right 'even to one another's body'.[15] It is significant that Hobbes thought it necessary to abandon an account of rights that amounts to a denial of duties in the transition from the state of nature to the civil condition, a condition that (even if not for Hobbes) invites the questions: How can I comply with the rights of *others*? How can *others* comply with my rights? By failing to situate these questions as part of their understanding of rights, proponents of the received approach devise a manifestly unreasonable account of rights; *unreasonable* as in contrary to sound practical reasoning in contemplation of action and what ought to be done.

The consequences of the received approach are familiar to students of human rights case law. Legally cognisable claims of rights under bills of rights are often said to be in conflict. In seeking to publish defamatory statements on another, one may be said to be acting pursuant to one's right to free expression, just as the other who is to be defamed may rely on his rights to privacy and reputation to block the publication.[16] So, too, with the accused person's right to make full answer and defence,

[14] Although this formulation is not found in the Universal Declaration, which speaks of the 'will of the people' (Art. 21(3)), it is found in other bills of rights: e.g. Canadian Charter, s. 3. On the European Convention on Human Rights and the 'right to vote', see Art. 3 of the First Protocol ('free expression of the opinion of the people in the choice of the legislature') and *Hirst* v. *United Kingdom (No. 2)* (2005) ECHR 681.

[15] Thomas Hobbes, *Leviathan* [1651] (Oxford, Oxford University Press 1996) 87 (Ch. 14).

[16] See e.g. *Chauvy* v. *France* App. no. 64915/01 (ECtHR, 29 June 2004), para. 70: 'two values guaranteed by the Convention which may come into conflict with each other in this type of case, namely, on the one hand, freedom of expression protected by Article 10 and, on the other, ... Article 8 of the Convention as part of the right to respect for private life'.

including the right to have counsel cross-examine the complainant on questions of sexual history, and the complainant's right to privacy not to be questioned in open court on matters of such an intimate nature.[17] The rights, we are told by judicial and academic proponents of the received approach, are in conflict; they compete. In its inattention to others who are in relationships with the right-holder, the case law struggles to resolve the conflict.

On this account, the source of duties is in the law. Rights conflict not only with each other, but also and regularly with a community's law. Given the conclusion of the interpretive approach to two-term rights – 'Yes: your action can be pursued in the name of your rights' – it can be said that rights necessarily conflict with much positive law, including those legal duties that are among the more settled parts of a community's legal order. For example, Aharon Barak explores how the case law supports his view that rights extend to 'the act of stealing' and other 'criminal activity', notwithstanding that these 'rights' conflict with the law's settled criminal and tortious prohibitions against such wrongful acts and activities.[18] Kai Möller, in turn, works out the implications of deep underlying premises in the case law to conclude in favour of a 'right to murder' (and by logical implication: to rape, to commit genocide, to kidnap, to torture, to get more than one's fair share by deception, etc.), again notwithstanding the law's settled prohibitions against such acts.[19] On this understanding, it follows that a community's law *both* recognises and affirms everyone's rights (in a bill of rights) *and* inevitably and invariably conflicts with the rights just awarded.

In both of these cases of conflict – between two rights or between one right and a legal requirement or restriction – the interpretation of two-term rights takes one only so far. In the case of a conflict between a law and a right, the received approach does not conclude that the right *must* prevail (little law would remain if such were the case); in the case of a conflict between two rights, the received approach could not conclude that 'the right' must prevail without begging the question. Thus, the received approach to interpreting human rights succeeds only in answering the question 'What rights do I have?', while emptying the answer of any practical significance. It provides no answer to the centrally practical question: 'May I *act* on my rights?'

How does the received approach to human rights law go about answering this practical question? Following the vocabulary of the Universal Declaration on Human

[17] See e.g. *R* v. *Mills* [1999] 3 SCR 668 (Supreme Court of Canada), para. 63: 'The conflict is resolved by considering *conflicting rights* in the factual context of each particular case' (emphasis added).

[18] Barak, *Proportionality* 42–3.

[19] For e.g., Möller, *Global Model* 77–9 and Kai Möller, 'Proportionality and Rights Inflation' in Grant Huscroft, Bradley W Miller, and Grégoire Webber (eds.), *Proportionality and the Rule of Law* (New York, Cambridge University Press 2014). For criticism, see Grégoire Webber, 'On the Loss of Rights' in Grant Huscroft, Bradley W Miller, and Grégoire Webber (eds.), *Proportionality and the Rule of Law* (New York, Cambridge University Press 2014).

Rights, the case law introduces a second evaluation, according to which: '[i]n the *exercise* of his [or her] rights and freedoms, everyone shall be subject only to such *limitations* as are determined by law solely for the purpose of securing due recognition and respect for the rights and freedoms of *others* and of meeting the just requirements of morality, public order and the general welfare in a democratic *society*'.[20] 'Others' and 'society' are acknowledged, but only in the inelegant language of a *limitation* on the *exercise* of one's rights. The European Convention carries this unwelcome distortion further by likening 'limitation' to an '*interference* by a public authority with the exercise of this right', to '*subjecting*' the 'exercise of these freedoms ... to such formalities, conditions, restrictions or penalties', and to '*restrictions*' placed 'on the exercise of these rights'.[21] To the legal mind, it is all rather uncraftsmanlike.

Here, the received approach suggests that contrary to the right itself, which is without limitation, the exercise of the right is subject to restrictions. Those restrictions are captured by a set of more or less interchangeable terms which identify the effect of limitations on various exercises of one's rights: 'infringement', 'interference', 'breach', 'contravention', 'encroachment', 'abridgement', and 'impairment'. As this vocabulary discloses, the received approach proceeds on the understanding that the legal restriction on the exercise of one's rights is *inconsistent* with one's rights even if such regulation is *for* 'the purpose of securing due recognition and respect for the rights and freedoms of others'. To this end, the received approach appeals to a second evaluation to assess the *justification* of the legal restriction's 'infringement', 'interference', etc. of the exercise of the right. The received approach does so by appealing to the standards of proportionality and balancing to arrive at an answer to the truly practical question: 'May I *act* on my right, notwithstanding the conflict with another right or with a legal regulation infringing the exercise of my right?'

Evaluation of the merits of balancing and proportionality reasoning will be deferred to Chapters 6 and 7,[22] but consider here the following: the exercise of rights must be in proportion with or balanced against ... what? Here, the jurisprudence of the received approach inserts 'public interest', 'state interest', or 'general interest' or 'collective goals', 'collective interests', 'social interests', 'community goals', or 'community values'. This opposition between one's rights and the public, the community, and so forth is revealing. It carries the concept of rights to the point where one's being in community is the *source* of the infringement of one's rights; it blinds one from viewing community as the foundation of any intelligible understanding of rights.

20 Universal Declaration, Art. 29(2) (emphasis added).

21 See Arts. 8(2), 9(2), 10(2), and 11(2).

22 For more general critical evaluations, see Francisco J. Urbina, *A Critique of Proportionality and Balancing* (Cambridge, Cambridge University Press 2017); Stavros Tsakyrakis 'Proportionality: An Assault on Human Rights?' (2009) 7 *International Journal of Constitutional Law* 468; Grégoire Webber, *The Negotiable Constitution: On the Limitation of Rights* (Cambridge, Cambridge University Press 2009), Ch. 3.

In every case asking whether the infringement of a right is justified, a court's reasoning appeals (sometimes cogently, often not) to the reality that one is not alone but in a community with others. Whereas the interpretation of two-term rights focuses on whether *my* act could be pursued in the name of *my* right, the justification of interferences with my act appeals to the rights, needs, goods, and responsibilities of *others* as members of a 'community in which alone the free and full development of [my] personality is possible'.[23] In so doing, the received approach confronts the question: 'Is the doing of this act in relation to *others* in keeping with what is justified in a free and democratic society?' In other words: 'Is the legally-recognised claim of right *in the right?*' So controlling is *this* question that courts sometimes altogether dismiss the preliminary interpretive question of what the right requires as a matter unworthy of serious investigation. The UK House of Lords has allowed itself to 'assume, *without deciding*', that a claimant's rights have been infringed even if the matter was 'doubtful' in some respects.[24] The European Court on Human Rights has proceeded to evaluate the proportionality of a ban on incest after accepting that the applicant's incestuous relations with his biological sister 'possibly' fell within the scope of the Article 8 right to respect for one's family life.[25] Other courts adopt this same practice.

The contrast between rights and *what is in the right* is present every time a court concludes that the infringement of a right is justified. In reviewing regulatory provisions prohibiting publications that expose or tend to expose persons to hatred, ridicule, or affronts to dignity, the Supreme Court of Canada began its analysis by affirming that *because* hate speech has 'expressive content', it *therefore* falls within the scope of the claimant's right to freedom of expression. The Court's conclusion that 'hate speech is, at its core, an effort to marginalize individuals' and an effort to 'reduce[e] their social standing and acceptance within society'[26] is an affirmation of the justice of the legislature's prohibition of hate speech. That affirmation is expressed in the conclusion that *it is right* to infringe the hate-promoter's *rights*. On this reading, respect both for rights and for justice is impossible because it will be, on a very regular basis, '*necessary* in a free and democratic society' to infringe rights.[27]

[23] Universal Declaration, Art. 29(1).

[24] See e.g. *Belfast City Council* v. *Miss Behavin' Limited* [2007] UKHL 19, para. 10: 'I am prepared to assume, *without deciding*, that freedom of expression includes the right to use particular premises to distribute pornographic books, videos and other articles and, *rather more doubtfully*, that a person who is denied the right to use his premises as a sex shop is thereby "deprived of his possessions"' (emphasis added).

[25] See *Stübing* v. *Germany* App. no. 43547/08 (ECtHR, 12 April 2012), para. 55 (emphasis added): 'The Court does not exclude that the applicant's criminal conviction [for incest] had an impact on his family life and, *possibly*, attracted protection under Article 8 of the Convention, as he was forbidden to have sexual intercourse with the mother of his four children'.

[26] *Saskatchewan (Human Rights Commission)* v. *Whatcott* [2013] 1 SCR 467 (Supreme Court of Canada), para. 71.

[27] Canadian Charter, s. 1 (emphasis added).

A similar, yet more emphatic confusion dominates the Supreme Court of Canada's evaluation of criminal prohibitions respecting child pornography. The analysis begins by recalling that while 'the prurient nature of most of the materials defined as "child pornography" may attenuate its constitutional worth, it does not negate it, since the guarantee of free expression extends even to offensive speech'.[28] On the question of the justification for the legislature's infringement of the child pornographer's freedom of expression, the Court not only accepts the justification but affirms that 'the possession of child pornography *must be forbidden* to prevent harm to children'.[29] In the Court's evaluation, there are conclusive reasons for acting *contrary* to the right: for the legislature to respect the pornographer's freedom of expression would be to act *unjustly* or *unjustifiably*. The child pornographer's right to free expression *must be* infringed because acting otherwise would be without justification and in the wrong, as in: *not in the right*. All of this suggests that matters have become rather confused.

The notion of a justified infringement of a right is equivalent to the affirmation that what one seeks to do in pursuit of one's right(s) is not just, not justified, not in the right. In each instance, the appeal to justification is an appeal to how one relates to others. Because the received approach awaits the infringement of one's rights before engaging with that central question, it allows for an understanding of rights to develop that divorces the right (the just, justice) from rights. The unsophisticated interpretation of two-term rights allows for a centred-on-self conception of rights to develop, with the consequence that unjustified claims of right have become cognisable in law and 'restricted', as they must, only by appealing to the perilous idea of a *legally justified* infringement of a *legally recognised* right. The confusion disclosed by such labelling is further compounded when one observes that legislatures are endorsing such confusion of thought. For example, one reads in the reports of the UK Parliament's Joint Committee on Human Rights and associated government responses explicit evaluations whether there is 'evidence ... of the claimed necessity to interfere with the affected right', discussion of 'the extent of the Bill's interference with the right', and analysis 'whether the justifications offered by the government for that interference are good enough to command Parliament's support'.[30] In evaluating the legislative merits of extending the offence of possession of extreme pornography to include possession of pornographic images depicting rape and other non-consensual sexual penetration, the Joint Committee reported that 'the Government accepts that the offence interferes with an individual's private life

[28] *R* v. *Sharpe*, [2001] 1 SCR 45 (Supreme Court of Canada), para. 27.

[29] Ibid., para. 29 (emphasis added). This latter affirmation is qualified by the majority's willingness to exempt 'a drawing made and kept exclusively by the accused' because, in the Court's undocumented assessment, such drawings 'appear[] to pose little real risk of harm to children': para. 59.

[30] See generally Murray Hunt, Hayley Hooper, and Paul Yowell, *Parliaments and Human Rights: Redressing the Democratic Deficit* (London: AHRC Public Policy Series no. 5, 2012) 34. One of the report's authors (Murray Hunt) is Legal Advisor to the Joint Committee on Human Rights.

(Article 8 ECHR) and with his or her right to freely receive and impart information (Article 10 ECHR)'.[31] After reviewing the evidence submitted by Government and other witnesses, the Committee concluded that the new offence would constitute a '*proportionate restriction* of individual rights', even as it welcomed the new provision as a 'human rights enhancing measure'.[32] This takes us some distance from understanding the legislature as an institution devoted to protecting human rights.[33]

The received approach instructs us that the law will recognise nearly all acts as done in the name of one's legally cognisable rights, but *also* that the law will and sometimes must justifiably infringe many of those rights. Such confusion – and the resulting division between rights and the right – inheres in the willingness to divorce rights from relationships between persons. This willingness leads much rights-talk to place rights and law in opposition, the latter (unlike the former) having relationships between persons as its concern. Rights, on the received approach, situate themselves in communities of persons only by conflicting with each other and by being infringed by positive law. They are the rights of 'egoistic man', of 'an individual withdrawn into himself ... and separated from the community'.[34]

2.4 INTERLUDE: PRINCIPLES WITHOUT RIGHTS

The lack of concern for relationships between persons within the received approach is further suggested by the increasingly common appeal in the vocabulary of lawyers and judges to *one*-term rights – 'The right to *x*' – without reference either to a right-holder or to the others who are, in some way, responsible to the right-holder. The willingness of the received approach to abstract away from persons is striking. Indeed, the very term 'right' often falls from view in judgments: conflicts between rights or between rights and 'the public interest' are regularly likened to conflicts between competing 'values', 'interests', or 'principles'. Evaluations of 'interferences' with such interests, values, and principles are then liable to proceed in abstraction from persons, as captured by the following formulation by a proponent of the received approach: '[t]he greater degree of non-satisfaction of, or detriment to, one

[31] Joint Committee on Human Rights, *Legislative Scrutiny: (1) Criminal Justice and Courts Bill and (2) Deregulation Bill* (2013–14, HL 189, HC 1293) para. 1.39

[32] Ibid. at para. 1.50 (emphasis added).

[33] cf. La déclaration des droits de l'homme et du citoyen de 1789, art 2: 'Le but de toute association politique est la conservation des droits naturels et imprescriptibles de l'homme'. (*The aim of all political association is the preservation of the natural and imprescriptible rights of man.*)

[34] See Karl Marx 'On the Jewish Question' in Jeremy Waldron (ed.), *Nonsense upon Stilts: Bentham, Burke, and Marx on the Rights of Man* (London, Methuen 1987) 147:

> None of the so-called rights of man, therefore, go beyond egoistic man, beyond man as a member of civil society – that is, an individual withdrawn into himself, into the confines of his private interests and private caprice, and separated from the community ... protect selfish desires of the acquisitive individual and presuppose an inherent conflict between the independent individual and the society which constrains his freedom.

principle, the greater must be the importance of satisfying the other [*principle*]'.[35] In evaluating the satisfaction of or detriment to a 'principle' ('value', 'interest') in abstraction of persons whose rights are implicated, one is invited to speak of balance and proportion without keeping one's focus firmly on persons.

Not only is this emerging one-term grammar of rights present in the vocabulary of lawyers and judges under the received approach, it has also begun to surface in human rights instruments. In its outline of fundamental *rights*, the EU Charter of Fundamental Rights not only omits reference to right-holders in affirming some rights, it sometimes omits reference to rights themselves, such as: 'Human dignity is inviolable' and 'must be respected and protected'.[36] While it is common to find no reference to *whom* is responsible for ensuring such respect and promotion,[37] there is reason to favour the Universal Declaration's explicit focus: '*All human beings* are born free and equal in dignity and rights'. The EU Charter also affirms that 'Academic freedom shall be respected' and that 'Intellectual property shall be protected'.[38] No attempt is here made to identify either a right-holder or a duty-bearer. In appealing to principles without mentioning persons, the EU Charter overshadows the persons who, traditionally even if imperfectly, have been situated in relationship to those subject matters that are *theirs by right*.

How might this philosophical regression be addressed? To re-orient this understanding of human rights to a proper focus on persons and relationships between persons, the two following sections situate rights in communities of persons.

2.5 THREE-TERM RIGHTS: RELATIONS BETWEEN PERSONS

The modern understanding of two-term rights engages in a long-standing tendency 'to treat the specific problem [of rights] as if it were far less complex than it really is'.[39] Writing a century ago, Hohfeld lamented how this tendency to simplify rights-talk 'furnished a serious obstacle to ... clear understanding'.[40] Whereas the problem confronting Hohfeld's conceptual undertaking was the indiscriminate use of the term 'right' to cover any one (or combination) of possible relations between persons, the challenge today is that relations between persons seem not to figure much at all in prevailing understandings of human rights.

35 Robert Alexy, *A Theory of Constitutional Rights* (Oxford, Oxford University Press 2002) 102 (footnote omitted).

36 EU Charter, Art. 1.

37 Cf. Basic Law for the Federal Republic of Germany, Art. 1(1) 'Human dignity shall be inviolable. To respect and protect it shall be *the duty of all state authority*' (emphasis added).

38 EU Charter, Arts. 13, 17(2). See further Art. 37 on '[a] high level of environmental protection' and Art. 38 on 'a high level of consumer protection'.

39 Wesley Newcomb Hohfeld, *Fundamental Legal Conceptions as Applied in Judicial Reasoning: and Other Legal Essays* in Walter Wheeler Cook (ed.), (New Haven, CT, Yale University Press 1919) 26.

40 Hohfeld, *Fundamental Legal Conceptions* 26.

Which account of rights promises to promote clear understanding? That is, which account (a) situates rights as relationships between persons, (b) resists the bifurcation between the right itself and its exercise by persons acting and doing, and (c) draws attention to the multiplicity of possible acts and arrangements that will realise the various 'subject matters' identified by bills of rights? It is, I think, this: a three-term relationship between one person, one act-description, and one other person. This account of a three-term right situates the right-holder in a relationship with another and some act-description. The corresponding rights structure requires one to situate each and every claim of right in community and to concern oneself with the justice of the claim of right made on or against another person. It situates rights as relationships between persons and invites evaluation of claims of right *both* from the perspective of the right-holder *and* from the perspective of the other who is responsible, in some way, to the right-holder.

What are the various relationships between persons contemplated by this three-term understanding of rights? For Hohfeld, the answers lay *in the law* and, more precisely, in existing jural relations between persons. To be sure, Hohfeld did not merely document an existing set of happily ordered legal relationships; his great contribution was in completing the work of his predecessors in parsing out 'chameleon-hued words' – principally 'right' and to a lesser extent 'duty' – to identify four different jural relations communicated by Anglo-American law under indiscriminate labels. What is more, Hohfeld insisted on highlighting that each of the eight jural incidents he identified is defined *by* its jural correlative and *against* its jural opposite. Central to the project as a whole was Hohfeld's focus on acts and deeds (and forbearances from acting and doing) to understand the various relations labelled 'rights' by the law.

Tracking Hohfeld's schema of jural relations, it can be said that all intelligible claims of right are one or a combination of the following four *jural correlatives*, where P and Q are persons and φ is an act-description signifying an action or forbearance:

1. P has a *claim-right* that Q should φ, if and only if Q has a *duty* to P to φ.
2. P has a *liberty* relative to Q to φ, if and only if Q has *no-claim-right* ('a no-right') that P should not φ.[41]
3. P has a *power* relative to Q to φ, if and only if Q has a *liability* to have his legal position changed by P's φ-ing.
4. P has an *immunity* relative to Q's φ-ing, if and only if Q has no power (a *disability*) to change P's legal position by φ-ing.[42]

[41] For important clarifications on the relationship between liberty and duty, see Granville Williams, 'The Concept of Legal Liberty' in Robert S Summers, *Essays in Legal Philosophy* (Berkeley, CA, University of California Press 1968).

[42] See John Finnis, *Natural Law and Natural Rights* (2nd edn., Oxford, Oxford University Press 2011) 199.

Much is captured by Hohfeld's relatively simple schema of jural relations. As already highlighted, each one of the four jural correlatives is a three-term relation between two persons and an act-description. The logical connective 'if and only if' in each of the four jural relations signifies how the same situation can be described *both* from the perspective of the right-holder P *and* again from the perspective of Q who stands in a relationship to the right-holder. Neither perspective may be omitted without loss of the relationship that is constitutive of the right: no rights without persons.

At the centre of the relationship between persons is one person's *acting* and *doing* (or forbearance from acting and doing). In the case of a liberty or power, the subject matter of a right is the right-holder's own act: what the right-holder may do in the name of his or her right. In turn, where the subject matter of a right is another's act or forbearance, then the right is a claim-right (correlative to *another's duty*) or an immunity (correlative to *another's absence of power (disability)*). Hohfeld showed how *acting* and *doing* are central to understanding rights while insisting that different relationships contemplate different persons acting and doing. Such acts and deeds can be natural acts (hitting, uttering), 'acts in the law' (enacting, selling, acquiring, sentencing), or 'acts in morality' (promising, forgiving).

Consider the Universal Declaration's affirmation, at Article 19, that 'Everyone has the right to freedom of ... expression'. A specification of this declaration of right is necessary before the claim can become directive of action. To this end, a series of acts and arrangements – a combination of Hohfeldian relationships – must be selected from among more or less reasonable alternatives and authoritatively established. The complexity of that selection process belies the *singularity* of '... has the right to ...'. To take a simple example, the declaration of right could mean that I have the *liberty* to criticise my government's foreign policy in a newspaper's opinion pages (correlatively: government officials have *no-claim-right* that I not do so). This does not imply that I have the *claim-right* that the newspaper publish my opinion-editorial (correlatively: the newspaper editors have no *duty* to do so). Rather, the newspaper has the *liberty* to select its editorial content (correlatively: I have *no-claim-right* to direct such content). However, in making its editorial selection, the newspaper's liberty is conditioned by its *liability* to be sued for certain content (correlatively: a person alleging defamation has the *power* to initiate a civil action). In the course of any defamation proceedings, the newspaper may benefit from a qualified *immunity* from requests to disclose its journalistic sources (correlatively: the suing party will be *disabled* in some respects from requiring such disclosure).

This simplified matrix of relationships between me and a newspaper, me and the government, and the newspaper and a suing party revolves around the subject matter 'expression', which 'everyone' is declared to have a 'right to'. The acts and arrangements revolving around this same subject matter will be multiplied countless times over as we venture to consider the range of relationships between persons and act-descriptions in relation to official state secrets, intellectual property and copyright, commercial advertisement, election advertisement, censorship, publication bans, blasphemy and incitement to religious hatred, press regulation, criminal conspiracy, etc. and the ambitious and complex range of associated criminal and civil responsibilities. Reason will not direct singular answers to all of the choices that must be made in designating which relationships between persons should govern in our community. Thus, it does not follow that if two jurisdictions arrive at different relationships between persons in specifying human rights, one of them is necessarily wrong. The *Universal* Declaration does not mandate a *universal* understanding of the specific relationships between persons that realise human rights.

This complexity is a function of how, for each and every specification of a 'subject matter' to which 'everyone' has a 'right to', far more than three terms (P, Q, φ) require specification. The person who is in a relationship with me in satisfaction of *my* rights also has rights, as does everyone, and so I will be in a series of relationships with them all in satisfaction of *their* rights, as they will be to each other. For these reasons, one must also contemplate and provide an evaluation whether the relationships and act-descriptions just specified cohere and are consistent with the family of relationships and act-descriptions *already* existing between P and Q and P and R and Q and R and ... so that each and every one *has* rights and can *respect* the rights of others.

This interdependence of rights across the range of human activity is acknowledged by a careful reading of the Universal Declaration and European Convention. In recognition that any right-holder has rights in concert with others, it should be acknowledged by all to be unreasonable to make claims of right that are not consistent with the same claim of right being made by another (claims, for example, that my right to vote awards me two ballots to your one; that my freedom of expression allows me to say whatever I want to whomever I want whenever I want in unqualified priority to you). Extrapolating from a responsible reading of *one* right held by everyone, the conscientious reader of the Declaration and Convention will conclude that because *all* human rights are held by 'everyone', no one person's claim of right should be acknowledged if doing so would deprive others of (and so conflict with) their rights. The interdependence of rights thus suggests that no one right – no one set of relationships and act-descriptions – may be contemplated without keeping in view the full range of other relationships and acts contemplated by other rights.

Inherent in all this is Hohfeld's notion of *jural opposites*, the term by which he communicates the idea that one cannot both have and not have a claim-right, both have and not have a duty, and so forth, in relation to the same relationship and act-description. The point would seem to be a basic demand of reason, and yet the received approach's troubled discourse of *justified infringements* of rights and bifurcation between rights and their exercise appears to proceed precisely on this contradiction. Whereas jural correlatives look both ways along the *same* relationship between persons, jural opposites look at two *different* relationships from the perspective of the same person.[43] Hohfeld helps us formulate options for adoption and choice: *either* I and every member of my class of persons (voter, parent, union member) have a claim-right correlative to your duty to φ *or*, because of and correlative to your liberty not to φ, we have no-claim-right; *either* I have a power to φ correlative to your liability *or*, because of and correlative to your immunity, I have no-power (a disability) to φ.

Hohfeld is correct to remind his reader that 'some caution is necessary at this point', lest attempts at clarification achieve their opposite goal: 'for, always, when it is said that a given privilege [liberty] is the mere negation of a *duty*, what is meant, of course, is a duty having a *content or tenor precisely opposite* to that of the privilege [liberty] in question'.[44] To appeal to an example favoured by Hohfeld: your privilege (liberty) to walk across my land is the negation of your duty *not* to do so. The opposite of my claim-right that you not walk across my land is my no-right that you not do so. Hohfeld's lesson is that these jural opposites should not be mistaken for answering any number of other questions, such as the reach of my claim-right that you not cast a shadow on my land, which is not negated by the negation of your duty not to walk across my land.

By inviting precision in identifying the 'content or tenor' of one's right, the troublesome distinction relied upon by the received approach between a right *itself* and the right *as exercised* can be dispensed with. At one basic level, that distinction falters in failing to recognise that the very purpose of a right is to be exercised.[45] To suggest that one can have a right but that the right cannot be exercised is simple confusion. Either I have a liberty or power to φ or I do not; either you have a duty or disability to φ or you do not. At another, fundamental level, the distinction falters in failing to acknowledge that not every right is to be exercised by *the right-holder*. What was for Hohfeld (and is for many others) the strict meaning of the term 'right' is a claim-right correlative to *another's duty*. To speak only of *the right-holder's exercise* of his right is to risk losing from view claim-rights and immunities, both of which are correlative to *another person's* act or forbearance.

By encouraging an understanding of rights focused on relationships between persons and the central practical question 'How should I act?', the Hohfeldian understanding remedies many of the ills associated with the received approach reviewed in Section 2.3. The confused divide between a right and its exercise, a right and its justified infringement, a right and its conflict with another right, comes about because of the failure to explore how right relations involve *more than one person*. Under the received approach, other persons are acknowledged only when the 'right' is adjudicated. And yet, when human rights law-in-action finds for the claimant or defendant,

[43] This simple but important point is helpfully put in Walter Wheeler Cook, 'Hohfeld's Contributions to the Science of Law' (1919) 28 *Yale Law Journal* 721–38, 727 and 728 n. 13.

[44] Hohfeld, *Fundamental Legal Conceptions* 39.

[45] I do not here address the philosophically rich question of an 'abuse of right' by the right-holder.

it determines a three-term relationship between plaintiff and defendant. In other words: despite the pretence that you were acting in the name of your right to free expression in defaming me, my successful civil suit settles (in law and, if justified, in morality) that you were not at liberty to do so. What sense is there in insisting that you did have the liberty to defame me when you did not? Hohfeld's jural opposites make clear the options for choice that are hidden from view under the received approach.

What guides selection between such options? Hohfeld tells us, concisely but correctly, that whether one or another jural relation between persons should obtain is 'ultimately a question of *justice and policy*; and it should be considered, as such, on its merits'.[46] It is to this relationship between rights and justice – to understanding the aim of rights not only as relations between persons but more exactly as *right relations between persons* – that we now turn.

2.6 RIGHTS AND IUS: RIGHT RELATIONS BETWEEN PERSONS

The preceding sections have developed the argument that the affirmation 'Everyone has a right to ...' must be subject to a process of specification before it can become what a right must be: directive of action. Starting from the two-term formulation of rights, one must reason in a way that moves towards three-term relations between persons and actions that are constitutive of rights. What, then, guides this process of reasoning? The academic career of the word 'right', alluded to in Section 2.1, provides a compass.

The English word 'right' translates the Latin *ius* (*jus*), being the root of the words 'justice' and 'justification'. In exploring the relationship of 'right' to 'justice', one could follow HLA Hart in tracing 'right' back to Plato and Aristotle, not in the sense of 'a right', but rather in the sense of 'the "right action" or "the right thing to do"'.[47] Hart's invitation to focus on 'acting' and 'doing' is welcome and is captured, albeit less transparently, in the uses to which 'right' (*ius*) was put by Aquinas and others.[48] In this frame, the historically primary meaning of *ius* was understood as 'the just thing itself', where 'thing' signals acts, arrangements, and states of affairs, all 'subject-matters of relationships of justice'.[49] In this usage, *ius* looks to such acts, arrangements, and states of affairs and evaluates them as just, in the right, or not. One may term this the 'objective' sense of *ius*, meaning that the acts, arrangements, and states

[46] Hohfeld, *Fundamental Legal Conceptions* 43.

[47] HLA Hart, 'Bentham on Legal Rights' in AWB Simpson (ed.), *Oxford Essays in Jurisprudence, Second Series* (Oxford, Clarendon Press 1973) 172.

[48] This account draws on Finnis, *Natural Law and Natural Rights* 206–10, 423–4, 465–6; John Finnis, *Aquinas: Moral, Political, and Legal Theory* (Oxford, Oxford University Press 1998) 133–8; John Finnis, 'Aquinas on *ius* and Hart on Rights' (2002) 64 *Review of Politics* 407; and John Tasioulas, 'Justice, Equality, and Rights' in Roger Crisp (ed.), *The Oxford Handbook of the History of Ethics* (Oxford, Oxford University Press 2013).

[49] Finnis, *Natural Law and Natural Rights* 206.

of affairs, with all of their contemplated and actualised interpersonal actions and forbearances, are 'themselves' right, as signalled by our modern language's expressions: 'the right decision', 'the right action', 'it is right that this be done'.

In usage over time, *ius* (is said to have) developed a second, now prevailing meaning: in alleged contrast to the 'objective' meaning, a second 'subjective' meaning refers to a right that someone (the subject) has. Here, *ius* is possessed by a person rather than attributed to a state of affairs, as captured by our modern language's recourse to the formulation: 'Everyone *has* the right to ...'. The qualification in this paragraph's opening sentence alludes to debates in academic circles questioning the extent to which these two meanings of *ius* can be neatly divorced, for reasons we will come to momentarily. Presently, it is important to note that some suggest that within *ius* lie two meanings, with one or the other favoured at different times in the history of ideas: first, an 'objective' evaluation of a state of affairs as just, 'in the right', and, second, a 'subjective' right which a 'subject' has, such as a claim against another's duty or a liberty from the claims of another.

Without doubt, there is reason to attend to the difference in usage between these two meanings of *ius*. The second meaning situates *ius* explicitly 'in the hands' of persons and provides a perspective (that of the right-holder) for evaluating states of affairs. It relates Aquinas's primary meaning of 'objective' *ius* 'exclusively to the beneficiary of the just relationship'.[50] In so doing, it provides for a way of expressing justice from the viewpoint of a single individual. Now, without discounting the importance of the differences between the 'objective' and 'subjective' meanings of *ius*, one will be led astray if one seeks to conclude too much from such differences, for example by suggesting that the 'subjective' sense focuses on persons whereas the 'objective' sense focuses on states of affairs. For what are the states of affairs that justice concerns itself with if not those implicating persons? Such states of affairs all revolve around relationships between persons and the interpersonal actions and forbearances provided for by different acts and arrangements that can be said to be ('objectively') *just* or *right* or not. It should therefore come as no great surprise that one can find in Aquinas's use of his primary meaning of *ius* traces of the second meaning, '[f]or *what is just* is what the virtue of justice requires the relevant person(s) to give to, or do for, or abstain from in relation to, someone else'.[51] In this frame, appeals to the modern usage of 'right' should not lose sight of the historically first meaning of the term, without which its conclusive and peremptory appeal is ungrounded. While attending to the special perspective of the beneficiary of a just relationship, one should keep in view the other who, together with the right-holder, constitutes that relationship.[52] Of course, one will appeal to a different vocabulary

[50] Ibid. 207 (emphasis omitted).

[51] Finnis, *Aquinas* 135 (emphasis in original).

[52] See Brian Tierney, *The Idea of Natural Rights* (Grand Rapids, MI, William B Eerdmans Publishing 1997) 70: 'the first rights theories were not derived from contemplation of the individual isolated from his fellows ... but from reflection on the right ordering of human relationships in emerging societies'.

to communicate the just relationship from the perspective of the other: duty, no-claim-right, liability, disability. But, as Roman legal thought well understood, 'one party's "part" in such an assignment might be a burden, not a benefit' and, notwithstanding this, nevertheless be labelled their *ius*.[53] Why? Precisely because evaluations of what is right ('in the right') look both ways along a relationship between persons. Even if it sounds foreign to present-day ears to affirm that the satisfaction of my debt to you is *my* right, no such discomfort accompanies the near equivalent affirmation that the satisfaction of my debt to you *is* right.

The subjective sense of *ius* will lead us astray if it is deployed without holding firmly in view the other who, together with the right-holder, constitutes the right relationship, even if that relationship is expressed with special reference to he or she who *has the right*. But this 'having', though expressed from the point of view of the right-holder, is 'held' in concert with the other who is in a relationship with the right-holder. On this account, there is no strong difference between the first ('objective') and second ('subjective') meanings of *ius*; indeed the two senses can converge: 'what justice is about, and what doing justice secures, is the *right* of some other person or persons – what is due to them, what they are entitled to, what is rightfully theirs'.[54]

The willingness to situate evaluations of justice from the first-person perspective is a welcome development, but one must guard against a possible tendency (observable within the received approach to human rights) to understand rights as that which benefits someone, *without more*. Indeed, while *ius* may properly be said to be related to the beneficiary of the just relationship (the right-holder), there is a danger – not present in the 'objective' sense of *ius* – to confuse all that is beneficial to a person as that person's right(s). The enduring importance of the historically primary meaning of *ius* is in its appeal to the perspectives of *all persons* affected by a state of affairs, for the evaluation that something is just holds only if it is true for all persons, even if the immediate state of affairs does not benefit all of them immediately or equally. If one loses perspective on the close relationship between the older and newer usages of *ius*, one risks employing rights in a way that renders them unable to express the requirements of justice in a community of persons. And in so doing, one risks abandoning the inter-definability of right(s) and justice traced from Roman jurists up to the drafters of the Universal Declaration on Human Rights. What is more, one risks underplaying the strength of rights, a strength that draws not only on

[53] Finnis, *NLNR* 209. See also Finnis, *Aquinas* 133–4: 'But Roman law, and still, vestigially, the language of Aquinas' time, accepted that a liability might also be a *ius*; to be given the appropriate penalty is a malefactor's *ius*' (footnote omitted). Analogously, see Barry Nichols, *An Introduction to Roman Law* (Oxford, Clarendon Press 1975) 158 (second emphasis added): 'The term *obligatio* denotes sometimes the right, sometimes the duty, but more properly it denotes *the whole relationship*'.

[54] Finnis is here paraphrasing Aquinas's *S.T.* II-II q. 58. See *Aquinas* 133. Finnis adds that Aquinas uses the formulae 'what is theirs' and 'what is their right' interchangeably.

the benefit the rights secure for the rights-holders, but also on the benefit the rights secure for all others.[55]

2.7 REASON AND CHOICE

The process of practical reasoning to specify the relationships between persons that will give to each and everyone what is theirs by right is both straightforward and not. As explored by Maris Köpcke in the following chapter, it confronts all of the complexities and challenges of setting out terms of collaboration and co-ordination between persons, some of whom will do right by their fellow community members and accept the burdens reciprocal to the benefits of their relations, while others will seek out only benefits and attempt to avoid all burdens. Adding to this complexity is the requirement that the series of right relations between persons be harmonious, such that one's rights co-exist (are not in conflict) with one's responsibilities as well as with the rights and responsibilities of each and every other member of the community. The process of practical reasoning will be guided and occasionally determined by deductions from what reason requires of persons in community; it will otherwise be guided but underdetermined by reason. Practical reason alone will not determine the whole of what human rights require.

Despite standing as imperfect (because incomplete) specifications of human rights, the Universal Declaration and European Convention sketch out some of the considerations that ought to be alive in the mind of each person who engages in the process of practical reasoning to specify the relationships between persons that realise rights in community. The various subject matters of justice regularly included in such instruments – life, liberty, security, culture, equality, expression, conscience, etc. – sketch out aspects of human goods and needs shared by 'everyone' and for whom right relations between persons are to be established. Bills of rights by no means exhaust the range of subject matters of concern to right relations. Draftsmen sometimes explicitly acknowledge as much either by affirming other 'just requirements' in a free and democratic society (e.g. morality, public order and the general welfare) or by affirming that the declaration of 'certain rights and freedoms shall not be construed as denying the existence of any other rights or freedoms'.[56]

A community (principally: those who have the authority and so responsibility to govern the community) confronts choice in many, but not all aspects of establishing right relations between persons. In some instances, acts, arrangements, and states of affairs stand to the subject matters of justice in community as a reasoned deduction. For example, the affirmation that 'Everyone has the right to life' directs one

[55] See Joseph Raz, 'Rights and Individual WellBeing' in *Ethics in the Public Domain: Essays in the Morality of Law and Politics* (revd edn, Oxford, Clarendon Press 1994) 55: 'part of the justifying reason for the right is its contribution to the common good'.

[56] See e.g. Canadian Charter of Rights and Freedoms, s. 26.

to conclude that genocide and the intentional killing of innocent persons really are inconsistent with right relations between persons oriented around the subject matter 'life'. The criminal law's prohibition of murder stands to the Universal Declaration's and European Convention's affirmation of 'life' as a conclusion deduced from the subject matter, which is itself indebted to the moral status of life as a good and need that 'everyone' shares and participates in ('has a right to'). Framed negatively: it would be unreasonable to conclude that right relations between persons around the subject matter of 'life' are consistent with the intentional killing of innocents. So, too, with the right to security of the person and criminal and tort prohibitions against rape, assault, and battery.

Specifications determined by reason are possible for other two-term affirmations of rights common to the subject matters of bills of rights. However, as further demonstrated in Chapter 5 by Paul Yowell, the greater part of the specification of three-term rights do not stand to the corresponding two-term declaration of rights as straightforward deductions, even when practical reasoning directs one most of the way. Even in those cases where the legislature can be understood unwaveringly to track the requirements of morality, legislation must realise those requirements in the technical language of the law. Legislative draftsmen do not ordinarily draft laws as moral injunctions: 'Do not kill or assault the innocent'. Even in the case of a straightforward deduction, translating the requirements of reason into positive law will require recourse to 'language coherent with the language of other parts of the law', language which seeks the artificial clarity and definiteness of the Rule of Law.[57]

The greater part of a community's positive settlement of right relations between persons will confront true choice, where conformity to practical reason will leave matters open for evaluation and decision. In Aquinas's account, a community's laws will relate to various subject matters of justice as *determinationes*, that is, as 'specifications and delimitations which when reasonable could nonetheless reasonably have been different, in some or many respects'.[58] What is the notion of *determinatio*? It is an 'intellectual process which is *not deductive* and does involve free choice … and yet is intelligent and directed [but not concluded] by reason'.[59] It obtains in practical reasoning when there are alternatives for choosing: where reason, having eliminated countless 'alternatives' as not-really-live because inconsistent with reason or inferior in all relevant respects to one or more other alternatives, nevertheless maintains multiple candidates for choosing. In such circumstances, the choice is guided but underdetermined by reason. One's choice – truly free choice – is in compliance with the requirements of reason, because each one of the alternatives

57 Finnis, *Natural Law and Natural Rights* 284. See further Grégoire Webber, 'Rights and the Rule of Law in the Balance' (2013) 129 *Law Quarterly Review* 399.

58 John Finnis, 'Introduction' in *Human Rights and Common Good: Collected Essays* (Oxford, Oxford University Press 2011) 3.

59 John Finnis, 'Critical Legal Studies' in *Philosophy of Law: Collected Essays, volume IV* (Oxford, Oxford University Press 2011) 301 (emphasis added). See also S.T. I-II q 95 a 2.

is supported by reasons that are not defeated *even if* no one alternative is supported by reasons that defeat all others. To appeal to the well-rehearsed example: given the need to secure the safe and efficient transport of persons and goods, there is need to decide which side of the road to travel even if there is no basis in reason (absent standing customary practice or other contingencies) to choose left or right. The example is especially telling because it identifies a scenario where choosing from among unranked reasonable alternatives is not a matter of optional advantage, but itself required: *not* choosing is an unreasonable alternative. A policy of *laissez-faire* is inferior to all driving on the left or all driving on the right, even if neither left nor right is superior to the other. Beyond requiring that a choice be made, reason does not identify which choice is to be made.

In the light of this process of specification guided but left open by reason, one appreciates why it was eminently reasonable for the drafters of the Universal Declaration to affirm rights without specifying which acts, arrangements, and states of affairs are to be selected to realise the various subject matters outlined in the Declaration. Recall that in 1948, the various communities of the world were *already situated* with positive regulation; there was no 'blank slate' from which to proceed. Without doubt, many instances of positive regulation were then, as many are now, unjust – in violation of the requirements of right relations between persons because adopted from among the not-live 'alternatives' confronting reasonable choice. But this did not warrant ranking the variously different and available (and imaginable) 'live' alternatives present in different communities (and in the minds of the drafters).

There are many ways to specify public health regulations to realise the 'right to life', the regulation of elections to realise the 'right to vote', parental and spousal duties to realise the 'right to family life', and so on. In selecting from among incompatible but live alternatives, there is 'no alternative but to hold in one's mind's eye some pattern, or range of patterns, of human character, conduct, and interaction in community, and then to choose such specification of rights as tends to favour that pattern, or range of patterns'.[60] The choice made is free, but – critically – this free choice is also *formative* because, in making it, one steps 'into a new world', a world now shaped by a choice that could reasonably have been different. The selected range of patterns that guides the specification of this and that right in this rather than another reasonable way now guides, as a requirement of reason, future choices. Why? Because a community's system of rights is to stand together coherently, with integrity and harmony, to 'speak with one voice', and to allow each and every member of the community to respect the rights of each and every other. In this way, a choice underdetermined by reason, once made, *stands* and *lasts*. It must stand and last if it is to yield the benefits of choice, of having decided this rather than that or no way forward. So, in making this choice, one has stepped into a world now shaped

[60] Finnis, *Natural Law and Natural Rights* 219.

by that choice even if the choice can be revisited. The process of *determinatio* for specifying other rights is henceforth less open. In next evaluating the range of live alternatives for evaluation and choice, one will reasonably rank some (even if not all) of the options as *more or less* in keeping with existing specifications of rights. The narrowing of options will also open up of new possibilities, including possibilities unavailable before the community was one where the common good and human rights were secured because specified by positive law.

None of this suggests that one cannot stand in a critical relationship to existing specifications and conclude that they do not establish *right* relations between persons and should be changed. Nevertheless, a community's patterns of human character, conduct, and interaction will and should warrant a place as guides to reasonable selection in the process of *determinatio*. Recall that in determining any one right relationship between persons centred on some action or forbearance, one must evaluate whether the relationship and act-descriptions being specified are consistent and cohere with the family of *already* existing relationships and act-descriptions. Each settlement by free choice of the specification of a right makes one's community different from the community-that-was prior to the choice. For, once made, the community becomes one that has made *that* choice rather than *another* and, having made that choice, the community now has reason to follow it up with other choices that will be less free because guided by the one just made. This idea is well captured in saying that what is settled by *determinatio* 'partly *reflect[s]* reasons, and partly *create[s]* new ones'.[61]

2.8 RIGHTS IN LAW

The discussion thus far has not maintained a firm distinction between rights in law (legal rights) and human (natural) rights. In this way, the discussion has tracked the ambiguity in the expression 'human rights law'. This ambiguity is welcome, perhaps inevitable.[62] Although it is rightly said that rights are superior to law in that legal authority and obligation fail insofar as they violate rights, the matter is more complex insofar as many human rights require law for their realisation. This relationship

[61] Maris Köpcke-Tinturé, 'Positive Law's Moral Purpose(s): Towards a New Consensus?' (2011) 56 *American Journal of Jurisprudence* 183, 191 (emphasis in original).

[62] For HLA Hart's views on this relationship, see 'Are There Any Natural Rights?' in Jeremy Waldron (ed.), *Theories of Rights* (Oxford, Oxford University Press 1984) 79: 'There is of course no simple identification to be made between moral and legal rights, but there is an intimate connection between the two' and HLA Hart, 'Natural Rights: Bentham and John Stuart Mill' in *Essays on Bentham: Studies in Jurisprudence and Political Theory* (Oxford, Clarendon Press 1982) 92: 'It is plain that an acceptable analysis of moral rights must be such as to allow sense though not necessarily truth to the statement that the existence of such a right is a good moral reason for having and maintaining a law or social convention conferring a [legal or conventional] right.'

of rights to positive law is disclosed by a careful reading of the Universal Declaration on Human Rights.

At one level, the class of persons ('Everyone ...', 'All ...', 'No one ...') to which the Declaration refers is no less universal a class than '[a]ll human persons' and 'all members of the human family', for we are all 'born free and equal in dignity and rights'.[63] In this frame, positive law is subordinate to our universal moral membership in the human family. However, the Declaration also frequently invokes that smaller class of persons: those *within my political community*. It does so with references to (domestic) 'law', 'tribunals',[64] and 'government',[65] and variously to 'the state', 'one's country', 'society', and 'the community'.[66] The necessity of the political community and its law, tribunals, and government does not overshadow the priority of the human person and our membership in the human family, but it does emphasise the special *need for law* to realise the rights that each and all have. There is a positive duty on the law-maker to instantiate and realise rights in community, a special responsibility that grounds the law-maker's authority. Thus, while law is properly measured against the requirements of human rights, it is also the case that, in the words of the Universal Declaration, 'human rights should be protected by the rule of law'.[67]

In the absence of law's determination of *this* rather than *that* state of affairs and *this* rather than *that* family of relationships, a community of persons has no authoritative determination of which state of affairs and which family of relations shall obtain where reason itself guides but does not determine choice. Without doubt, many legal acts, arrangements, and states of affairs establish *wrong* relations between persons. However, this does not detract from the truth that, absent a set of acts or arrangements, many rights in community would be unrealised because no one would be *given* what is his or hers by right and violations of the rights of the weak by the strong would go uncorrected in justice.

In analysing the exaggerated opposition between rights and law in Section 2.3, I appealed to how the English term 'law' is expressed in other languages in a way that signals the relationship between right(s) and law. The French, Spanish, Italian, and German vocabularies all signal how the corpus of legal rules, even if with many failings, aspires to the right, the just; that is, aspires to respect and comply with, *by authoritatively establishing*, everyone's rights. In this frame, it is no surprise to discover that the same Latin root *ius* also gives us the lawyer's terms 'jurist', 'juridical', and 'jurisprudence'. Law can achieve justice in community more authoritatively

63 Universal Declaration, Art. 1, preamble.

64 Universal Declaration, Arts. 6, 7, 8, 10, 11, 12, 29.

65 Universal Declaration, Art. 21.

66 Universal Declaration, Arts. 12, 13, 14, 15, 16, 18, 19, 27, 28, 29, 30.

67 Universal Declaration, preamble. The preamble qualifies this affirmation with: 'if man is not to be compelled to have recourse, as a last resort, to rebellion against tyranny and oppression'. The qualification is too narrow.

and more perfectly than custom, practice, or other possible sources of rules setting out relations between persons. Law can perfect the appeal to the universal by establishing right relations not only between individuals but, critically, between classes of persons. HLA Hart reminds us that law 'must predominantly, but by no means exclusively, refer to *classes* of person, and to *classes* of acts, things, and circumstances'.[68] For Hart, such need was a function of the inability, in 'any large group', to provide 'particular directions' to individuals separately.[69] But the need can be related more generally to law's distinctive ability to ensure that 'everyone' and 'all members of the human family' within our self-governing community are 'entitled to all the rights and freedoms ... without distinction of any kind'.[70]

Where are the rights in law that perfect right relations between persons? There is no need to repeat the reasons for concluding that they are not to be found in bills of rights modelled on the Universal Declaration or the European Convention. One stays on the right path in following Hohfeld, whose juristic analysis of rights-talk invited us to study tort and contract and property, among other fields of law. The common law and the civil law traditions refer to these fields of law as the law of obligations (synonymously, the law of duties) and not as the law of rights. However, Hohfeld's lesson reminds us that everything in law can be seen from the point of view of two persons in a relationship, so that what is one person's duty is another person's right.[71] So: your duty under tort and criminal law to refrain from assaulting me is correlative to my claim-right that you not assault me, and your duty is qualified by your liberty and my no-right in cases of self-defence, etc. Your obligation under contract to perform the terms of our agreement is correlative to my claim-right that you perform those terms of agreement, and your obligation is qualified by my power to relieve you and by the law respecting abusive terms of contract, *force majeure*, etc. Your duties under property law not to trespass are correlative to my claim-right that you not trespass on my land, as qualified by public rights-of-way and the like. Although the vocabulary of duty and obligation is often preferred in the law to the vocabulary of right, it is nonetheless intelligible to affirm that human rights law is not a special category of positive law, but rather inherent to all reasonable positive law. The law of obligations, on this account, is the law of rights.

Now, there is good reason why the law treats the concept of duty as having 'a more strategic explanatory role than the concept of rights'.[72] Hohfeld's jural correlatives can (almost) all neatly be oriented around (but not reduced to) the concept of duty: (a) as

[68] HLA Hart, *The Concept of Law* (2nd edn, Oxford, Oxford University Press 1994) 124. Hart thought that 'in the bare notion of applying a general rule of law [we have] the germ at least of justice': 206.

[69] Hart, *Concept of Law* 124.

[70] Universal Declaration, Art. 2.

[71] I take no side in the debate between the 'will' vs. 'interest' theories of rights on the directionality of duties. For an overview, see Matthew H Kramer, Nigel E Simmonds, and Hillel Steiner, *A Debate Over Rights: Philosophical Enquiries* (Oxford, Oxford University Press 1998).

[72] Finnis, *Natural Law and Natural Rights* 210.

correlative to one's claim-right (claim-right/duty), (b) as the absence of duty (liberty/no-right), (c) as the authority to establish new duties or extinguish existing duties (power/liability), and (d) as protected from the authority of another to create or extinguish duties (immunity/disability). But the point is even more fundamental. For duties correlative to claim-rights must in near all instances be *associated with* or *attributed to* the other three Hohfeldian relationships so as to secure and maintain right relations between persons. Thus, a Hohfeldian liberty correlative to another's no-right will, in many instances of that relationship, be supported by what Hart helpfully termed a 'protective perimeter': duties of non-interference by others owed to the liberty-holder.[73] Also: a Hohfeldian power will be promoted and effected by the 'duty of officials and others to recognize and effectuate one's acts-in-the-law', just as a Hohfeldian immunity will be 'protected by a similar duty of officials and others not to recognize another's juridical acts as it purportedly bears on my position'.[74] The law of obligations helps situate rights in the family of standing legal relations that support them.

2.9 CONCLUSION

Law is needed to specify rights. This idea has been introduced and partially defended in this chapter, but it receives thoroughgoing analysis by Maris Köpcke in the next chapter. Together, our chapters help frame the argument that the legislature has primary responsibility to the community to think and act in law. This responsibility includes legislating with full awareness of the existing set of right relationships between persons established in law and custom, and a commitment to harmony within the corpus of legal materials and the acts and deeds and forbearances they require of each and every member of the community. To be sure, legislatures and courts share in the on-going plan for setting out right relations between persons in the community. But the legislature bears the first responsibility to settle which among the near countless possible meanings contemplated by the two-term declarations of rights found in bills of rights is to be *the* meaning for *this* community. Legislation perfects the artificial clarity and univocality that the law seeks to achieve by seeking to answer *both* the question 'is this my right?' *and* the question 'can I act on my right?' with the *same answer* because, as legislation specifying right relations between persons makes clear, they are both the same question. This action-directing quality of justified positive law is at the core of the law's claim on my conscience when contemplating the practical question: How should I act?

[73] HLA Hart, 'Legal Rights' in *Essays on Bentham: Studies in Jurisprudence and Political Theory* (Oxford, Clarendon Press 1982) 173. Hart adds, 'it is not at all clear that lawyers or anyone else would speak of a completely naked or unprotected liberty as a right, or that any useful purpose would be served if they did'.

[74] John Finnis, 'Natural Law: The Classical Tradition' in Jules L Coleman, Kenneth Einar Himma, and Scott J Shapiro (eds.), *The Oxford Handbook of Jurisprudence and Philosophy of Law* (Oxford, Oxford University Press 2004) 24.

3

Why It Takes Law to Realise Human Rights

Maris Köpcke

3.1 INTRODUCTION

The previous chapter has argued that only rights specified into three-term relations – identifying *who* is (not) to do *what* in relation to *whom* – are directive of action and thus rights properly so called. For duly specified rights shape the kind of right relations between persons which must hold if a community is to realise justice, to give everyone what is theirs by right. Rights can only be realised if they are specified. And it takes law properly to carry out the process of *determinatio*, of specification of rights. It takes law to realise human rights.

This final proposition might well strike some as perplexing. It is implicit in rights declarations, as the previous chapter has shown, although it is at best insufficiently articulated by the literature on human rights, which presents (two-term) 'rights' as being amenable to justified infringement by law. Indeed, the proposition is by no means self-evident. How can it take a legal system – a community-specific, complex set of changing arrangements – to realise requirements of justice that hold universally and prior to any such social arrangements? Consider what this proposition entails. It entails that a legal decision such as a legislative enactment or a judicial resolution can render it the case that somebody is morally entitled (has a right) to something she would have otherwise not have been entitled to. And, correlatively, that another person is subject to a moral duty that would otherwise not have been incumbent upon him. Law is made and unmade and, in so being made and unmade, the proposition holds, law can alter our moral positions. And not only *can* law alter our moral positions, but in many ways it is the irreplaceable tool with which to do so, for justice's sake.

This chapter provides an argument in support of the above proposition. Sections 3.2 and 3.3 unpack the idea of specification of rights by showing that it involves generating what will be called specific convergence – that is, collective convergent conduct following specific patterns settled through rationally underdetermined choice. In countless respects, as Section 3.4 shows, only conduct integrated in an appropriate scheme of specific convergence can make a genuinely apt contribution to realising justice and rights in the community, and in that sense become morally necessary and obligatory conduct, due to somebody else by right. Section 3.5 goes on to explain what it takes to generate specific convergence in large diverse human communities, namely publicly marking and fairly enforcing the conduct due; and Sections 3.6 to 3.8, in turn, demonstrate why a system of positive law is a privileged tool for this purpose. These latter sections, respectively, spell out how central features of a system of positive law are ideally suited to help a community create and sustain (i) widely salient, (ii) dynamic, and (iii) systemically coherent schemes of specific convergence, and so allow a community to transform the human rights of the Universal Declaration, European Convention, and like instruments into truly action-guiding, practical, and ultimately actionable claims of right that take their place in a legally scripted network of just relations between persons.

3.2 SPECIFYING RIGHTS: A CLOSER LOOK

Exactly what is involved in *specifying a right*? The starting point of an answer is to recall the reason why we look to rights as things to be specified and realised in the first place. Human rights identify morally valuable aspects of human wellbeing, such as life, liberty, health, expression, or personal security – aspects which, to be protected and furthered, require in various ways the cooperation of other persons, whether through acts or abstentions.[1] We all have reason to contribute to furthering the wellbeing of others. But sometimes our reason to do so is of a particularly strong kind, namely a *duty* – a duty to undertake specific conduct for the sake of somebody else's wellbeing. Where that is so, the person whose wellbeing is at stake has a corresponding *right*, a genuine, specified, three-term right. The existence of a specified right entails the existence of a duty. In an important sense, therefore, it is true to say that what it takes to specify human rights is precisely what it takes to transform our generic, context-dependent and defeasible reasons to advance other people's wellbeing into specific, and thus action-guiding, moral duties.

A moral duty or obligation[2] is helpfully understood in terms of the *necessity*, given certain facts, to undertake determinate conduct as a means to a morally valuable end.[3] Morally obligatory conduct is not merely desirable but necessary all things considered – and the things to be considered include the moral importance of the end, the conduct's effectiveness as means to this end, available alternative means,

[1] This chapter will not discuss duties towards oneself and their possible relevance to justice in community.

[2] Throughout the text, the terms 'obligation' and 'duty' are treated as coextensive (likewise 'due', 'owed', 'obligatory', etc.).

[3] John Finnis, *Natural Law and Natural Rights* (2nd edn, Oxford, Oxford University Press 2011) 307.

and side-effects and associated costs to the individual and others.[4] Some very fundamental moral duties hold in all times and places, as they can be discerned using right reason alone without the need for specification through social arrangements. Such is, for example, our duty not to intentionally kill or injure another person without justification, or our duty to perform an 'easy rescue' by taking a proportionate step that is primarily in our own hands. These kinds of abstentions or acts are always necessary means, all things considered, to preserve the life or health of others. But adequately protecting and advancing human wellbeing further requires manifold forms of conduct the description of which cannot be similarly 'deduced' from a general reflection on human needs.

Consider a person's health, a crucial aspect of a person's wellbeing, captured by Article 25 of the Universal Declaration and closely related to other rights such as the rights to life, liberty, and personal security. In order to protect a person's health, it is not sufficient (though it is necessary) that others refrain from intentionally causing that person unjustified injury or that they single-handedly perform an 'easy rescue' when, if ever, an opportunity arises. Health can likewise be impaired by accidental injury, inadequate food quality or intake, water and air pollution, or the consumption of harmful drugs. Impaired health may, in turn, further call for professional treatment, medication, and various other forms of assistance and facilities. We all have reason not to impair, and to improve, the health of others. But this insight alone will in many contexts not yield a conclusion concerning which *concrete* form of conduct, if any, one ought to undertake, say, to avoid accidentally injuring others or to help them get medical assistance. And not just any kind of concretisation will do, as not any kind of concretisation will establish a means distinctly suited to advance those ends. Were a well-off person to resolve, for his own part, to hand exactly 10 percent of his annual income to a randomly chosen homeless person 'for medicines', he would probably not, through this concrete action, significantly assist even the health of the receiver, who might buy the wrong drugs given the lack of medical guidance, get robbed, have pretended to be homeless, or waste the resources – and who may in fact have a lesser need for medical care than others who remain unassisted. *Specification* of rights involves more than identifying *specific*, concrete tasks as due from someone and to someone else.

Contributions towards the medical care of the least well-off can become especially fit for purpose in being part of a more general – collective – pattern of convergent conduct, involving many contributors and beneficiaries organised according

4 See further Timothy Endicott, 'The Infant in the Snow' in Timothy Endicott, Joshua Getzler, and Edwin Peel (eds.), *Properties of Law: Essays in Honour of Jim Harris* (Oxford, Oxford University Press 2006) 358, 363 on how human rights and correlative duties (particularly on welfare matters) are 'conditional' on capacity, circumstances, and need; and John Tasioulas, 'On the Foundations of Human Rights' in Rowan Cruft, Matthew Liao and Massimo Renzo (eds.), *Philosophical Foundations of Human Rights* (Oxford, Oxford University Press, 2015) 51, 56–61, disaggregating several factors speaking to practical necessity (duty).

to reasonable means- and need-relative rates, with centralised mechanisms to collect, manage and distribute the aid and monitor its use in connection with medical advice, coupled with checks and guarantees against various forms of fraud and defection. Such a model resembles the national health insurance systems of some countries. A well-functioning redistribution scheme is liable to render any individual contribution a particularly apt and available means to promote the health of needy persons, and thus a morally obligatory action – and, consequently, to bestow on needy persons moral rights to specific forms of assistance that will realise (an aspect of) their 'right to health'. Note that, under such a scheme, our original contributor's share might well amount to precisely 10 percent of his annual income (collected, perhaps, through a combination of income tax and employees' national insurance deductions). What makes a decisive moral difference is the presence of a collective redistribution scheme, of which the individual contribution is part.

We find a similar predicament in other everyday contexts, for example traffic regulations, which (if sound) specify another crucial aspect of the right to health. Even in the absence of traffic regulations, drivers would be morally obligated not to, for example, intentionally run over other persons. But in an environment of many moving vehicles and multiple intersections, drivers will acquire new, specific duties to the extent that their community takes steps, as it should, to reduce the incidence of accidental or negligent injuries by setting speed limits for particular road sections, requiring driving licenses conditional on skills testing, establishing crossings and traffic lights, etc. Of course, the existence of such new duties (and correlative new rights of other drivers and pedestrians) presupposes that the relevant traffic regulations are indeed collectively followed and expected to be. If drivers did not generally stop at red, any given driver would have little reason to do so and, in heavy traffic, strong reason *not* to. While a driver's duty not to intentionally run others over holds regardless of what other drivers do, the duty to stop at red, like so many traffic duties, only holds against the background of a relevant kind of collective, convergent conduct.

We can extract from the preceding reflections a preliminary sense of what is involved in specifying rights. In the above scenarios where new, specified duties (and rights) arise, the conduct due has the following features: it (i) is part of a *collective* scheme, (ii) is *specific* to the point that it could have reasonably been different, and (iii) is to occur in a context of *actual* behavioural convergence. Let us briefly dwell on each of these features.

First, the collective nature of a scheme of resource pooling or traffic order contributes to its effectiveness – so long, that is, as the reach of the scheme does not exceed a manageable size which in practice tends to coincide, for a number of reasons, with that of membership in a political community. Relatedly, the collective nature of the scheme also enhances its fairness. The fact that the relevant conduct is due from all those members of a political community who are in a comparable position to contribute and have like reason to do so (all those similarly well-off, say, or all drivers) reflects their moral equality and by the same token fortifies the moral reason they each individually have to do their part. Additional, crucial fortification of their moral reason to contribute will be provided by adequate monitoring and checks against defection or fraud, rendered possible by extending the collective reach of the scheme in a yet further sense, namely to encompass the ancillary tasks of persons in roles such as health officers, tax inspectors, traffic police, or licensing agents. Finally, as the very existence of such oversight tasks partly presupposes, a good scheme of resource pooling or traffic will be synchronised (including by sharing of information) with numerous other realms of the community's collective life, such as revenue collection, welfare services, immigration control, and liability insurance – not to mention the protection of the relevant interests, including financial and property interests, of tax payers and car users, as an essential counterpart to their demanded contribution, which it both enables and goes to justify as an exercise of fair play.

Second, assigning intelligible tasks to such a multitude of persons in different roles calls for a significant level of precision, of *specificity*, in the task-descriptions – more detail than, at most junctures, right reason alone can yield. Right reason might well underdetermine, for instance, the exact distribution of tax bands, the financial (and other) eligibility criteria for each kind of health service, the calibration of speed limits, the frequency of license renewals and the quantum and scaling of fines. But in the absence of reasonably precise determinations, in many cases of a numerical kind, the relevant enterprises will hardly be workable, let alone fair, because lacking in Rule of Law virtues that would enable participants reliably to plan and enable checks and correctives to be applied impartially and consistently.

The design of (i) collective schemes of conduct made up of (ii) specific tasks is still not enough to specify the right to health. Our original contributor, instead of handing over the cash, might have masterminded a detailed and sound community-wide redistribution scheme under which his contribution amounted to precisely 10 percent of his income. But unless that scheme was the one actually adopted and generally followed by his fellow community members, to the exclusion of alternative schemes, he might have no more reason to contribute than under his original plan. Only by figuring in (iii) an *actual* pattern of specific convergent conduct is one's contribution in the above contexts genuinely apt to serve as a means to protecting the health of others – a point mostly implicit in the discussion so far but that bears bringing out. For it highlights that specifying human rights is not just a matter of 'working out the specifics', of scripting a network of relations between persons. It is, in many ways, a matter of attaining what will henceforth be called *specific convergence*. It is primarily specific convergence that specifies and realises rights.

The next section explains the idea of specific convergence, and Section 3.4 shows that it is needed across the board, rather than just in isolated contexts, in order to realise justice in a political community.

3.3 SPECIFIC CONVERGENCE

The need for specific convergence arises where some state of affairs required by justice can most effectively and fairly be brought about through the convergent conduct of a large number of persons, and that conduct could in principle follow any one of several available and appropriate but incompatible patterns. The underlying means-ends relation can be formalised as follows:

E (End): As a matter of justice, some state of affairs concerning human wellbeing needs to be brought about.

M (Means):

M1. The state of affairs can effectively and fairly be brought about only through convergent conduct of a large number of persons.

M2. The convergent conduct could in principle follow any one of several available and appropriate but incompatible patterns.

A few comments on each leg. The 'state of affairs' referred to in *E* can involve either the presence of something good, i.e. conducive to wellbeing, or the absence of something bad, i.e. detrimental to wellbeing. Indeed, often one and the same situation can be construed either way (e.g. maintaining health entails preventing illness and injury). Accordingly, the reference to 'bringing about' must likewise be understood broadly, to include preserving, creating, changing, preventing, forestalling, etc., as the case may be.

The means, as *M1* captures, must be not only collective by design but also collective in *actual fact*: convergent conduct must occur. The idea of convergence further stresses two crucial points that will be central to this chapter's argument. First, the conduct of the relevant people need not be identical: it needs to converge, but it is not necessary that it coincide in every particular. In fact, few meaningful enterprises can be sustained by identical conduct on the part of the persons constituting the collective. Even military marches have their leaders and musicians. Our above examples have charted how protecting (some aspects of) personal health takes complex combinations of different kinds of acts, abstentions, dispositions, and expectations. Public healthcare for the needy requires that taxpayers make contributions (not identical but income-relative), that qualifying persons receive assistance (not identical but condition- and means-relative), that non-qualifying persons are refused assistance, that expenses are monitored, and so on. A single set of traffic lights directs drivers and pedestrians to perform more or less the opposite kinds of conduct: some proceeding on their way while others stop, and vice versa. It might be thought that, in the case of wrongful acts that should be avoided by all, justice *does* call for identical collective conduct – in the form of simultaneous universal abstention. However, attaining a state of affairs that comes anywhere near such collective abstention, in a large human community, and doing so fairly, will call for intricate tasks of surveillance, inspection, prosecution, judgment, punishment, and rehabilitation, all involving very diverse (non-identical) yet complementary conduct by a multitude of agents.

This last reminder that persons may be unwilling to discharge their responsibilities towards others introduces the second point brought out by the idea of behavioural convergence. Bringing about the needed state of affairs does not require unity of aim but only convergence of conduct. Resource pooling and road safety require that people do their part, be it out of the good will to cooperate, unreflective mimicking of the crowd, in response to a perceived threat of punishment or disadvantage, or even, in surrogate form, through another's forceful intervention (e.g. compulsory seizure to pay tax debts or imprisonment of serious traffic offenders). Individual motivations for performing the conduct due are not part of what specific convergence consists in, although, as Section 3.5 will show, they affect the *strategy* to generate it.

The second leg of the means, *M2*, speaks to the rational underdetermination of the nature and contours of the required convergent conduct. As has been noted above, complex patterns of convergent conduct involving numerous persons will call for sufficiently specific – precise, concrete, detailed – descriptions of the conduct due. Right reason will furnish at most junctures only a range of reasonable alternative patterns none of which is superior to the others in terms of its effectiveness and fairness. But to insist that the pattern settled on must be specific should not mislead one into thinking that the way to settle on it will typically involve no more than a 'merely technical', low-stakes choice amongst fine variations to which agents can be expected to be broadly indifferent, such as fixing the upper limit of a parking fine at £100 (rather than £90, or £110), or setting the deadline for requesting subsidised medication at ten calendar days from the date of prescription (rather than eight working days or eleven calendar days).

Quite the contrary: establishing just relations between persons persistently calls for decisions that, in some circumscribed respect at least, prioritise some aspect(s) of human wellbeing over others, or favour certain justified demands over others, where it is not possible simultaneously to realise all relevant goods and justified demands. Such decisions can be anything but trivial. Even narrowing down on a speed limit, before a concrete figure starts to crystallise, involves an often difficult trade-off between, on the one hand, safety, and, on the other, the many benefits of speedy transport for drivers and perhaps the region at large – a predicament not unlike that faced by most decisions setting safety standards in industry, workplace, transport, and many other environments. Tax bands in a redistribution scheme, in turn, allocate burdens and benefits to, respectively, contributors and beneficiaries, as do eligibility criteria that determine which health benefits, if any, undocumented migrants can apply for; all of which decisions presuppose the earlier choice to provide healthcare to the needy through a public healthcare system rather than, say, by subsidising access to private care. In the case of each decision, even with all the relevant factual and statistical information at hand, there can hardly be one metric that would yield an 'optimal' option, 'maximising' the goods at stake, because these goods, these aspects of wellbeing, are irreducibly different and incommensurably valuable, as is each person's entitlement to participate in them.[5] So the ultimate decision may well come down to a choice between various similarly reasonable (sets of) options, each of which strikes a different balance between the relevant goods and entitlements – a rationally underdetermined choice, and a high-stakes choice at that. Therefore, where *M2* speaks of 'several' patterns available, this may be either because the choice is indifferent or because it involves incommensurable variables. Or, as will often be the case, a combination of the two.

Where *E*, *M1*, and *M2* apply, there is need for specific convergence, that is, for collective convergent conduct in a specific pattern that could reasonably have been different but that through its effective implementation becomes a privileged means to bring about a requirement of justice. Specific convergence is, in that context, the means needed to realise justice. Therefore individual conduct becomes part of this means insofar as it participates in the pattern of convergence. Indeed, from the point of view of the individual, his own conduct is *the* means in his power for realising (an aspect of) justice, and hence is morally obligatory for him.

It is worth noting that the need for specific convergence, the need to generate it, is logically prior to the need for any given individual to undertake the conduct specified by the pattern, *once adopted*. Precisely because there is more than one eligible shape the pattern could in principle take (*M2*), the specific content of anyone's due contribution (and correlatively of anyone else's right to it) cannot be established until a choice of pattern has been made. In fact, in many respects there will be no genuinely due contribution (and no genuine right to it) in the absence of a pattern of convergence (actual or expected) that renders it possible in the first place effectively to foster the relevant aspect of human wellbeing. This is, however, not to say that in the absence of an organised social practice in the relevant domain individuals cannot have strong moral reasons, even moral duties, to promote the wellbeing of others. But the strength of those reasons, particularly the reasons to perform positive acts for others' sake, will critically depend on each person's ability to help in any given situation in ways both effective and proportionate to the burdens involved. Because the ability thus to help is bound to be limited in the case of most individuals acting on their own accord, in practice those reasons to act will largely become absorbed in the role-related moral responsibilities those same individuals hold by virtue of being parents, friends, neighbours, and so on. Not so, however, in the case of persons who, as a matter of fact, are in a position to generate specific convergence in a community, whether because of their standing, resources, international stature,

[5] This sound meta-ethical position is expounded, for example, in Joseph Raz, *The Morality of Freedom* (Oxford, Oxford University Press 1986), Ch. 13; Finnis, *Natural Law and Natural Rights* Sec. V6; and John Finnis, *Fundamentals of Ethics* (Washington, DC, Georgetown University Press 1983) Sec. IV. 2–3.

or for any other reason. Their moral reasons to help others will crystallise into moral duties to set up and maintain suitable schemes of specific convergence in the realms where justice would thereby most securely be realised.[6]

In which realms is justice most securely realised through specific convergence? The next section argues that in virtually all realms of community life, justice requires the direct or indirect operation of a scheme of specific convergence. What *kind* of scheme of specific convergence is fit for this purpose? In many respects, only that which a legal system can provide, for reasons Sections 3.6–3.8 explain.

3.4 JUSTICE AND SPECIFIC CONVERGENCE

Realising justice and human rights in a political community involves adequately protecting and promoting the wellbeing of all community members. Our examples so far have primarily focused on some aspects of the human right to health. Providing healthcare to the needy and avoiding traffic collisions require widespread practices of convergence following specific patterns that could have reasonably been different. The same is obviously true of any other kind of benefit or assistance, of any nature, that is best provided directly through resource pooling, either to persons severally (public education, retirement pensions, unemployment subsidies, etc., whether or not on a redistributive basis) or indistinctly (police force, infrastructure, water quality, and many other so-called public goods).[7] The regulation of immigration, residence, and nationality, which in a sense are gateways to the above benefits, also requires practices of specific convergence. As does any sound policy on the private use of firearms, having settled on one amongst various reasonable schemes, which depending on context might include permitting licensed private use or banning possession while fortifying police control. And likewise in other realms, realms as varied as pollution and recycling, patent protection, workplace safety, minimum annual leave, and restrictions on campaign advertising, specific patterns of mutual restraints based on underdetermined choices may be constitutive of duties of businesses and private individuals in a reasonably just community.

In all these contexts, the conduct due by some persons (to others by right) has a description that could have reasonably been different, as *M2* reflects, and it is also due by others within the same class (e.g. all adult citizens, all pharmaceutical businesses, all lorry drivers, etc.); hence it plainly belongs to a (typically large)

6 In this spirit, see Leslie Green, 'The Duty to Govern' (2007) 13 *Legal Theory* 165 and Finnis, *Natural Law and Natural Rights* Sec. IX.4, especially 246. To the extent that others have the ability to support the tasks of such persons (by joining campaigns, lobbying, publishing news, raising public awareness, etc.) they *pro tanto* have reason to do so.

7 Public goods 'are *non-rival* (the quantity of them consumed by any one does not perceptibly limit the consumption by others) and *inexcludable* (if the good is provided for some it is available for others and none may feasibly be excluded from enjoying it)': Leslie Green, *The Authority of the State* (Oxford, Oxford University Press 1988) 128.

multi-person pattern of the kind *M1* describes. The conduct that is due realises, in the most focal sense, an obligation that is both *specified* (*M2*) and part of an actual *collective* pattern (*M1*). The obligation is directly and immediately constituted through specific convergence. However, this is not, at least apparently, the case with other duties (and rights) that speak to important aspects of wellbeing such as the duties not to kill, injure, or rape and generally to abstain from performing what are known as *mala in se* – that is to say, acts wrongful in all times and places, independently of social arrangements, and therefore morally prohibited without the need for specification. Refraining from *mala in se* is conduct due by everyone, so in this sense is *collective*, but is not of a description that could have reasonably been different: *M2* does not seem fulfilled. The converse is true of numerous duties (and correlative rights) we find in any community that fosters and respects individual autonomy in shaping personal relations in realms such as commerce and family. The duties and rights constituted by contracts, marriage settlements, wills and the exercise of other private powers are eminently *specified* but, in their main contours, they are privy to those directly involved in the relevant transaction or agreement: *M1* does not seem adequately satisfied. Someone might think, therefore, that the role of specific convergence in promoting justice is not nearly as central as this book holds it to be: specific convergence, it might be felt, is needed in a few – important – realms, but not across the board as a standard means to realise human rights.

But this impression would be mistaken. For one thing, protecting the aspects of wellbeing compromised by *mala in se* imperatively requires, as our earlier discussion has foreshadowed, a diverse range of efforts of prevention, control, and correction – efforts that ought to be structured so as to involve specific convergence on their own accord. For instance, all basic elements of offences and torts (causation, *mens rea*, negligence, etc.), penalty ranges, compensation measurements, and so on, ought to be, and be followed, alike in like cases. This means that they should be part of a large convergent pattern (*M1*) and to that end enshrined in advance in parameters specific enough that they could have reasonably been different (*M2*). At this point our objector might insist that these specifications leave intact the duties not to commit the relevant *mala in se*. Just because the victim's death cannot be causally attributed to the defendant, or the custodial sentence is twenty years rather than twenty-five, it does not mean the defendant was any less obligated to refrain from stabbing the victim in the first place. These specifications, it is true, bear in the first instance on the normative positions of those administering the relevant processes, notably judges. But through the proxy of judicial intervention, these specifications come to bear, crucially, on the normative positions of those who have breached their obligation to refrain from *mala in se* and on that account become subject to a range of new, ancillary duties – for example, to submit to a given penalty, to pay a certain compensation, or to provide specific redress – which duties are no less requirements of justice.

At any rate, the objector's concern misunderstands this chapter's point about the role of specific convergence in realising human rights. Of course in *mala in se*, as opposed to *mala prohibita*, specific convergence does not determine the primary duty to refrain from wrongdoing. To the extent that morality determines what kinds of conduct a community can rightfully exact from its members, there is no room for *determinationes*. Pure *mala in se* relevant to justice in community are relatively few in number but of fundamental importance.[8] These considerations, however, are relevant only from the point of view of duty-bearers and right-holders and the content of their respective duties and rights. Specific convergence indeed does not shape the content of those duties and rights. *But specific convergence remains key to meeting the human needs for the sake of which* mala in se *must be avoided*. The aspects of wellbeing compromised by *mala in se* can only adequately be protected and fostered through specific convergent practices that in turn give rise to specified duties and rights – duties and rights that will hold alongside, supporting and complementing, the duties to abstain from *mala in se*. Therefore, once the focus is placed on what it takes to realise human rights, on what is needed effectively and fairly to bring about states of affairs required by justice, as propositions *E-M1-M2* do, specific convergence is shown to be of decisive importance, perhaps especially in the case of *mala in se*, as means through which justly to foster critical aspects of human wellbeing.

These reflections serve, *a fortiori*, to deflect the objection regarding the duties and rights arising from contracts and other forms of individualised decision-making. Here as well, the reaction to the *breach* of the relevant duties ought in many circumstances to be determined, handled, and responded to through procedures and arrangements akin to those noted above. But moreover the very *constitution* of such duties and rights is, in an important sense, determined by specific convergence. It is not determined directly, but at one step removed. Although it is the parties to a contract who decide how they wish to structure their relations, something else, other than their sheer decision, must take place for that very decision to genuinely constitute 'a contract'. Not every agreement to contract or to marry, not every decision to bequeath or donate, succeeds in bringing about that which it purports to bring about. Not every 'hereby I bequeath', thereby bequeaths. What additionally is needed is conformity to the requirements accepted in the community for constituting *valid* contracts, marriages, wills, etc., often involving steps such as a written form, consideration, or a signed deed. Validity criteria are themselves determined by specific convergence, as Section 3.6 will show. Therefore specific convergence, in providing validity criteria, provides the framework that enables the creation of particular duties and rights through private transactions and associations. Specific

[8] They are smaller in number even than the set of so-called 'core' criminal offences: for example, elements of the offence of rape may reasonably take account of cultural sensitivities (see Joseph Raz, 'On the Authority and Interpretation of Constitutions: Some Preliminaries' in Larry Alexander (ed.), *Constitutionalism: Philosophical Foundations* (Cambridge, Cambridge University Press 1998) 166) and the definition of property offences presupposes concepts of ownership and related rights shaped through *determinationes* in the relevant regime of private law.

convergence thus is decisive even in realms of social life in which the task of forging human relations is best left to the initiative and happenstance of private autonomy, personal choice and private bargaining, where specific convergence plays an essential background role as both a facilitator and a guarantee (not least against exploitation and abuse).

In short: Barring forms of conduct that, because of overriding privacy concerns or other limits of proportionate intervention, are best left out of the bounds of the collectivity's organised jurisdiction, such as intimate betrayals, specific convergence is a tool of choice to realise justice in community – whether operating in the foreground or background, whether constituting duties or reacting to their breach, whether determining their contours directly or mediately, and either way no less indispensably.

3.5 MARKING AND ENFORCING

But specific convergence does not arise out of the blue. Conduct of thousands, indeed millions of persons, following specific patterns from among numerous eligible alternative patterns, is in many contexts unlikely to occur and endure spontaneously – that is, without some kind of deliberate and targeted, more or less centralised, more or less organised human intervention to that end. There are, to be sure, some familiar contexts where specific convergence arises and endures relatively spontaneously, even amongst thousands or millions. Natural languages are made up, amongst other things, of patterns of sound-sense relations. Calling the furry being that barks a 'dog', 'chien' or 'gos' is, you might say, largely a matter of indifference. All three represent viable alternatives, involving recognisable combinations of human sounds of a length and distinctness adequate to communication. There are countless further possibilities. The fact that in English we say 'dog' depends, ultimately, on the sheer fact that this is what is, and has long been, done by all those who regard themselves as English speakers, who in turn expect other English speakers to do likewise. 'Dog' is, in this sense, a specification: it is one of several alternative patterns of conduct each of which could fulfil the same purpose if generally followed to the exclusion of alternative strings of sounds. Specifications of this kind, in their systematic interplay, jointly enable persons to share their thoughts with one another at a level of precision and depth that would otherwise not be open to them. And the more persons participate in the relevant practice, the wider and more effective (and reliable) their opportunities to communicate. In speaking a language, one joins a pattern of specific convergence. Sound-sense relations are specifications that fulfil a morally valuable end. And typically, as noted above, they come about spontaneously as communities happen gradually to converge on speaking one way rather than another across time, a convergence usefully sustained and enhanced by casting the language in symbolic, written form and registering in dictionaries any developments of the underlying social practice.

But the set of specialised, interlinked specifications needed to realise justice across manifold realms of a community's life cannot be expected to come about as a result of the kind of haphazard, gradually overlapping series of acceptances characteristic of spontaneous or 'customary' forms of behavioural convergence. For one thing, the specifications required will be much larger in volume and will be subject to much more frequent change in order to adjust to rapidly evolving needs. It is enough to recall that it is not uncommon for persons to accomplish proficient mastery of the rules of their language(s), whereas the most studious lawyer could not conceivably retain the totality of provisions of a legal system, even as it is at a single point in time.

For another thing, the kinds of conduct needed to realise justice, although ultimately for the sake of all, will often most immediately require the subject to bear some form of burden or restraint or to forsake some kind of advantage that many persons might not be disposed to bear or forsake, whether out of sheer egoism or lack of reassurance that others will do their part. Indeed, many collective endeavours needed to realise justice are such that, by their very nature, they encourage free-riding. That is, they involve predicaments in which it 'pays', selfishly speaking, for an individual agent to abstain from shouldering the relevant burdens or costs, as doing so will not tangibly restrict, and might even enhance, that agent's own enjoyment of the associated benefits or goods, provided most others do comply. Cases in point include evading tax while benefitting from public infrastructures or services, stealing but not being stolen from, or edging out business competitors by outsourcing production to foreign factories deploying child labour in order to avoid paying minimum wage. Situations of this kind have a structure significantly different from that of situations resembling the predicament of drivers deciding on which side of the road drive, or speakers choosing whether to adhere to an intelligible linguistic pattern.[9] The latter kinds of situations have no built-in incentive to free-ride, as there is normally nothing to be gained, and much to be lost, even from a selfish

[9] The distinction between these two predicaments echoes the one drawn in game-theory between 'coordination problems' and 'prisoners dilemmas' (on the contrast, see e.g. Edna Ullmann-Margalit, *The Emergence of Norms* (Oxford, Oxford University Press 1977) 114ff), except that game-theory measures each player's 'pay-offs' in terms of selfish 'interests' amenable to being 'maximised' and transitively ranked, and so does not distinguish between what morally ought to be done and what certain persons are in fact inclined to do (R Duncan Luce and Howard Raiffa, *Games and Decisions: Introduction and Critical Survey* (New York, Wiley 1957) 25). Efforts to import into legal theory some of the game-theoretical insights (particularly on 'coordination games', based *inter alia* on Thomas C Schelling, *The Strategy of Conflict* (New York, Oxford University Press 1963) 81ff; David Lewis, *Convention: A Philosophical Study* (Oxford, Blackwell 2002) 8ff; Ullmann-Margalit, *The Emergence of Norms* 78ff), with relevant qualifications, have on the whole not succeeded in distinctly articulating, through that language, the key issues at stake when reflecting on the moral need for law to realise justice. See e.g. John Finnis, *Philosophy of Law: Collected Essays, Volume IV* (Oxford, Oxford University Press 2011), Ch. 3, especially 69; Joseph Raz, 'Facing Up: A Reply' (1989) 62 *Southern California Law Review* 1153, 1189–93, especially 1189; Jeremy Waldron, *Law and Disagreement* (Oxford, Oxford University Press 1999), Ch. 5; Samantha Besson, *The Morality of Conflict: Reasonable Disagreement and the Law* (Oxford, Hart 2005), Ch. 6.

point of view, by deviating from the group. But these latter kinds of situations are the exception, rather than the rule, in the enterprise of organising and allocating just shares in sensitive aspects of human wellbeing amongst millions of strangers with clashing preferences, differing world-views, uneven abilities, and large degrees of mutual distrust.

Where specific convergence cannot spontaneously arise and endure, but is morally needed, it must be brought about. By whom? By those who are in a position to do so, and thus hold the primary responsibility, as explained in Section 3.3. How? The answer to this question follows from the above considerations on the various kinds of pitfalls that potentially stand in the way of spontaneous convergence. These pitfalls, broadly speaking, concern, on the one hand, an absence of *information* concerning what, if anything, the relevant subjects should do; and, on the other hand, an absence of ready *willingness* by persons to do it. The primary way to tackle the latter problem, in its many varieties and manifestations, is through the operation of tasks of prevention, control and correction to which we have variously referred, which can increase the individual 'cost' of defection (e.g. punishment, tax), inculcate a willingness to forego selfish advantage (e.g. rehabilitation), or in extreme cases altogether prevent ill-will, weakness of the will or folly from crystallising in harmful action (e.g. imprisonment, professional incapacitation). Here success builds upon itself, as an effective functioning of these processes will bring reassurance to those conditionally disposed to do their part by demonstrating to them that they will not be contributing without reciprocal advantage. These tasks and processes will jointly be referred to as *enforcement mechanisms*, their object being to make it the case that behavioural convergence actually occurs. They track the need expressed in *M1* for convergent conduct of a large number of persons.

Tackling the problem about lack of information, in turn, involves two important steps. First, if the relevant group does not spontaneously settle on one specific pattern of conduct, *one* has to be chosen. Where, as normally, there are several available and appropriate but incompatible patterns (*M2*), the choice in question will be rationally underdetermined on grounds of indifference or incommensurability (Section 3.3). And, second, that choice, once made, has to be adequately marked, flagged up, publicised, so as to be accessible to all those concerned, meaning: the subjects who owe the specific conduct; those to whom it is owed and who might otherwise be affected by it, including in the near or distant future; those responsible for managing the conduct or its consequences; and those in charge of seeing to its performance and reacting to the duty's breach. Note that this second step, publicly marking the choice, is not merely a requirement of effectiveness of the enterprise. The fact that the choice will be publicly marked and known is part of what renders the choice morally relevant in the first place, capable of effecting a genuine specification of new moral duties and rights as opposed to being a well-meant effort to design a collective plan of action that might languish on somebody's shelf. For, in the contexts under discussion, one person's conduct can be an effective and available means to a valuable end, and thus morally required, and thus owed by right, to the extent that it slots into an *actual*, as opposed to merely possible, pattern of collective conduct. The existence of adequate *marking mechanisms*, as they will be called, goes to establish the adequacy of the means thereby marked. Marking is, to some extent, self-fulfilling. Marking conduct *as* due can make it the case that conduct truly (morally) *is* due.

In many contexts, however, effective marking is not enough, although it is necessary, to bring about actual convergence. The mark may have to be supported by enforcement mechanisms. Thanks to effective enforcement, for example, the information provided by marks such as speed limit signs is not merely that a choice has been made to render certain specific conduct obligatory, but also, albeit implicitly, that that choice will, by and large, be paid heed to by others (e.g. because traffic police are known to be alert). And it is this joint understanding which entitles drivers to treat the sign, the chosen conduct, the thing marked, as imposing a genuine moral obligation here and now. This shows that enforcement mechanisms crucially reinforce marking mechanisms. But the converse is also true. Marking mechanisms bolster enforcement mechanisms, in terms of both their effectiveness and fairness. The better a choice is marked, and thus the more determinate and prospectively knowable its content, in short the more Rule-of-Law compliant the choice is, the fairer any subsequent enforcement procedures will be and the more exact the guidance offered to those administering them.

Marking and enforcement mechanisms are closely interdependent and, in their combined interplay, they constitute the strategy to generate the kind of specific convergence needed to realise human rights in many social domains. There is no logical priority between marking and enforcing. On the one hand, enforcement presupposes the existence of something to be enforced, which ought to be marked clearly in advance. On the other hand, no mark truly *marks* in the eyes of many, across territory and time, unless it is of a kind that many diverse persons have standing reason to look out for, a reason supplied, to a large extent, by the awareness and prospect of general enforcement. Specification of human rights requires marking and enforcement, operating hand in hand.

3.6 LAW'S MARKING: LEGAL VALIDITY

The remainder of this chapter will argue that the most sophisticated combination of marking and enforcement mechanisms, the one most apt to help realise justice across central areas of community life, is that which only a system of positive law can supply. In this sense, law is the means of choice to specify rights, so much so that in the preceding discussion it has become inevitable to refer to various kinds of legal processes and institutions (e.g. tax, judges, offences). Our goal here is to outline the extent to which, and the general limits within which, there is good sense in realising rights through a legal order. The law's tools may be studied from the point of view of either marking or enforcement, as the two are bound up together. But our primary focus will be on marking, as this sheds the clearest light on the idea of rights specification. Law's marking has numerous intriguing features that can be discovered at work in familiar concepts and presuppositions of legal reasoning that are rarely, if ever, associated with the object of study called 'human rights law'.[10] Let us therefore revisit the idea of marking, and consider precisely why and how law is in a position to fulfil this task.

The thing to be marked, it will be remembered, is a choice. It is somebody's decision concerning what certain persons should do (and others are entitled to or should claim, enforce, tolerate, etc.). Characteristically it will be a choice underdetermined by reason – a *choice* properly so called. A selection from amongst alternatives, neither of which, on the whole, is rationally superior the others. A settlement of a morally urgent question that morality, however, does not fully answer. A choice, a decision, is a human act. Where morality runs out, but its gap needs filling, doing so is down to human agency. And law is fundamentally a product of human agency in this important sense: our normative positions in law (i.e. the rights, duties, powers, etc. we hold as a matter of law) are determined only by human acts. (They are determined in various ways and by various kinds of act, of which the primary one will be our focus of discussion.)[11] It is acts that make law, and it is acts that are needed to supplement morality where the latter's directives are not precise enough to help organise a collective pursuit of justice.

A choice is a special kind of human act. It is a deliberate act with propositional content. In the case of marking, the content of the choice is (chiefly and ultimately)[12] that a certain pattern of conduct is required from some persons (and due to others, etc.). The thing to be marked, strictly speaking, is that content: the required conduct-description. It is *that* which should be rendered salient to all those concerned. What needs flagging is the choice in the sense of the thing chosen, rather than the act of choosing as such ('choice' is ambiguous between these meanings). But how to flag up a conduct-description? How to make it stand out to members of the group, present and future, who, in their daily lives, are presented with a plethora of required or recommended conduct-descriptions, of do's and don'ts, by interlocutors as varied as educators, media, family, and commercial and religious institutions? How to convey that it is *this* conduct-description, and not those others, which is part of a network of specific convergence required by justice and backed up by enforcement? The *content* of the conduct-description, in and of itself, would not suffice to set it apart in the necessary way. All the above sources may recommend or

[10] This and other central themes of this chapter are expounded in Maris Köpcke, *Legal Validity: The Fabric of Justice* (Oxford, Hart 2018).

[11] On the related contrast between legislated law ('paradigmatic law'), case law, and customary law, see John Gardner, *Law as a Leap of Faith* (Oxford, Oxford University Press 2012), Ch. 3.

[12] The bracketed phrase makes allowance for the existence of (*inter alia*) legal empowerments, dealt with under Section 3.7.

command conduct on all kinds of subject-matters, which are likely to overlap as well as conflict. Nor would it help if subjects sought to discriminate amongst directives according to their moral merits, asking themselves which one is sounder. For one thing, an option picked out by an underdetermined choice may not be (at least on its face) superior to other alternatives on offer. For another thing, even where an option *is* superior, because morality does yield a best answer, that answer might not attract consensus within the relevant group, particularly in a culturally and ideologically diverse community.

This points to an important truth. A conduct-description will not be salient, and so not successfully marked, if its identification primarily turns on judgments that group members cannot be expected to share. For salience has to do with predicting the behaviour of others, knowing that they are trying to predict one's own on the same basis.[13] It has to do with providing a focus for mutual expectations. An option is truly salient within our group, and so adequately marked, only if I can correctly predict that most others likewise regard it salient, for all I know about them. And often that is not much.

It follows that the cues to identify and thus mark the relevant option must be such that they can be relatively easily and uniformly spotted by persons of different backgrounds, sensitivities, and skills. The primary strategy is to rely on cues concerning the *source* of the relevant directive. Features, that is, of the act of choosing as manifested in physical action, rather than of the thing chosen. Cues such as by whom and through what procedure the choice was made, or in what form it was cast or publicised. Of course not all conceivable features of the manifested act of choosing will be easy to identify by a large population, the greatest part of which will not have witnessed the act and may hold clashing views about even its procedural and formal propriety. Features primarily to be relied on, to generate salience, should be relatively easy to ascertain by many and through time. Stamps, signatures, written records of voting results, deeds, and so on, are in appropriate circumstances apt to perform this task.

Any mature legal system provides a systematic arrangement of such kinds of cues. Those cues, in law, serve to identify acts that change legal positions, and so shape or modify legal duties, rights or powers that persons hold at any point in time. The acts in question change legal positions in a special *way*. They manifest a choice to change legal positions by means of that very manifestation. They change legal positions, as it were, by saying so. This modus operandi is rendered more or less explicit in certain well-known formulae such as 'be it hereby enacted that ...', 'you are declared bankrupt ...', 'I hereby bequeath ...', etc. Such acts, such exercises of legal power, may be performed by public institutions or by private individuals. In the first case they may take the form of legislation, judicial pronouncements, license

[13] On the idea of salience, see Lewis, *Convention* 35; Schelling, *The Strategy of Conflict* 111ff ('focal point').

renewals, patent awards, and so on. In the second case they typically take the form of transactions, whether realised by persons in concert (such as contracts or marriages) or individually (such as wills). Notwithstanding the many radical differences amongst all these kinds of exercises of power, they have a common quality: they are *legally valid*. Indeed all legally valid acts are exercises of legal power in the above sense. The acts, the decisions, the choices in question would not change legal positions but for the fact that they are legally valid. An oral agreement to sell a piece of land, though possibly intended to change the buyer's and seller's legal positions, even *manifestly* so intended, will in many jurisdictions not succeed in doing so unless and until it is recorded in a deed and an official registry. It is not the content of the decision, as such and exclusively, which determines its legal validity. Valid acts are chiefly *marked* by a set of cues concerning procedural and formal features of the act of choosing, the source of the choice.

Such procedural cues can be very simple or tiresomely intricate. Either way, some of them are bound to concern the person or institution making the choice (e.g. a certain majority of MPs, the competent council, or a licensed doctor). Typically they will also make relevant certain factual circumstances in which the choice was made (e.g. in Parliament upon third reading, in a ceremony presided by a judge, or in the presence of witnesses), and perhaps the mode in which it was recorded (e.g. in an official gazette, in a notarial deed, as a registry entry, or as a stamp on a passport). Procedural cues of this kind, subject to additional publicising measures (e.g. access to registries or a governmental website), can be more or less uniformly spotted and ascertained by very diverse persons, directly or through the aid of lawyers. Ideological enemies can easily agree that a tax bill was voted on by a majority, even if they disagree whether the tax rates are fair.

The cues under discussion are none other than what legal theorists call (in a helpful if simplifying jargon) criteria of legal validity. It is important to stress that criteria of legal validity can, do, and should virtually always also make reference to the *substance* of a decision – to what it is about – as opposed to its mere procedure. The next section will illustrate this. Moreover, the very distinction between criteria referring to procedure and criteria referring to substance cannot be sharp. And criteria of both kinds may be more or less controversial, particularly (though not only) where they are evaluatively circumscribed (e.g. 'reasonable time', 'unfair contract terms').[14] On the whole, however, criteria primarily concerned with procedure include some of the least controversial and, importantly, most distinctive kinds of cues which enable legal systems saliently to mark conduct-descriptions stemming from very different sources (Section 3.8) and addressed to a very miscellaneous audience. This is why procedural criteria of validity are a chief tool to generate specific convergence.

[14] Criteria are evaluatively circumscribed to the extent that evaluative terms (not further specified in law) have a morally determinate meaning. Cf. Joseph Raz, *The Authority of Law* (Oxford, Oxford University Press 1979) 75; Gardner, *Law as a Leap of Faith* 22.

To the extent that a decision is marked independently of its subject-matter and any moral concerns bearing on it, it can be identified without engaging one's own or anyone else's view on the questions of justice that are the object of the decision – underdetermined and controversial as they may be.[15]

The marking effected by legal validity has a special sophistication. Criteria of validity, we have noted, will normally make reference to just a few aspects or features of the act of choosing. But even these features, once the valid act is performed, may change without in the least affecting the act's continuing validity, that is, the continuing legal relevance of the change of normative positions that the act has effected. Statutes remain valid long after the persons voting for them have left office or died, indeed even in the face of changes of mind or of heart subsequent to casting a valid vote. And one may be bound by a mortgage or pledge no matter how much one comes to regret having signed it. The technique of validity isolates certain features of an act not only from other aspects of the act's originating context and circumstances, but also from ulterior changes in those features, and from shifting views about the act's point or value. It freezes the original choice, as it were, thereby rendering it identifiable through time, precisely as a choice, as a deliberately introduced legal change, and yet relatively detached from the original act of choosing. The technique of legal validity makes it possible for choices, for legal specifications, to circulate through time and many hands. This is so almost in a physical sense, given the tendency of legal thought towards objectifying the product of the valid choice (the statute, the contract), attaching to it the predicate 'valid', and sometimes even verbally likening it to its physical record ('I was not carrying the license') or its proof ('no entry without a valid ticket').

Validity thus furnishes a shared grammar in which demands, disagreements, conflicts, and claims can be cast. As with any grammar, it must be easier to share it than to share the arguments and claims therein articulated. Law's grammar is made of rules which determine when a choice speaks the law's language; when, in other words, it is the law speaking and choosing, or, what is the same, when one is speaking and choosing on the law's behalf. As legal theorists have long insisted, the legal rules that determine when an act is legally valid can be distinguished from the legal duties and rights changed in following such rules. The rules of law's grammar are the device whereby law, as it were, regulates it own creation and change. It is law about law. It is law taking care of its own identification, and – we can now add – of its own *marking*. It is law establishing how to mark certain kinds of choice.

But note that the way to mark saliently, that is, the precise combination of cues to be used in each case to the exclusion of other possibilities, is itself largely an underdetermined question. Although the nature of some criteria of validity is anything but rationally indifferent (consider, for example, who should consent to a marriage,

[15] Raz's understanding of legitimate practical authority (e.g. Joseph Raz, *Ethics in the Public Domain* (Oxford, Oxford University Press 1994) Ch. 10) runs in some ways parallel to this argument.

or whether a criminal trial judge need give reasons for judgment), many others would have appropriate alternatives, including those procedural or formal criteria that most contribute to the act's salience. Yet *one* set of cues has to be widely converged on and deployed, in each domain, in order for it to be *the* way unmistakably to mark, and to spot, a successful legal change. Legal systems, by regulating validity criteria, generate specific convergence *on the question of identifying law*, a question ancillary to the manifold questions of justice that law is needed to settle. Legal validity therefore makes up, so to speak, a secondary level of specific convergence. That secondary level is relatively independent of, but it decisively bolsters, convergence at the primary level. We must settle on a way to make and identify valid statutes and regulations in order to settle on tax rates. Validity perfects the law's marking, and marking is part of what it takes to generate specific convergence and thus to specify genuine moral duties and rights. Validity criteria are aids to identifying law, and identifying law, in turn, is an aid to realising justice.

Because law – reflexively – determines its own identification, legal rules establishing when an act is legally valid characteristically exist before the relevant act is performed. They anticipate its occurrence. That is why the act in question can effect a legal change more or less *by so saying*. It can help generate convergence deliberately, in a relatively on-off way that stands in sharp contrast to the nature of slowly aggregative custom formation. The legal 'performative'[16] effect of the choice, the doing by saying, the correspondingly self-fulfilling description of the legal change, the 'hereby': all occur against the background of a standing framework of legal rules, of validity criteria, that bestow on the act its legal meaning and force.

The immediate framework of rules that regulates an act, say the way to file an administrative appeal, is very often *itself* the product of further exercises of legal power (regulations, decrees, etc.), iterated in complex ways that only in metaphorical language can be cast as strictly hierarchical or chain-like. Of course, ultimately the iteration of rules about other rules culminates, along the lines perhaps Hart best explained, in a stable collective custom of treating certain acts or kinds of act, such as legislative enactments or supreme court rulings, as highest sources of law and thus, amongst other things, as salient ways to generate legal salience.[17] For legal systems generate salience by using tools, validity criteria, that are themselves salient – at bottom in a spontaneous, non-derivative way, but otherwise characteristically by virtue of deliberate choice. And these iterations of deliberate *marking* choices, of legal empowerments, are in fact key to the enterprise of realising justice through specific convergence. They enable the kind of gradual, step-by-step, dynamic specification of rights that the next section vindicates and charts.

[16] The idea of 'performatives' was famously introduced in JL Austin, *How to do Things with Words*, JO Urmson and M Sbisa (eds.), (2nd edn, Cambridge, MA, Harvard University Press 1975).

[17] Hart's doctrine of the rule of recognition is expounded in HLA Hart, *The Concept of Law* (2nd edn, Oxford, Oxford University Press 1994), Ch. 6.

3.7 DYNAMIC SPECIFICATION

Up to this point, this chapter has characterised the specification of human rights as involving focally underdetermined choices of specific patterns of collective conduct, marked and enforced so as to guarantee their actual fulfilment. The previous section has fastened on law's powerful technique for marking such choices: legal validity. But the discussion so far has for the most part eluded the important question of *who* should make the relevant choices and *when*. The previous section has already hinted at the fact that many different kinds of agents can and do perform valid acts. But it remains to be explained whether, and if so how, it can be a requirement of justice to have such multiplicity of interlocking sources. For there is nothing in the idea of specification of rights, as such, that would be incompatible with all specifications being simultaneously made by a single agent working out, and saliently marking, down its finest details, a complex collective strategy for advancing human wellbeing in a political community. The obvious fact that such endeavour well exceeds the capacities of any person or institution[18] is, as we will see, by no means the most important reason why the specification of almost any human right should be effected gradually, dynamically, as a *process*, through the choices of different agents adding up over time and related in ways that only the technique of validity can fashion.

The present section takes a look at what we might call chains of specification. It takes – loosely speaking – a vertical look. It shows, by reference to a representative kind of legal regime, why it takes iterations of choices, choices deriving from one another, to transform certain generic claims of justice (two-term rights) into genuine (three-term) rights and duties (Chapter 2), and how legal systems have sophisticated tools to render such dynamic specification possible. Building on this, Section 3.8 looks – horizontally as it were – at the relations between different chains of specification, which only law can render systemically coherent in their radical diversity reigned in by legislative oversight.

Let us, to that end, return to the specification of the generic right to health. One reasonable way to specify it, one reasonable strategy to realise some aspects of it, we have noted, is to arrange a public, means-tested provision of healthcare to the needy, funded principally through income tax. Setting up and running such a system will, in turn, call for numerous and familiar kinds of further specifications, including: the nature and scope of treatments provided in public hospitals and practices (for all conditions? with some exclusions?); the requirements for the supply of subsidised medicines (upon prescription by any doctor? by a public doctor only? generic brands only?) and for reimbursement of pharmacies (every month? every three months?); the kinds of available assistance and care for the elderly, disabled, and ill (only old

[18] It is exceptional, though perhaps possible, for substantial bodies of law to be single-handedly masterminded, as noted in Chapter 6, Section 6.8.

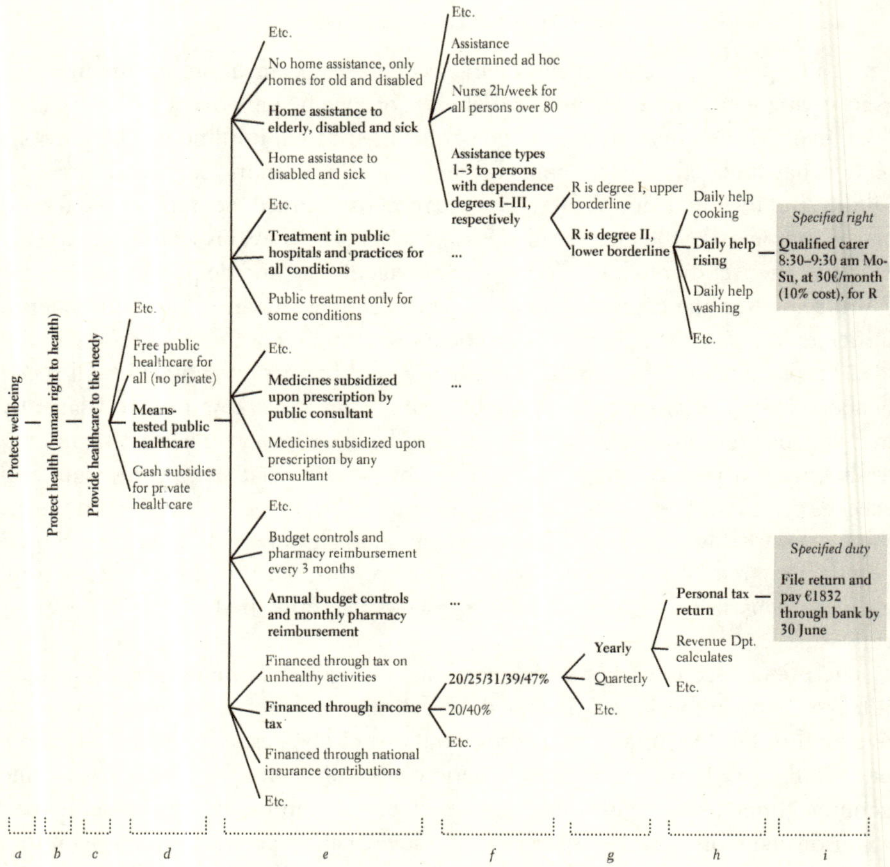

FIGURE 3.1. Progressive specification

and disabled people's homes? home assistance for some or all of them?); the frequency and procedures of budgetary control (annual? by which commission?); and, not least, the parameters for determining income tax liability and collecting contributions. Figure 3.1 sketches this set of specifications in highly simplified form. In so doing, it follows two conceivable chains of specification all the way down to the determination of, respectively, a concrete right and a concrete duty: the right to a specific kind of daily home assistance from a public scheme, and the duty to pay a specific amount of income tax by a certain date. This right and this duty are not strictly correlative because resource pooling is involved, but that is the very ground of their respective rational strength.

The sample specifications are modelled on the Spanish public healthcare system, particularly on the System for Autonomy and Attention to Dependence, created in 2006, which channels the provision, on a means-tested basis, of various kinds of assistance, including home assistance by qualified carers, to persons who by reason of age, disability, or illness are 'dependent' on the help of others in the performance of basic daily tasks. The statute creating the System establishes that the assistance a person is entitled to receive depends both on the 'degree of dependence' the person is certified to have (ranging from I, moderate, to III, great),[19] and on the 'individual attention programme' subsequently drawn up by social services in light of the person's needs and preferences,[20] all in following a process that the statute outlines and leaves to territorial authorities to flesh out.[21] (In Figure 3.1, the statute corresponds to stages *e* and *f* of the rights specification.)

It is worth dwelling briefly on the process whereby persons become legally entitled to assistance. In Catalonia,[22] the process (i) begins with the person's application,[23] whereupon (ii) a specialised evaluation team visits the person to determine the degree of their dependence. The specialists apply an official assessment test (approved by the Spanish government for the whole of Spain) which, in the course of over hundred pages, calls for quantifying the degree, frequency, nature, and cause of a person's dependence in discharging up to fifty-nine different kinds of activities, including 'fastening a button or similar' or 'cleaning and caring for the home'.[24] (iii) The resulting dependence degree[25] is confirmed in an administrative resolution[26] that lists the types and maximum amounts of eligible assistance corresponding to that degree, as per the service catalogue approved by the Spanish government.[27] For example, a person certified to have dependence degree II, which is severe dependence, is entitled, amongst other things, to twenty to forty-five monthly hours of home assistance[28] (the resolution on the dependence degree corresponds to stage g in Figure 3.1). (v) The most appropriate kind of assistance, from within this eligible range, is to be selected and fully concretised in the 'individual attention programme' drafted by a social worker of the municipal social services of the person's neighbourhood or town, having visited the person and discussed that person's preferences as between available local resources.[29] (vi) This plan is in turn approved by a second

19 Law 39/2006 Arts. 26–8.

20 Art. 29.

21 Arts. 27–9, based on 'common criteria' agreed by a federal council (created by Art. 8).

22 According to Spanish law, presently one of Spain's seventeen regions ('autonomous communities', Spanish Constitution Art. 137).

23 Accompanied by an official medical report (Law 39/2006 Art. 28.1, Royal Decree 1051/2013 Art. 3). The application is handled by a sub-unit (*Servei d'Atenció a les Persones*) of the Catalan government's Social Services Department (Decree 115/2007 of the Catalan Government Arts. 2.2 and 3.1.a)).

24 Royal Decree 174/2011 Annexes I–IV.

25 Proposed by the specialist team and at least one government official (the 'Assessment Commission') in a written report (Law 39/2006 Art. 27.1).

26 By the *Servei d'Atenció a les Persones* (Law 39/2006 Art. 28.3, Decree 115/2007 of the Catalan Government Art. 3.1.a).

27 Royal Decree 1051/2013, based on Law 39/2006 Arts. 14 and 15.

28 Royal Decree 1051/2013 Annex II.

29 Law 39/2006 Art. 29, Decree 115/2007 of the Catalan Government Art. 4.3, Law 12/2007 of the Catalan Parliament (on Social Services) Art. 17 d and additional provision 1.2. Official guidelines to social workers (*Protocol de Procediments del Programa Individual d'Atenció, Informe Social de Suport del PIA*; both available online) specifically instruct them to take into account a person's

administrative resolution,[30] which generates an enforceable legal right to the specified assistance (the second administrative resolution corresponds to stages *h* and *i*).

This scheme, like so many equivalent ones in countless legal domains, articulates one of numerous reasonable ways whereby a community can facilitate the provision of assistance to vulnerable persons.[31] If the scheme is effective, the legal right to specific assistance realises a very important aspect of the right-holder's (R's) human right to health and is therefore also R's *moral* right.

Did R always have this right? Looking at Figure 3.1, it is possible to answer both Yes and No. On the one hand, R's wellbeing, and therefore R's health, always mattered morally. We may express this by saying that R always had a human right to health, declared (not created) by various international instruments. The Spanish 1978 Constitution gives legal formulation to this human right ('right to the protection of health'),[32] entrusts public authorities with 'organis[ing] public healthcare',[33] and summons the legislature to determine the corresponding duties and rights,[34] all while noting everyone's 'equality before the law'[35] as well as everyone's duty fairly to contribute to public expenditure.[36] The constitution further requires that public authorities promote the enjoyment of rights by disabled persons[37] and arrange specialised health assistance for the elderly.[38] But – on the other hand – the 2006 statute setting up the System for Autonomy and Attention to Dependence, in its Article 4, *bestows* on such persons the 'right ... to accede ... to the services ... set out in this law, in the terms therein provided'. Therefore, when R is certified by the first administrative resolution as having dependence degree II, R thereby *becomes* eligible to receive some service(s) within a specified range.[39] Then again, he becomes so eligible subject to the concretisation of the service(s) in the second administrative resolution. For it is only *upon* that second resolution, at the very end of the decision chain, that R is both legally and morally entitled (has a Hohfeldian claim-right) to receive a

environment (including e.g. 'rotation amongst [their] children') and preferences, as well as locally available resources, and make numerous recommendations concerning procedure (e.g. what to do if the beneficiary refuses to sign).

30 Decree 115/2007 of the Catalan Government Art. 3.1.b.

31 Alternative reasonable ways might include subsidised insurance or more private forms of service selection; in the System under discussion, economic assistance is only awarded where assistance in kind (public service) is not available or feasible (Law 39/2006 Arts. 14, 17, and 18.1).

32 Spanish Constitution Art. 43.1.

33 Art. 43.1.

34 Art. 43.2.

35 Art. 14.

36 Art. 31.1.

37 Art. 49.

38 Art. 50.

39 According to Law 39/2006 Art. 28.3, the first administrative resolution will determine the services to which the applicant, depending on his dependence degree, is 'entitled'; Royal Decree 1051/2006, which provides the lists of services, uses the more cautious language of 'intensity of protection' (e.g. Art. 1) and 'intensity of service' (e.g. Annex II) and so avoids talking of entitlements or rights.

specific service from specific individuals and institutions, who have correlative legal and moral duties (for example, duties to provide the service, to seek a replacement carer, etc., duties in turn supported by an array of liberties, powers, etc.).

In this example, and assuming, as we do, that the system is operative and reasonably fair, the presence and completion of a chain of decisions makes a moral difference. One might wonder, however, whether it is essential to this moral difference that the decisions in question are mostly taken, as in the example, by different persons or bodies and at relatively separate points in time. Could the chain be fruitfully collapsed, so as to involve fewer decisions and, crucially, fewer agents? Conceivably, the statute, or even the constitution, might bestow a legal right to a blanket form of assistance, say to one weekly hour of nursing care, on all persons fulfilling a characteristic that requires no additional ascertainment procedure, such as being aged eighty or above or being certified as disabled for the purposes of tax deductions. But this arrangement would surely be too blunt: those characteristics are relatively poor indicators or proxies for the kinds of needs assistance is meant to address (captured by the radically vague notion of 'dependence'). And at any rate, the conditions of eligibility and service would require periodic adjustment in light of, for example, fluctuations in revenue. An alternative way of compacting the chain might be for the statute, or even the constitution, to empower municipal social workers to determine on an *ad hoc* basis whether, and if so which, public assistance is to be given to each person, by making an overall judgment on the perceived needs and available resources. Unlike the previous option, this type of specification would be overly particularised and wholly dependent on the open-ended judgments of an exorbitant number of social workers, resulting in a likely inequitable allocation of resources and possible waste thereof, not to mention increased occasions for corruption and manipulation, and little if any transparency and predictability.

As against these options, it is better to distinguish amongst several dependence degrees, established for each person by a specialised team using uniform criteria, themselves drawn up with professional input.[40] Likewise it is better for there to be a uniform range of services corresponding to each dependence degree, devised and updated centrally in light of available budgets.[41] And, rather than automatically assigning a fixed form of assistance pursuant to dependence degree, it is better that the assistance be particularised by professionals familiar with the person's immediate situation and surroundings as well as with the resources locally on offer. In what sense, exactly, are the latter arrangements *better*? They yield a more effective protection of the health of vulnerable persons. They mark courses of conduct more

[40] The dependence assessment test (Royal Decree 174/2011) acknowledges (Annex III.2) the input of twenty-seven expert advisers.

[41] The current service catalogue, as the preamble of Royal Decree 1051/2013 suggests, is the result of numerous adjustments to earlier service catalogues to reflect budgetary constraints in times of economic recession.

apt to serve human wellbeing. They generate convergence better suited to bring about a valuable state of affairs. And that has to do with the fact that those taking the decisions, those marking at each stage, are better placed to identify and select appropriate options. Having dependence assessed by specialised teams, rather than by government officials or local social workers, increases homogeneity, prevents bias and error, and allows targeted training. A local social worker, in turn, is best able to evaluate whether R can draw greater benefit from a weekly hour of nurse care than, say, from half an hour of physiotherapy coupled with an electronic alarm device. Although most of the choices to be made along the chain will be rationally underdetermined to an extent (e.g. why three dependence degrees and not four? is a magnetic clasp 'similar' to a button?), the relevant agents are more likely correctly to identify the rationally determined aspects of the respective choice, and thus to arrive, as it were, at a better shortlist of options.

We can extract from this example an important set of general *reasons* that warrant adding new links – decisions by others – to chains of specification. (Where these reasons point the other way, they warrant *not* adding links.) The reasons primarily concern *expertise*, *proximity*, and *time*. First, those having specialised knowledge are more likely to get right any question on which that knowledge bears; therefore, health experts should advise the government on configuring the assessment test and service catalogue, and the application of these instruments should likewise be in professional hands. Second, where reaching a just decision requires close acquaintance with an environment, the better arbiter is the one nearest to the relevant facts; thus, it is appropriate that local social workers have the final word on assistance, and the Spanish legislature does well to empower territorial governments to determine their respective part of the process. Third, where the criteria bearing on a decision will change over time (e.g. revenue and resources), or indeed where the factors calling for decision will, if at all, arise in the future (e.g. a new person's dependence), the relevant decisions cannot adequately be taken in advance.

Those general reasons why certain decisions are best entrusted to certain agents rather than others apply in many realms relevant to justice, often in combination and along with several additional reasons, including expediency and the intrinsic value of someone's choice. Expediency, like all the other reasons, can support either adding or removing links of a chain. The Spanish dependence system, for example, has notoriously led to unreasonable (even catastrophic) delays in processing claims of assistance, and it is at least possible that dispensing with the second administrative resolution (and corresponding potential legal challenges), and having the 'individual attention programme' drawn up by the very team that assesses dependence, might yield a gain in speed not outweighed by the shortcomings in decision calibration. Conversely, the fact that certain technical questions have been specified by administrative decree, rather than settled in the original statute, no doubt expedited the latter's enactment and thus the system's set-up. Sometimes, however, it matters intrinsically, rather than instrumentally, that a certain agent decides on a certain question. It matters not so much because the agent is more likely to get it right, or to decide more quickly, but primarily because the decision would lose at least part of its point were it not adopted by that agent in particular. This applies to almost all exercises of private power, such as marriages, wills, or contracts, as well as to citizens' political participation in the running of the state. On some conceptions of democracy at least, this reason alone can recommend that certain questions be tackled legislatively rather than by bureaucrats, however competent ('no taxation without representation').

All the above reasons, insofar as they weigh in favour of choices being made *later* and *by others*, support specifying rights *dynamically*. In the idea of entrusting someone else with deciding on some matter, of letting another's say-so occupy a place that it could otherwise not have occupied, of settling a question not directly but vicariously, by settling *who is to settle it* – in this idea lies the germ of the notion of legal empowerment. In our sample chain, as in any other legal decision-making chain, any step in which an agent bestows on another the capacity to decide on some matter, typically determining the conditions for doing so, is a legal empowerment. Our chain involves the constitution's empowerment of the legislature, the legislature's empowerment of territorial governments, those governments' empowerment of administrative organs, those organs' empowerment of applicants and service teams, and so on. A legal empowerment confers on an agent a faculty, a power, to do something the agent would otherwise not be *able* to do: namely, to change legal positions (legal rights, duties, etc.) by manifesting the agent's own decision that those legal positions be thereby changed. Unlike natural abilities, which are inherent in a person, the ability deliberately to change legal positions – legal power – is essentially vicarious. It is *conferred* on a subject, by someone else.

The tools to confer legal power have been surveyed in the previous section. The tools to confer legal power are (chiefly) criteria of legal validity. Every legally valid act changes legal positions because it involves the exercise of a faculty conferred on the subject to do so. Empowering an agent is determining who is to decide on what – and how, and when, and on what not, etc. Criteria of validity, procedural and substantive, create and shape the scope of a legal empowerment. They regulate the amount of freedom (discretion) or constraint incumbent on the agent ('organise public health', 'fastening a button'), in both the form and content of the choice, and in so doing they render the latter identifiable as part of the relevant legal chain. For, clearly, the judgment that one daily hour of home care is the kind of assistance most useful to R at this point in his life will not engender a legal right to this care in being uttered, however justifiably, by R's spouse, a friend, or R himself. It engenders a legal right only in being expressed by the competent social worker in a duly stamped report, subject to official approval. The local social worker has the power to change the legal positions of R (and of others) insofar as she fulfils the applicable criteria of validity, which both confer on her the power and determine its constraints. Her decision will be *ultra vires*, for instance, if she picks a service that does not correspond to the relevant dependence degree. And it may be formally defective if she fails to (try to) visit the patient prior to issuing the resolution.

As a matter of law, legal power is a *vicarious* ability because only by acting in accordance with the provisions in a pre-existing legal framework can one's say-so have the relevant legal meaning and import. Analogous reasoning applies with respect to that ability's possible *moral* import. For, in the many domains and respects in which large-scale patterns of specific convergence are called for adequately to meet human needs, it is only by slotting into one such pattern (e.g. paying 10 percent of one's income through tax) that a person's contribution is genuinely apt justly to make a difference, and may therefore be owed by right. The ability to determine and *mark* such patterns of conduct, on a wide or narrow scale, can therefore amount to an ability to, as it were, craft moral duties and rights. And that capacity to mark, to craft requirements of justice, is often only had precisely by speaking in the law's voice, typically as one link within a chain of legal empowerment. This is so whenever, as explained in this section, cogent considerations of justice require that the specification of rights be effected gradually and in the course of a process that allocates appropriate freedom to those best placed to decide, and at the same time circumscribes their choices in keeping with existing rational constraints, including the constraint that what has already been settled cannot, so far forth, be reopened or undone by those further down the chain.

3.8 SYSTEMIC SPECIFICATION

But talk of a 'chain' is a simplification, not least because Figure 3.1 shows at best a slice of a vast and complex *network* of specifications, which speak in sometimes overlapping and conflicting ways to subject-matters and needs that extend well beyond healthcare. Even the questions opened up for decision at stage *e* of the chart, all of them relevant to setting up a network of public healthcare, are but a small depiction of the extraordinarily wide pool of intersecting realms that specific convergence must simultaneously extend to in a community if justice is to be adequately realised in *any* of these realms.

To some extent, the legal technique we have charted in the last two sections – legal validity – contributes, in and of itself, to sustaining, to rendering viable, this vast network of coexisting decisions and determinations. It does so primarily in two, partly opposing, ways. The first way has to do with ensuring that the relevant decisions are *severally identifiable* – identifiable as made on the law's behalf, as legally binding on their own terms, as legally valid. Validity's capacity saliently to mark, to mark relatively independently of subject-matter, indeed to simplify the recognition of the legal positions marked through tangible forms of record or proof, is all the more pressingly called for the more varied the decisions and legal areas in question. Such relative detachment of the system of marking from the system marked, of the secondary from the primary level of convergence, can and must become nearly complete in those exceptional situations in which certainty is paramount, to the point that even a breach of substantive criteria of validity can be outweighed, *as a matter of law*, by a proper fulfilment of procedure: in many legal systems this is the case with some property registry entries, notarial deeds, and with (other) legally final resolutions (*res judicata*).

By and large, however, and conversely, compliance with applicable validity criteria will by itself secure a degree of coherence, or even just non-contradiction, *amongst* the acts setting validity criteria and the acts fulfilling those criteria, particularly criteria of the substantive sort. That is the second way in which the technique of validity helps to render manageable the jungle of valid acts, a jungle that legal professionals learn to make their way through by deploying a range of interpretative tools that generalise what certain well-entrenched kinds of validity criteria need not always explicitly state: for instance, that later or more special provisions supersede earlier or more general ones; that certain sets of rules are default regimes; that presumptions or burdens of proof may apply across whole areas of regulation; and that also in other respects legal materials are to be construed consistently with one another, almost as if devised by a single author – something law students are quick to pick up as they begin to be summoned to state 'what the law is' on some issue.[42] This incomplete but still significant degree of coherence amongst legally valid acts within a legal system has, as its natural counterpart, the fact that the persons performing those valid acts are not fully in control of the legal meaning of their acts. This may be expressed by saying that legal meaning is *systemic*: an act's legal meaning, the change in legal positions it introduces, is potentially co-determined by the legal meaning of the valid acts by other persons and institutions (which bear on its validity).[43] Consenting to marry a person already married, settling on a clause in breach of a legally implied term, or allocating dependence services beyond the eligible range – these acts may claim to change legal positions, but will not change them by so claiming. That there is a settled grammar for speaking the law's language entails that those who do not correctly use it may not be understood, or indeed not be taken to have spoken. This is a price we pay for the systemic and *pro tanto* harmonising character of legal meaning.

But a sound community-wide pursuit of justice does not only require that valid decisions be individually identifiable and relatively consistent with one another. Much more strategic, positive links must be devised and forged between areas of

[42] Some of these interpretative devices or postulates are usefully articulated in Frederick Schauer, *Thinking Like a Lawyer* (Cambridge, MA, Harvard University Press 2009). Kelsen spoke of presuppositions of legal cognition: Hans Kelsen, *General Theory of Law and State*, Anders Wedberg (tr) (New York, Russell 1945) 406–7; Hans Kelsen, *The Pure Theory of Law*, 2nd ed, Max Knight (tr) (Berkeley, CA, University of California Press 1967) 206. The 'single author' aspiration is reflected (though overstated) in Dworkin's portrait of the 'interpretive judgment': Ronald Dworkin, *Law's Empire* (Oxford, Hart 1998), Ch. 7.

[43] See further, Köpcke, *Legal Validity: The Fabric of Justice*, Ch. 6.

legal regulation in order to channel sensitive relations between the subject-matters they regulate. These relations may be called for as a result of the fact, for example, that some undertakings serve as means to further undertakings (as in the case of resource pooling or public tender), or the need to demarcate prerequisites for holding certain cross-cutting general kinds of legal status (such as nationality, full age, or bankruptcy), or the standing need for ancillary tasks of oversight, control, and fraud prevention (including everything from safety standards and licensing, to tort and criminal responsibility). In our example alone, the needed connections between (as it were) different chains of specification will be manifested in adequate income tax regulation and collection and transparent budgeting; administrative access to tax data for the purposes of means-testing; business incentives for hiring dependent persons; labour rules governing the government's or R's employment of the carer; professional licensing of pharmacists, social workers, and doctors; the eligibility of non-nationals for assistance; and all corresponding regimes of offences and procedural pathways and guarantees.

These strategic connections should for the most part be formulated centrally and by an agent well placed to design and deliberately to introduce potentially far-reaching general legal changes across a range of topics, an agent with appropriate resources and information, but also appropriate legal hierarchy. For reasons that the next chapter will explain, this task is primarily incumbent on the legislature. While not even a legislature is typically in full control of the legal meaning of its own decisions, it has a comparably wide freedom or discretion to mould them, coupled with a pre-eminent technique to mark them. It therefore has a key role in leading and organising the specification of human rights, not despite the systemic nature of legal meaning but because of it.

3.9 CONCLUSION

Good law-making is craftsmanship of human rights. The point of law is not merely to give effect to or enforce previously existing rights; even less is it to infringe them. In an important sense, good law-making brings rights into being. Genuine, actionable rights exist insofar as other persons hold correlative duties. Conduct is due, is owed for another's sake, where it is an especially suited, available, and thus necessary means to advance a critical aspect of that other person's wellbeing. But the critical aspects of human wellbeing enshrined in human rights can, in significant respects, only adequately be advanced through organised convergent conduct, including the mutual restraint, of large numbers of persons, following patterns specific enough that they could have reasonably been different but that, once settled, become privileged and necessary means to foster justice. Setting up and maintaining such schemes of convergent conduct is primarily the responsibility of those who are in a position saliently to mark, and justly to enforce, suitably comprehensive strategies by deploying tools that only legal systems can supply.

For it takes the grammar of legal validity to cast the chosen strategies in a language understandable by persons far apart in space, time, and moral outlook. It takes legal empowerments to allocate the task of choosing, of crafting duties and rights, amongst those best placed to decide at each juncture. And it takes the resources of a legal *system*, both at the level of reasoning and institutional design, as the rest of this book elaborates, to weave the freedom of choice of multiple actors into a reasonably coherent, targeted pursuit of justice in human relations that expresses the self-direction of individuals and of the community as a whole. It takes positive law to specify, to craft, to realise human rights.

4

Legislation as Reasoned Action

Richard Ekins

4.1 INTRODUCTION

The main way in which rights are and should be secured in law is through legislation. The legislature is a type of institution structured to protect and promote rights. These claims run against the grain of much scholarship, which maintains that the legislature is disposed, at best, to maximise the general welfare, not to reason about rights. The burden of this chapter is to explain how the legislature is capable of reasoning and how it reasons about rights, such that legislation may be a set of reasoned choices that specify rights. The chapter opens by considering the misconception that while courts reason about principle, the legislature does not reason, but is instead a machine that is driven by popular preferences. This is a familiar but misleading account of how legislators reason and act and an unsound theory of the objects of reasonable legislative action. The better view is that the point of legislation is to change the law reasonably, which requires the exercise of rational agency, and hence an agent. The legislative assembly is an institution that is structured to exercise such agency. In legislating well, legislators consider what should be done, relying on a complex mix of moral, empirical, and technical reasoning, and choose a course of action. Rights are central to good legislative deliberation, being the ends for which the legislature acts or bearing on the means it chooses to some other end. The well-formed legislative assembly reproduces the community in a form fit to reason and choose, such that legislation is intelligibly thought the choice of the self-governing community. This understanding of the legislature should inform how limits on legislative authority are framed.

4.2 MISCONCEIVING THE LEGISLATURE

The legislature, many scholars argue or assume, is an institution that is incapable of reasoning, except in service to the preferences or interests of (a majority of) voters. These scholars argue or assume, in sharp contrast, that the judiciary is an institution that is capable of responding to reason. This disjuncture is taken to have an obvious implication for the separation of powers – legislation, in which legislators assert majority preferences, should be limited by judicial review, in which judges reason and protect rights.

This line of argument is developed with particular force in Dworkin's work. Dworkin takes his distinction between principle and policy to entail an institutional division of labour.[1] He signals this in the preface to *Taking Rights Seriously*, where he says:

> the promotion of the highest average welfare ... might be advanced more securely by assigning different types of questions to different institutions according to some theory of institutional competence, rather than by supposing that all institutions are equally able to calculate the impact on overall welfare of any particular political decision.[2]

Later Dworkin argues that the judiciary is the forum of principle.[3] The implication is that the legislature is the forum of policy.[4] That is, the judiciary settles questions of principle and right and the legislature settles questions of policy and general interest – and judicial review is the mechanism by which rights qualify the general interest. This contrast between judicial and legislative power is found throughout Dworkin's early formulation of rights, where he says that 'the institutions of political democracy ... enforce overall or unrefined utilitarianism'[5] and that '[t]he political process is a machine which is calculated, though imperfectly, to reach decisions such that ... the *overall* preferences of all the people, considered neutrally with the same consideration for the preferences of each, is improved'.[6] The courts refine the legislature's utilitarian calculation by enforcing rights.

In his subsequent work on resource-egalitarianism, Dworkin abandons utilitarianism but continues to define the public interest and sound policy in terms of what members of the community want, viz. by reference to the distribution of preferences.[7] This is consistent with his distinction between choice-sensitive and choice-insensitive issues, which corresponds to policy and principle.[8] Hence,

1 See BW Miller, 'Justification and Rights Limitations' in G Huscroft (ed.), *Expounding the Constitution* (New York, Cambridge University Press 2008), 93, 101.

2 R Dworkin, *Taking Rights Seriously* (London, Duckworth 1977), ix.

3 R Dworkin, *A Matter of Principle* (Cambridge, MA, Harvard University Press 1985), 69–72.

4 See P Yowell, 'A Critical Examination of Dworkin's Theory of Rights' (2007) 52 *American Journal of Jurisprudence* 93, 108.

5 Dworkin, *Taking Rights Seriously*, 277.

6 R Dworkin, 'Social Sciences and Constitutional Rights – the Consequences of Uncertainty' (1977) 6 *Journal of Law and Education* 3, 10.

7 R Dworkin, *Law's Empire* (London, Fontana 1985), 384; see further Yowell, 'A Critical Examination of Dworkin's Theory of Rights' at 116–20.

8 Dworkin, *Sovereign Virtue: The Theory and Practice of Equality* (Cambridge, MA, Harvard University Press 2000), 204–5.

he argues that courts should resolve choice-insensitive issues, in which the object is moral truth, whereas the legislature should resolve choice-sensitive issues, for which preference distribution is decisive.

The institutional advantage of the legislature, for Dworkin, is its capacity 'to produce an accurate expression of the different interests that should be taken into account'.[9] This advantage is realised by way of the legislator's responsiveness to voters and by way of the competition and bargaining amongst legislators. But this advantage effectively disables the legislature from responding to arguments of principle:

> [A]n argument of principle fixes on some interest presented by the proponent of the right it describes, an interest alleged to be of such a character as to make irrelevant the fine discriminations of any argument of policy that might oppose it. A judge who is insulated from the demands of the political majority whose interests the right would trump is therefore in a better position to evaluate the argument.[10]

Judicial reasoning concerns principle, but 'ordinary politics [turns on] the weight of numbers or the balance of political influence'.[11] Hence Dworkin's conclusion that '[j]udicial review insures that the most fundamental issues of political morality will finally be set out and debated as issues of principle and not political power alone, a transformation that cannot succeed, in any case not fully, within the legislature itself'.[12] In the final chapter of *Freedom's Law*, he explains how he thinks legislatures make decisions:

> when political controversies are decided by legislatures ... the decision is likely to be governed by what most people want. That is desirable when an issue turns on what is in the best interests of the community as a whole, and the gains to some groups are balanced by losses to others. In such matters, numbers should count. But they need not count, at least not for that reason, in matters of fundamental principle ...[13]
>
> Ordinary politics generally aims ... at a political compromise that gives all powerful groups enough of what they want to prevent their disaffection, and reasoned argument elaborating underlying moral principles is rarely part of or even congenial to such compromises.[14]

Thus, while the judiciary is structured to reason about principle, the legislature responds to numbers. The legislature's general incapacity to reason about principle follows from the fact that the point of the legislature is to aggregate preferences,

[9] Dworkin, *A Matter of Principle*, 85.

[10] Dworkin, *Taking Rights Seriously*, 85.

[11] R Dworkin, *Freedom's Law: The Moral Reading of the American Constitution* (Cambridge, MA, Harvard University Press 1996), 30.

[12] Dworkin, *A Matter of Principle*, 70.

[13] Dworkin, *Freedom's Law*, 344.

[14] Ibid. 344–5.

which is a complex exercise in counting what others think, and it is therefore structured to treat points of principle as if they were questions of preference. Instead of reasoning directly about what should be done, legislators instead invoke the fact of majority preference as if it were a reason.[15]

This analysis of the nature of the legislature is problematic. It fundamentally mistakes the capacities of legislatures, capacities that are to be understood by reflecting on the point of legislating – the reason to legislate – and on how legislators pursue that end.

The inadequacy of Dworkin's account of legislating is made clear by a sympathetic argument in its defence. Dimitrios Kyritsis maintains that 'it must be false to say that principle-based justifications don't figure in legislative proposals'.[16] I agree. He goes on to say that Dworkin acknowledges this when he says that '[t]he justification of a legislative program of any complexity will ordinarily require both sorts of argument'.[17] One might add that Dworkin says that legislators have a duty to advance the integrity of the law.[18] Kyritsis also says that 'it would cast legislatures in an irredeemably bad light to suggest that all they are institutionally bound to do is to aggregate interests'.[19] Legislators, he contends, would fail to do their duty if they ignored principle or rights; it is at least as much part of their institutional function to consider such questions as it is to debate issues of policy. It would be deeply counterintuitive to think that legislators had discharged their duty if they made considered policy judgments but were insensitive to rights and principle.[20]

Kyritsis is quite right about the centrality of questions of principle to legislating, on which I say more below. And it is true that from time to time Dworkin concedes this. But this does not entail that one should understand Dworkin to think legislatures and courts both capable of responding to reasons. Rather, these concessions, and their plausibility, undercut the main body of his argument, which is clearly for a conception of the legislature in which principle, and indeed reason, has no place. His understanding of how and why legislators act and how their interaction produces policy is inconsistent with legislators reasoning about principle. Indeed, for Dworkin the point of the legislature is to aggregate preferences, which makes the legislature incapable of addressing questions of principle by reasoning rather than by counting.

Dworkin reasons that legislators seek re-election and hence aim to do as their constituents please. In this way, he adopts the public choice conception of the legislator, a passive agent who responds to stimuli, and defends, in modified form, the

15 Dworkin, *A Matter of Principle*, 368.

16 D Kyritsis, 'Principles, Policies and the Powers of Courts' (2007) 20 *Canadian Journal of Law and Jurisprudence* 379, 386–7.

17 Dworkin, *Taking Rights Seriously*, 83.

18 Dworkin, *Freedom's Law*, 31, 345 and *Law's Empire*, Ch. 6.

19 Kyritsis, 'Principles, Policies and the Powers of Courts', 386–7.

20 Ibid.

idea that the legislative process is a machine that produces legislation.[21] This conception is reductive and indeed empirically false. Legislators are not passive agents, but persons acting for ends that explain their action, sometimes justifiable (the common good of their community) and other times not (personal enrichment or career advancement).[22] The public choice conception fails to ground a general theory of the legislative process, as a type of social reality, precisely because it does not explain adequately the good reasons there are to legislate, reasons that frame how legislators understand what they do together.

The point of the legislature is not to aggregate majority preferences. There is very often no unique, stable majority preference. More importantly, the reason for authorising a legislature is not to maximise preference satisfaction but to make provision for the common good, which requires that whoever legislates responds to good reasons for or against changing the law. Dworkin's focus on preferences is grounded in his presupposition that fairness requires that one avoid grounding law in true judgments about what should be done. No legislator should disable herself in this way: she should respond to good reasons for law-making, not merely find and give effect to the preferences of citizens.[23]

One sees the mistake in Dworkin's example of a choice-sensitive question, viz. whether to build a new road system or a sports centre.[24] Dworkin argues that 'information about how many citizens want or will use or will benefit directly or indirectly from each of the rival facilities is plainly relevant, and may well be decisive' to building the road system or the sports centre.[25] He then restates this as the question of 'whether a new sports stadium or a new road system will better match the needs and desires of the population as a whole'.[26] Therefore, he concludes, questions of this kind are most accurately decided by 'a process in which the wishes of most people are recorded directly, as through a referendum, or indirectly through the decisions of representatives elected and re-elected by popular majorities'.[27] This discussion

[21] D Rodriguez, 'Legislative Intent' in P Newman (ed.), *The New Palgrave Dictionary of Economics and the Law* (London, Macmillan 1998), Vol. 2, 563, 565 (Rodriguez does not endorse the public choice conception); see R Tollinson, 'Public Choice and Legislation' (1988) 74 *Virginia Law Review* 339–71.

[22] K Shepsle, 'Congress is a "They", Not an "It": Legislative Intent as Oxymoron' (1992) 12 *International Journal of Law and Economics* 239, 240.

[23] Nothing in this paragraph denies that compromise is an important part of legislative craft and prudent politics. The right way to secure the common good is very often to make stable, reasoned provision for what is to be done by articulating a plan that is capable of being supported by a wide range of legislators and citizens notwithstanding their many disagreements. See further Section 4.5 below and Chapter 6.

[24] The example trades to some extent on the possibility that there are good reasons for either choice, so that the options are in some sense incommensurable. However, the reasons should be irrelevant for Dworkin, so I set this reading aside.

[25] Dworkin, *Sovereign Virtue*, 204.

[26] Ibid. 205.

[27] Ibid.

equivocates between what citizens want, what they will use, what will benefit them, what their needs are, and what their desires are. Only the first of these are preferences in the strict sense. One need not prefer what one desires, or vice versa, and what one needs or will benefit from are not settled by what one prefers. If the question should be decided by reference to *need*, as is plausible, then what citizens prefer does not settle what should be done. The aggregate preference of citizens, even if it existed, would not constitute the standard for sound legislative action.

In outlining this example, Dworkin notes that 'a variety of issues may merge in that decision, from issues of distributive justice to those of sound environmental policy'.[28] How does sound environmental policy relate to what people want? In *Law's Empire*, Dworkin asserts that whether to conserve another species is paradigmatically a question that should turn on what people want, that is, on their preferences.[29] This assertion makes stark the truth that counting preferences treats each person equally at the cost of failing to respect anyone's reasons. Someone might oppose a policy on the grounds that there are good reasons to prevent the extinction of species where possible. Dworkin's account renders the legislature indifferent to these reasons, entailing that legislatures should act on even ignorant, confused, and vicious preferences.[30] No well-formed legislature, responsible for the common good, acts in this way.[31]

Likewise, Dworkin's analysis takes for granted that the decision of a representative legislature is indistinguishable from the outcome of a referendum.[32] This indifference is consistent with his public choice premises and his reductive account of legislative action. If preference satisfaction is the point, then legislators are delegates, relaying the preferences of their constituents or, at best, negotiating on behalf of their principals (the voters), who have already formed their preferences about what is to be done. This analysis again misconceives what it is to legislate and what it is to be a legislature. The reasons for legislating, which is to say the reasons why reasonable persons conceive there to be a distinct form of governing that is legislating, entail that there should be a legislature. The legislature should not be a mere conduit for an existing preference set, but should instead form a stable, coherent agent that deliberates and chooses what is to be done.

Dworkin's analysis fails to explain legislating, as two quite different examples make clear. In enacting the Suicide Act 1961, Parliament set aside the rule of criminal law prohibiting suicide and introduced a new rule of criminal law prohibiting

[28] Ibid. 204.

[29] Dworkin, *Law's Empire*, 340.

[30] See Yowell, 'A Critical Examination of Dworkin's Theory of Rights', at 100–1 and citations therein. In his early work, Dworkin excludes certain kinds of vicious preferences, e.g. racist preferences, not on the ground of their content but on the formal ground that they involve 'double-counting' of preferences.

[31] Together with other claims in this chapter, this is not an empirical claim about how all legislatures act, but a claim about the central case of a legislature. See the discussion of the central case in Chapter 1.

[32] Dworkin, *Sovereign Virtue*, 205.

the assistance of suicide. This statute is not well understood if one approaches Parliament as an institution that is incapable of responding to reasons, which merely aggregates popular preferences. The law-making act is an intelligible response to a set of related principles: affirming the sanctity of life (and the proposition that suicide is a tragedy to be avoided), taking it to be imperative to protect the vulnerable from abuse, and rejecting a broad understanding of autonomy as a justification for freedom to be assisted in one's suicide. Similarly, in enacting the Freedom of Information Act 2000, Parliament introduced an elaborate scheme to require public officials to disclose information on request, subjecting these duties to a complex enforcement arrangement. Again, this statute is misunderstood if assumed to be an unthinking expression of popular preference, even if the public was broadly supportive of, or even insistent on, such reform. In devising and adopting the scheme in question, Parliament took transparency in government (and indeed in public life generally) to be a sound principle, tempered by recognition of many other principles, including most obviously the importance of effective government.

4.3 THE ENDS OF LEGISLATIVE ACTION

It is a mistake to conceive of the legislature as a machine or process, as if the interaction of legislators somehow combined to produce outcomes through aggregating popular preferences or as a result of competition amongst lobbyists. The root cause of the misconception is a failure to take the legislature seriously, to follow the reasoning and choice of those members of the legislature who aim to legislate well. Not every legislator does his or her duty, but the way to perceive a stable type of institution, recognisably present in more or less developed forms here and there, is to see the reasons that warrant introducing and maintaining such an institution in the first place. The reasons to legislate call for a certain kind of action, which in turn requires a certain kind of institution.

The reasons to legislate are plainly closely related to the reasons for law, for legislation is a central source of law. The authority of law does not turn on the consent of the governed, even if the legal and political authorities should often maintain this consent. Rather, authority turns on the capacity to secure the common good, which state of affairs is an intelligible reason for those who can act to coordinate others and for others to accept and support their efforts to coordinate.[33] The object of authoritative action is this common good, not some aggregate of the preferences of members of the community. What is true of government and law in general is true likewise of the subsidiary act of legislating, which is that part of governing involving the deliberate making and changing of the law.

In legislating, some person or body exercises authority and acts to change the existing law, whether by introducing into the legal system some entirely new (set of)

[33] See Chapter 3.

propositions, or by amending or repealing existing propositions. The reason to make provision for such deliberate legal change – that is, to recognise or introduce legislative authority – is not that it is fair to give effect to what people want, as Dworkin and others maintain. The reason is that the common good requires that such provision be made, which common good is the object of the exercise of legislative authority and makes the act of legislating intelligible.

Why is this provision necessary? Not all law is deliberately made by acts intended to make or change the law: custom is a source of law that lacks this character and so too is case law, at least to the extent that it is made indirectly, in the wake of adjudication. In one (secondary) sense, a political community may have law without legislation. However, much of the value of legal order lies in the standing possibility that legal rules may be changed by deliberate, clear and reasoned action. A community would be in bad shape if it had no means to modify – deliberately, clearly – the content of the rules that directed social life. Thus, as Hart recognised, there is good reason to introduce the particular secondary rule that is a rule of change,[34] which authorises some person or body to repeal rules that are (or which have become) unreasonable, to introduce rules that would help realise some aspect of the common good, or to amend and improve existing rules.

The community's need for clear, deliberate legal change provides good reason to institute a body to make law deliberately. It does not follow that this body – the legislature – must legislate frequently. It may be that the legislature may not have to act often or that it has to act repeatedly and radically. It may often be reasonable for the legislature to permit secondary forms of legal change, case law and custom, to proceed. The legislature is able to correct or to supplement case law or customary legal rules and the reasonable exercise of legislative authority involves overseeing the law and changing it when need be.

The key advantage of the capacity to make law deliberately is that the law-maker is able to respond directly to the reasons that bear on changing the law. If there is good reason to repeal a law, for example if it is obsolete, unworkable, or pernicious, then one may repeal it; if there is good reason to introduce a new rule, in that it helps restrain wrongful action or opens up valuable new opportunities, then one may act on those reasons to adopt law to that effect. This direct and open responsiveness to all relevant reasons distinguishes legislating from law-making by other means. A judge deciding a case responds to that dispute and his decision is limited by the existing legal materials. It is not open to him simply to change the law to be as he thinks it should be if it were open to him to posit the law anew. The judge understands that he is not a legislator and that it is not his task to oversee the content of the law and to act freely to change it as is required to instantiate the common good.

The well-formed legislature responds to the reasons to change the law. That is, it decides when there is good reason to act and how, if it acts, the law is to change.

[34] HLA Hart, *The Concept of Law* (2nd edn, Oxford, Clarendon Press 1994) 92–3.

The capacity to legislate entails the freedom to settle the content of the law by acting for that end. Freedom does not mean that legislating is arbitrary. Rather, it means that the way in which the legislature acts, including whether it acts and the content of the law it makes, is settled not by rules but by how the persons exercising legislative authority choose to respond to the reasons that they perceive. The legislature is thus self-starting and self-directing. It need not wait for a case to adjudicate or a petition to arrive before it acts and within jurisdiction it may legislate as it sees fit. The exercise of legislative authority is under the voluntary control of the institution itself.[35] For the legislature to act in this way it must have the capacity to formulate proposals for legislative action, and to evaluate and revise them in response to the reasons that bear on the common good. To legislate, one must consider the common good, propose a legislative response, reason about its merits and perhaps modify it accordingly, before deciding whether to adopt the response.

An institution free to deliberate and to act as and when it chooses is well placed to make good law. The legislature responds directly to the complexity of the common good in that its deliberation is open to whatever is relevant to the good of the community. The reasons for change may justify a complex, comprehensive decision as to what shall be done. The legislature is able to act to introduce a detailed set of legal rules that addresses an aspect of the common good in this comprehensive way. Legislation is posited at a certain point in time in a canonical formulation and is prospective in effect. It is a form of law suited to the Rule of Law. Public promulgation and canonical formulation make the legal change easier to locate and grasp than that found in unwritten custom or in the best understanding of a line of cases. This advantage is contingent, but the structure of the legislative act is directed towards positing law in the best form possible, by way of a public, canonical text, which is the focus of legal reasoning.

4.4 THE SOCIAL REALITY OF LEGISLATIVE AGENCY

Who should legislate? The common good requires a legal order in which particular rules, whether rules of custom or case law or legislation, are subject to deliberate, intelligent change when there is good reason for such change. Thus, the well-formed legislative act is the making of an intelligent choice about how to change the law: it is not mechanical preference aggregation. It follows that authority to legislate should only be exercised by a person or body that is capable of responding to reasons: legislative authority requires agency. The reason to authorise a legislative assembly to legislate is not that it aggregates preferences but rather that it is a body that is formed to be an agent.

[35] J Raz, 'Intention in Interpretation' in R P George (ed.), *The Autonomy of Law* (Oxford, Oxford University Press 1996) 293, 299–301.

In a small community, an assembly of all adult citizens might reasonably meet to decide what the content of the law shall be. They would legislate in their official capacity as members of this assembly, with the decision of the assembly settling how they would act as ordinary members of the community.[36] The assembly would represent the community in the sense that it constitutes an agent distinct from the members of the assembly as individuals, and also because it would act for the common good of *all* citizens, including those outside the assembly, such as children and the mentally ill.

In most communities, an assembly of all is not possible. There are far too many citizens to meet together in one location and even if all were to assemble in some physical or virtual location, the resulting group would be far too large to deliberate intelligibly and to act together rationally. The members of this assembly of all would be unable to talk to one another or to coordinate their action and so would be unable to form, evaluate, and revise proposals for legislative action. Also, most citizens would not be sufficiently well informed to participate as equals in the assembly's decision-making process. The members of a small community, say the medieval Icelandic Commonwealth, are more likely to have direct acquaintance with, and thus to engage rationally with, the limited number of issues that fall to be decided. They are also likely to hold one another to account for how they vote,[37] with the relative size of the community making each vote stand out. In a large, modern society, by contrast, each vote is less weighty and legislative issues are complex, such that voters are likely to lack knowledge about much that is relevant to legislating well.[38]

The electorate is not a reasonable substitute for a legislative assembly. Imagine the electorate were to exercise legislative authority by way of a series of plebiscites. The electorate would not be well placed to make law by responding to referendum proposals precisely because the electorate, unlike the assembly of all citizens, is not a rational agent. A plebiscite or referendum puts a proposal to the electorate, to be adopted or not. The electorate obviously has no capacity to formulate proposals itself, as a body. And it also has no capacity to revise a proposal, or to amend or improve it after due deliberation. The electorate is also unable to evaluate proposals as a body. Individual voters each evaluate proposals but the outcome of the plebiscite is just the aggregation of the responses of individual voters. That is, the electorate does not jointly argue about a proposal, change it, and then choose it. The plebiscite aggregates the individual responses of voters to a yes/no question over which they have no control, setting aside other possibilities. The electorate's incapacity to frame proposals has another consequence. Voters are not well-placed to consider

[36] J Finnis, *Natural Law and Natural Rights* (2nd edn, Oxford, Oxford University Press 2011) 252–4.

[37] G Brennan and A Hamlin, *Democratic Devices and Desires* (Cambridge, Cambridge University Press 2000) 198–9.

[38] Ibid. 172–3; R Hardin, 'Democratic Epistemology and Accountability' (2000) 17 *Social Philosophy and Policy* 110, 115–7.

how various proposals relate to one another. That is, the decision whether to adopt or reject this proposal is often made without considering the further consequences that this decision has. The electorate is made up of individual voters with very different priorities. Each voter may act perfectly rationally and yet the electorate as a whole may approve a series of proposals that are jointly incoherent. The electorate is not capable of ordering its decisions over time in the way that reason may demand.[39]

Legislation by plebiscite is not a good way to make general provision for legal change, and its drawbacks help illuminate the need for law-making by a deliberative assembly. Circumstances change and many laws require updating or repeal. It is difficult for voters to monitor the statute books and note outdated laws. And often those who promoted the initial referendum and benefit from it have no interest in sponsoring a subsequent referendum to update or repeal it. The difficulty of revisiting past decisions raises a further point. If the electorate makes law directly, then the law-maker cannot be held to account. Assuming anonymous voting in elections and in referendums, it is impossible to discipline a majority of the electorate for bad or incompetent decisions. In other words, there is no public decision-maker who is obliged to explain its acts. What this means is that while plebiscitary law-making is directly responsive to what a majority wants, it is undisciplined and unaccountable. Pettit concludes that the electorate is not conversable: it does not respond to reasons like a person and cannot be held to account for irrationality.[40]

Legislating well requires the exercise of rational agency. The agent who legislates cannot be the electorate at large, but should instead be some group or body that is capable of deliberation and decision. The modern legislative assembly is an institution that is framed to meet this need, with legislators jointly deciding how or if to change the law. The size and structure of the legislative assembly turn on maintaining this capacity. The assembly is not so large that its members, suitably coordinated, are unable to meet and converse. The assembly's stable membership makes it possible for it to deliberate over time about the merits of changing the law in this or that way, about alternative ways of changing the law, and about the implications one decision has for another. The ongoing, extended public argument about how to change the law that characterises the legislative process involves the development, evaluation and revision of proposals for legal change. In contrast to an electorate deciding by way of a succession of plebiscites, the legislative assembly is well positioned to make law deliberately rather than haphazardly.

Many scholars doubt that the legislature is capable of responding to reasons with intelligent choice.[41] The doubts centre on how a group of many legislators, who

39 P Pettit, 'Deliberative Democracy, the Discursive Dilemma, and Republican Theory', Ch. 7 in J Fishkin and P Laslett (eds.), *Debating Deliberative Democracy* (Oxford, Blackwell 2003) 138, 148–9.

40 Ibid. 154–5.

41 For discussion and references, see further R Ekins, *The Nature of Legislative Intent* (Oxford, Oxford University Press 2012), Ch. 1.

disagree with one another about what is to be done, could possibly respond to reason and choose as one. That is, while it seems plausible that the interaction of legislators might produce outcomes, these outcomes (which is to say: statutes) should not be thought to be the *decisions* of any single agent, for no such agent exists. I now explain – very briefly – how the well-formed legislative assembly is an agent that is capable of exercising rational agency.[42]

The legislative assembly is a complex social group. Its members enjoy decision-making equality in voting, but not in agenda-control, and the group structures their interaction in various stages by detailed procedural rules, in which majority voting looms large. The purpose of the legislature is to make law deliberately and for good reasons, which is to say for the common good. That is the purpose for which legislators act jointly and it is also the purpose that defines the enduring institution of the legislature, which particular legislators join for a time. The legislature stands ready to change the law, when there is good reason to do so. Again, it may be that it can act well without legislating frequently. The secondary or standing intention of the group, which defines the institution, and which all legislators share, is to stand ready to legislate when need be, acting on particular occasions in accordance with the legislative process. This standing intention is grounded in the unanimous interlocking intention of all legislators, who intend to act jointly to legislate.

The legislature acts to change the law. The act of the legislature, the exercise of its capacity to legislate, is the enactment of this or that statute, or of some far-reaching legislative code. The legislature acts on a proposal for legislative action – a bill – the content of which is the particular plan on which the legislature acts, and thus its primary intention (to be distinguished from the secondary intention noted above). The bill is a proposal for legislative action because it is a plan for how to change the law. It is a detailed text setting out how the law will change if it is enacted. This is the plan that coordinates legislators, which explains their joint action. The detail of the proposal is the focal point for argument and action. It is the proposal that legislators deliberate about and which, if they assent, they will act to introduce. That is, the proposal is what legislators hold in common. They act together by reference to that proposal and the legislature acts when they act to adopt it (a proposal that is rejected is not adopted and so there is no legislative act).

The plans of action that the legislature introduces should be coherent and grounded in an intelligible chain of reasoning. The proposals that legislators form and move and eventually adopt are considered for their suitability to be adopted by the legislature as a whole – that is, by the intelligent agent that the legislators jointly aim to constitute. If the legislative process truly were a machine, then it would be extremely difficult for legislators to attend to the shape of the proposal put before them (strictly speaking, no unified proposal for action would be put before them;

42 Ibid. Ch. 8.

this would instead arise as a side-effect of their interaction). However, there is good reason instead for the legislative process to be structured otherwise, as indeed it is in most modern legal systems. Proposals for legislative action are developed over time in stages at which the coherence and intelligibility of the whole plan of action is before legislators (whether in committee or in plenary session). Importantly, a subset of legislators, especially party leaders, the mover of the bill, and committee leaders, enjoy unequal control over the shape and content of the proposal, which helps make it possible for rational plans to be formed notwithstanding the possibly conflicting intentions of the many legislators. (Thus, the division of legislators into political parties and the creation of legislative offices help the many legislators deliberate and decide together, helping order and coordinate their joint action.) These plans of action, which may indeed be no legislator's first choice but which constitute complex, coherent means to intelligible ends, are then adopted by the legislature as a group in the act of enactment.

Far from legislative action being a side-effect, or even the overlap or coincidence, of the individual action of legislators,[43] legislating by assembly is the joint act of the members of the institution. The particular actions of legislators are unified by the rational order of their standing intention to form an institution that acts rationally and by the rational order of their particular intention to choose to change the law in some specific ways for some specific reasons, which reasoned choice is made out in the proposal open to all. The social reality of the well-formed legislature is thus that it exercises rational agency, being structured to form and adopt reasoned plans and to reflect on their coherence. The assembly thus stands ready to legislate well and in its particular actions exercises its capacity to respond to reasons for changing the law by making reasoned choices.

To be clear, the use of majority voting in the legislative process does not support Dworkin's assertion that the legislature responds to power and numbers whereas the judiciary responds to reasons.[44] The use of a rule of majority vote tells one little about how members of the group decide. Judges should decide cases for the right reasons, namely that the law requires, or at least is consistent with, a particular decision. Yet as Waldron argues the balance of reasons does not settle the outcome in a multi-member appellate court: instead, the outcome is settled by the vote amongst judges, each of whom should have voted for reasons they found persuasive.[45] Likewise in the legislature, the outcome of the process, the question of whether a particular proposal is enacted, is settled by a majority vote, but the reasonable legislator, like the reasonable judge, acts for reasons. Like the judge in dissent, the legislator who is in the minority opposes the legislature's decision, but can and should (at least often) recognise that the majority had reasons for supporting the decision and that this is a

[43] John Gardner, Joseph Raz, Larry Alexander, and Andrei Marmor each conceive of it in this way.
[44] Dworkin, *A Matter of Principle*, 70.
[45] J Waldron, *Law and Disagreement* (Oxford, Oxford University Press 1999) 90–1.

decision, an act, of the whole social group in the same way that a judgment is an act of the whole court and not only of the majority.

4.5 DELIBERATION AND CHOICE

To legislate is to choose. For the legislature to act well, its members must think carefully about the existing law and about whether it ought to be changed. If they conclude that changing the law in some way, whether by introducing new propositions or amending or repealing existing propositions, will help realise the common good then they ought to choose jointly to change the law in that specific way. When the legislature enacts a statute, it exercises its capacity to change the law for good reasons, which is to say it exercises its will to adopt some reasoned proposal for legal change. The legislative act is the decision about what should be done. The form of the act is the utterance of the statutory text that promulgates the legislature's reasoned law-making choice.

Legislative deliberation is reasoning about how or if to change the law, reasoning which culminates in the working up of proposals for change that are *chosen*. This reasoning is complex. Reflection on the common good may provide reasons to develop a proposal to change the law in some way, which proposal is a complex means to the ends that constitute the relevant aspect(s) of the common good. This proposal the legislators will develop and evaluate, revising it to avoid some (not all) foreseen but unintended consequences and to make it a means capable of securing some other intelligible end(s). The legislators develop this proposal and may choose it – acting jointly as the *legislature* – if they conclude that it is fit to be chosen, such that there is good reason for the legal changes it introduces.

The legislative act is a moral choice made in response to reasons: a choice about the propositions that ought to frame our common life. It follows that one cannot legislate well without sound moral judgment. However, sound moral reflection does not reveal an ideal legal code, which the legislature may transcribe or translate. Reasonable legislators will perceive that there are many goods which do not reduce to any one master-value and which may be realised in the lives of the many persons for whose common good they should act. Legislators will recognise further that while some sound intermediary principles and absolute prohibitions frame how persons should live, moral norms alone are insufficient. The legislature's action is framed by general moral truths but its duty is very often to specify these truths, choosing in what particular forms they shall be given effect in the law of his community.[46]

Legislative deliberation is not abstract moral reflection. It is informed by empirical reasoning, in which legislators aim to discern the relevant facts about the state of the world, such that they may change the law in a way that introduces certain patterns of

[46] See Maris Köpcke, Section 3.3 in this book.

social life (say, an end to violent assault; or fair and thriving commerce). Legislating well (or indeed even at all) also requires technical reasoning – about the existing law and about how one's proposed law-making act is to work to change the law and the world. The craft of legislating involves developing proposals in a form fit to change the law and the life of the community as intended. The elaboration of a set of legal rules, which is intended to capture the moral conclusion that a problem ought to be addressed in a certain type of way, may suggest alternative ends for which the legislature should act or may even warrant revising or abandoning that prior moral conclusion.

Part of the craft of legislating is attending to how and why the persons one aims to coordinate are likely to act. The law the legislature enacts will appeal to the reasonable, while often compelling the unreasonable to comply. The legislators may foresee that many persons are likely to fail to comply with the legal rules they introduce and yet rightly refrain from choosing some alternative means of compliance if, for example, it is too harsh or costly. Here, the legislature chooses some particular (complex) means to the end(s) for which it acts, not on the limited grounds of instrumental rationality but rather by considering the range of valuable goods in play.

The reasoning of legislators is an extended reflection on the position of their community, its common good, and the opportunities they have to act for that good. The legislature's deliberation involves the formation, refinement, and scrutiny of proposals for how to change the law in ways that are supported by good reasons: that is, which support, protect, or instantiate some aspect of the common good. Legislators may begin with relatively abstract ends, such as maintaining a clean environment or a social order free from violence, but their reflection on those ends involves their specification, identifying more particular states of affairs that are attractive elaborations of the more abstract ends and which are fit to be chosen.[47] Thinking about means to those states of affairs may in turn reveal further ends that warrant the legislature's response (or at least its intelligent consideration), and particular means to further ends may constitute partial ends in their own right. The final proposal for legislative action in which deliberation culminates is a complex scheme of means-end relations, which the legislature may choose, in which case it acts intending the means and the ends.

The legislature legislates when it communicates or promulgates its choice that certain propositions shall be law. The legislative act thus adopts a canonical text and authoritatively introduces into the law the propositions the text formulates. The legislative act is first and foremost the act of settling on those propositions. That is, just as law in general is seen most clearly in the bearing it has on – the meaning and force it has in – the deliberation and action of those it addresses, so too the primary reality of legislating is in the practical reasoning and choice of the legislature.

[47] On specification, see H Richardson, *Democratic Autonomy: Public Reasoning about the Ends of Policy* (Oxford, Oxford University Press 2002), especially 104, 108–10, 127.

The central aspect of the act of legislating, then, is the exercise of reason and the response of will, which culminates in choice.

This analysis is consistent with the truth that compromise has an important place in legislative reasoning, which does not hold (at least in anything like the same way) in judicial reasoning. But, *pace* Dworkin, this is not a difference that tracks one institution's openness to reason and another's capture by preference and power. The courts act in response to cases brought before them and the options open to them are or should be narrowly curtailed by doctrine, in the ordinary case. The legislature, by contrast, acts on its own initiative and has a very wide range of possible courses of action open to it. In working up proposals for choice, legislators should aim to make decisions that, *inter alia*, will not provoke insurrection, that are capable of keeping the peace, that avoid unnecessary social strife, and that may enjoy sufficiently broad popular and elite support so as to be unlikely later to be repealed. That is, legislators often have good reason to try to compromise, to secure widespread support for changes in the law. Indeed, the Rule of Law requires as much, per the desideratum of stability. Importantly, that legislating often involves compromise does *not* entail that it does not involve principle, or that it is somehow divorced from reason. The legislature often – rightly – chooses a principled, reasoned compromise.

4.6 RIGHTS IN LEGISLATIVE REASONING

The legislature should not attempt to balance the common good *against* the rights of any member of the community. Any such attempt at balance would be incoherent. The reason for this is not that rights do not place moral limits on the legislator (and all authorities) – they do – but rather that rights are constitutive elements in the common good, such that reasonable reflection on the common good involves judgment about what persons are entitled to. The common good, which is the set of conditions under which members of the community are able to flourish, consists in large part of the securing to each person that to which each is entitled from all other persons.[48] What each person is entitled to is that person's rights, which take various forms: a liberty to act or refrain from acting in some way (free from a duty of the countervailing form), a claim-right that some person or body perform or refrain from some act, a power to change some person's legal position, or an immunity from one's legal position being changed in some way by another.

The reasonable legislature does not set out to secure some public benefit, the pursuit of which involves intentional or incidental interference with people's rights and which 'infringement' (or worse, 'violation') of rights is justified if reasonable (or 'proportionate'). Rather, the legislature deliberates about what rights citizens have, which is to say to what each should be entitled. This deliberation is moral reasoning

[48] See Chapter 2.

informed and framed by empirical and technical reasoning and often calls for the exercise of free choice amongst reasonable alternatives. That is, legislative reasoning about rights is central to legislative reason in general. The reasonable legislator, like any other person, should recognise that there are some absolute moral rights, including the right not to be intentionally killed or tortured, which impose duties on all other persons. The legislature has good reason to proscribe, punish, and deter such violations of duty, and should act to protect in law the absolute rights that are central to sound morality.

This recognition of absolute moral rights turns on recognition of the intelligible human goods that are the objects of reasonable action and insight into the principles that frame how one should realise these goods in one's life and the lives of others. More generally, this course of reflection, which is fundamental to practical reasoning and choice, informs all legislative choice, including in relation to rights. The legislature's reasoning culminates in the choice of some legal propositions, which very often specify some pattern of claim-rights, liberties, powers, and immunities and thus jointly constitute a series of defined relationships amongst persons. This set of relationships, which are three-term rights (some action and two persons), constitutes the legal rights of the persons in question.[49] Thus, rights are legislated: they are given form and content in legislation.[50]

How do two-term rights – a person's right to some subject-matter, whether life or free speech or equality – feature in legislative deliberation? These rights unify, loosely, some set (perhaps an incomplete, yet to be fully specified set) of three-term rights, in which form they must be extended to be *legal* rights in the full sense of the term. Two-term rights are useful in legislative deliberation to the extent that they help legislators keep in view an aspect of human wellbeing and perhaps a mode of action that is consistent with, or well suited to, supporting or realising that aspect.

It follows that rights feature in legislative reasoning in a number of ways. The legislature aims to identify and give effect to the rights that citizens have, which requires in part reasoning about the general facets of human wellbeing and/or general propositions that serve them. Thus, the legislature may both act to realise – introduce, support – the right in question, which means that it is an end for which it acts, and also act consistently with the right, which disciplines the means one may choose to other ends. More precisely, rights may be the end(s) of legislative action, the means the legislature adopts to some end(s), and side-constraints on the means that may be adopted to some end(s).

One sees this variety in the example of the Suicide Act 1961. The Act cancels the duty in criminal law not to commit suicide, hence creating a liberty, at least so far as the criminal law is concerned, to *attempt* to commit suicide. The Act imposes a new duty

[49] See Chapter 2 and G Webber, *The Negotiable Constitution* (Cambridge, Cambridge University Press 2009).

[50] And in rules of the common law, although very often displaced by statute.

not to assist another in his suicide, which makes it a criminal wrong to invite another to assist one in one's own suicide and means that each person has a claim-right that others not encourage or incite them to commit suicide. This series of legal relationships cannot be simply read off from the right to life or from a principle of autonomy. They are particular choices about how the law should be framed to protect the lives of members of the community, about the pattern of legal relationships that should govern someone who attempts suicide and those who encourage or assist others in suicide. Reasonable people disagree about the merits of this pattern, but it should be clear that it is the conclusion of reasoning that aims to take rights and principle seriously.

Affirming the right to life, or the freedom of speech, for example, highlights the importance of some interest and measures that may tend to support it, which in turn enables right-holders to call attention to their interests and to ground argument about what should be done. However, determining precisely how this underdetermined aspect of human wellbeing is to be given legal effect requires specification. That is, the incomplete affirmation of the right is made complete by specifying the particular states of affairs to which it generally refers that are in truth valuable and to be protected, and also to specify the types of action that are to be prohibited, permitted, or enabled to that end. This specification requires the law-maker to make more concrete the distinctions on which the general affirmation is silent, for example, between worthwhile, protected speech and false, pernicious speech. This process of specification involves focusing in detail on how the abstract value affirmed in the general right is or is not valuable in particular contexts and less abstract instantiations. It also involves careful attention to whether some particular type or action, which might be a possible concrete specification, is truly reasonable, which turns on whether it would remain the object of the reasonable person's choice when the detail of this specification and its impact on the lives of others is known. (The reasonable person in all his or her deliberations and choices is open to, and actively wills, the flourishing of all persons.)

When one deliberates about the common good, one should be aiming to pick out worthwhile states of affairs, realised in the lives of individual members of the community and in their interaction as members of one community. More precisely, the states of affairs constitute the set of conditions that make possible human flourishing, in which each person may live well. Hence the good of each person, and the opportunities for each person to flourish, are constitutive of the common good. There is no space on this account to exploit some few (or many), deliberately harming them, for some greater good or collective interest. All collective interests, properly understood, are goods for individual persons and should be sought in ways that keep the good of each person in view. That is, the neglect, through ignorance or contempt, of the good of some is unreasonable. Rights affirmed in general terms, which pick out and make salient some aspect of the wellbeing of each person, may help authorities to avoid acting either against the good of some for the good of others or neglecting the good of some. Thus, rights certainly express a constraint on how authority may be exercised, for rights point out particular aspects of the wellbeing of persons whose opportunities to flourish constitute part of the common good. However, the rights that constrain and constitute the common good, and so warrant choice, protection, and support, are not the general, incomplete rights but the rights duly specified, picking out particular states of affairs and types of action.

There is no general formula for specifying general rights to particular states of affairs and actions. The task is to choose how to secure the conditions that make possible the flourishing of members of the community. Finnis frames the task well when he argues that one should have in one mind's eye some attractive pattern of social life and action, in which persons may live well, and then choose those particular rights that favour and support this pattern.[51] This process, which involves specification and which confronts multiple irreducible goods, is framed by reason but not settled by reason. Once reason has framed the options for choice, ruling out the many unreasonable options, what is required is choice, led by imagination, empathy, and insight, and made by one whose character is sound.

4.7 TWO EXAMPLES

Let me outline further, by way of two examples, this sketch of the way in which the legislature specifies rights by enacting legislation.

Consider first the right of any person charged with a criminal offence to be presumed innocent until proved guilty (Art. 6(2) of the European Convention on Human Rights, for example). The right is a sound normative proposition, which follows from the charitable disposition the community should adopt in determining whether its members have committed serious wrongs. The point of the proposition is also in part to minimise the risk of miscarriages of justice, in which innocent persons are wrongly (mistakenly) found guilty, which risk turns in part on the general inequality of arms between prosecution and defence. This right is a closely specified proposition, which is fit for adoption as a legal proposition in its own right. The legislature would depart from the right were it to abrogate the presumption in relation to some offence, replacing the presumption (and its related formula that a finding of guilt should be beyond reasonable doubt) with another standard, say proof on the balance of probabilities. For the adjudication of *criminal* charges, any such departure is unjustified.

The proposition requires specification, however, in relation to some questions. In many jurisdictions, the legislature provides that a person found in possession of some quantity of a proscribed drug shall be presumed to intend to supply that drug to others.[52] The presumption is defeasible, but the onus is on the defendant to prove, on the balance of probabilities, that he did not intend to supply the drug to others.

[51] Finnis, *Natural Law and Natural Rights*, 219.

[52] For example, in the UK, see Misuse of Drugs Act 1971, s. 5, and in NZ, see Misuse of Drugs Act 1975, s. 6(6).

Is this inconsistent with the presumption of innocence? The House of Lords and the New Zealand Supreme Court have each answered yes, reasoning that the legislature had chosen to lower the standard of proof in order to make it easier to secure convictions in drug trafficking cases.[53] That is, Parliament was prepared to risk convicting the innocent in order to convict more of the guilty and to deter others from such crimes. This judicial reasoning is a little hasty. The provision directs triers of fact to draw certain inferences from certain facts, viz. possession of some amount of drugs entails that the possessor intends to supply the drug to others. The provision should track the inferences that a sound trier of fact should in any case make, with the point of the provision being to frame the reasoning of *all* triers of fact in this same way. This is itself a means to two ends: making true judgments about guilt and making such judgments without undue cost and complexity. The latter is no utilitarian regression. Rules of evidence should be chosen in part to make possible efficient trials, for costly, complex criminal trials may frustrate the ends of the criminal law, not to mention obstructing reasonable action for other aspects of the common good.

The inference that the reverse onus provision directs, and the conditions under which it may be defeated, are reasonable to the extent that they are likely to direct triers of fact to make true judgments about whether the accused in fact intended to supply. In deciding whether to enact a provision of this kind, and in specifying its content (especially the relevant amount of the proscribed drug), the legislature should keep in view the prospect of triers of fact acting well, which here means distinguishing the guilty from the innocent and maintaining that charitable disposition towards the accused that is warranted. The legislature would go wrong either if it chose amounts that failed to distinguish supply from personal use, effectively deeming many or all instances of the latter to be the former, or if it failed to consider the difficulties the defendant might face in proving he had no intention to supply. The legislature's clear delineation between amounts that ground the inference and amounts that do not has another salutary effect, which is in part an end for which it acts. That end is the clarification to would-be users of some proscribed drug that they are likely (reasonably!) to be understood to intend to supply the drug if they possess a certain amount. Hence, these users, who by definition act unreasonably in flouting laws forbidding possession of proscribed drugs, are encouraged to think again about possessing any amount, especially an amount above the threshold. This may help dissuade some users from subsequently forming the intent to supply or from stockpiling proscribed drugs. This clarification, which is in part a deterrent, is arguably reasonable because it is made by way of an inference that in fact tracks truth.

Consider next the right to a fair trial (Art. 6(1) of the European Convention on Human Rights, for example). This captures, loosely, an important aspect of human wellbeing and articulates, in incomplete form, a sound normative proposition. The

[53] *R* v. *Lambert* [2002] 2 AC 545; *R* v. *Hansen* [2007] 3 NZLR 1.

legislature should specify the right. The rape-shield legislation in question in *R* v. *A (No. 2)* attempted this, sharply limiting the circumstances in which rape defendants (and their counsel) could cross-examine complainants on their sexual history.[54] The legislature aimed to change the law of evidence in a way that would make it possible for defendants to contest the charges against them, without putting in question that which the legislature judged irrelevant, viz. the sexual history of the complainant, a focus on which might often compromise the integrity of the trial. Further, the legislature aimed to protect complainants from, and would-be complainants from the prospect of, intrusive, degrading questions about their sexual history. That is, the legislature acted to give effect to its judgment of what constitutes a fair rape trial, in which the trial does not, save in exceptional circumstances, extend to the complainant's sexual history.

Perhaps the complainant's sexual history is often relevant evidence. Still, the decision that some evidence that is in principle relevant should be excluded is not novel. The right to a fair trial need not entail an absolute rule that all relevant evidence should be admissible (or compellable). The various limits on the introduction of evidence (say, the immunity to compulsion of priests or doctors or lawyers who have relevant information) are not *limits on the right to a fair trial* but are rather particular specifications of that right, which constitute part of what it is to have a fair trial, specifically, that one may introduce any evidence that is relevant that there is not otherwise a good reason to exclude. There is more than one form of fair trial. The length and thoroughness of criminal trials turns in part on the resources made available. Any modern legal system should make provision for defendants to be legally represented, but this turns on the premise that this is affordable, which entails further (alas) that the quality of representation is limited also.

The legislature acts to protect complainants from brutal cross-examination in part because it perceives that it is wrong, again absent exceptional circumstances (where there are reasons why the complainant's character should be put in issue), to permit complainants, who are likely to be victims, to be treated thus. The legislature also, quite reasonably, has its eye on the consequences of the status quo, in which many victims of serious sexual crime fail to report or to proceed to trial because of their (justified) fear of what they may endure in the witness box. The legislature has good reason to address this state of affairs, for the sake of the just order that is an absence of sexual crime and for the vindication of the integrity of the rights of the particular victims in questions (to be free from sexual assault). Thus, the pitiful figures regarding rape reporting and conviction rightly inform the legislature's deliberation about what constitutes a fair trial. True, a narrow focus on this consideration alone would derail that deliberation, for the legislature might lose sight of the importance of the open, truth-telling process that a trial should be or, that which is related, of the prospect of unsound convictions being entered. The legislature might act unreasonably

[54] *R* v. *A (No. 2)* [2002] 1 AC 45; Youth Justice and Criminal Evidence Act 1999 (UK), s. 41.

in its specification in this domain. Still, it is not trading away the right to a fair trial against other interests when it undertakes this deliberation and chooses as it does. Its choice is of what is a fair trial, to which the considerations outlined above (and doubtless many others) are relevant.

In enacting a rape-shield law, the legislature may specify the right to a fair trial. The law-making act may be a reasonable means to the set of related ends for which the legislature acts: finding the truth relevant to the charges against the defendant, protecting (likely) rape victims from unfair treatment in the witness box, encouraging victims to come forward, avoiding excessive costs, and maintaining the charity towards defendants that grounds the presumption of innocence. These ends all warrant consideration and are incommensurable. The legislature develops and evaluates proposals to change the law by reference to these ends. The legislature should think carefully about the relevant facts and possibilities (uncertainties), rejecting proposals that are cavalier or ineffective, and then *choosing* to act for some state of affairs, because it is judged valuable.

4.8 SELF-GOVERNMENT BY LEGISLATION

I return now to the question of *who* legislates. There are worse things than being ruled by a (beneficent) foreign power or a (well-meaning, competent) committee – not being ruled at all or being ruled by a tyrant. Still, much is lost when the community does not rule itself, when citizens do not share in government. Just as one lives well by exercising one's capacity to choose for reasons, formulating a coherent plan of life and so on, the community lives well when citizens jointly settle how they shall live, constituting themselves in a certain way and responding to the many reasonable courses of action open to them with intelligent choice. That is, self-government is valuable.

Legislating is one of the community's central acts of self-government. The legislative assembly is a representative and deliberative body, which acts on behalf of the community in reasoning about what should be done and then in choosing to change the law. True, whoever exercises legislative authority, whether monarch, committee, or assembly, represents the community in its law-making acts, for that person or body acts for the good of all and citizens owe a duty to obey the laws in question not to the ruler but to each other. However, the legislative assembly represents the community in a further sense, constituting an agent, the reasoning and choice of which helps realise collective self-government.

The assembly is a type of institution uniquely well placed to represent the whole community. It is a large group, whose members are selected in such a way that the assembly acts not just for but also on behalf of all citizens. With several hundred members, individual legislators may represent particular groups or districts.[55]

[55] This line of thought is implicit in Waldron's work but he does not discuss representation in any detail: Waldron 54, 109–10, n. 60.

The assembly may 'represent more accurately [than a president] the range of diversity in the polity and ... foster closer connections between representatives and voters'.[56] Still, the assembly's size is limited by its point, which is to legislate well: the representative assembly is structured to reproduce the community in a form that can reason and act well.

My understanding of the capacities of the legislature stands in sharp contrast to Christopher Eisgruber's argument that the legislative assembly is not capable of representing the whole people and that it is unfit for constitutional self-government, save when disciplined by judicial review of legislation. The structure of his argument is to note that while the people should rule themselves, majorities should not dominate minorities. Democratic government, Eisgruber insists, 'must respond to the interest and opinions of all the people, rather than merely serving the majority, or some other fraction of the people'.[57] That is, he says, it must be impartial. This has institutional implications:

> If constitution-makers want to establish a democratic system of government, they should design institutions that are impartial rather than majoritarian. They might therefore reject the British model of an omnipotent national Parliament. They might choose instead to fragment power in order to increase the likelihood that the government will be responsive to the interests of minorities as well as majorities. To that end, they might wish to set up a variety of institutions with differing constituencies and responsibilities. Rather than locating all power in a single national legislative body, they might create a federalist structure, or a bicameral legislature (in which differently constituted majorities could check one another), or an independent executive with policy-making responsibilities, or ... an independent judiciary with special responsibility for protecting individual rights.[58]

Notwithstanding the nod to federalism, bicameralism, and a presidential executive, it is to judicial review that Eisgruber looks to discipline the (British) legislature, which he asserts is more or less inevitably majoritarian rather than impartial.

There are several problems with this analysis. Parliament is not the only institution in the Westminster constitution, but retains authority over others. And Parliament is not unitary in the sense that there are no politics internal to its action (it is also, one should add, *bicameral*). The facts of periodic election and parliamentary government (that is, the executive's dependence on continued parliamentary support) do not entail that the institution is simply the plaything of a univocal majority. Notably, Parliament comprises hundreds of elected representatives (and hundreds of peers), formed into political parties, which support a government or outline an alternative

[56] J Carey, 'Legislative Organization', Ch. 22 in R Rhodes, S Binder and B Rockman (eds.), *Oxford Handbook of Political Institutions* (Oxford, Oxford University Press2006) 431, 432.

[57] C Eisgruber, *Constitutional Self-Government* (Cambridge, MA, Harvard University Press 2001), 19.

[58] Ibid.

government in waiting, and which stand ready to contest the next election. The political community, in Britain as elsewhere, is complex and assembling a majority in the legislature standardly requires one to maintain the support of a coalition of minorities *and* to campaign on a plan for governing in the interests of the whole community.

The legislature's use of majority voting procedures does not entail disdain for, or neglect of, the good of the minority, any more than an appellate court's use of such procedures. The question that falls to be decided may often turn on a disagreement about what that good is (and, one should add, the majority may be entirely right), with majority voting being a fair procedure to reach a decision. Whoever rules should not rule for the good only of a majority of citizens, but this tells us nothing about the merits of majority rule as a decision procedure.

Reasonable legislating is not the transmission of popular preferences. Likewise, representation does not require the set of judgments and preferences of legislators to reflect in direct proportion the set of judgments or preferences of the voters. Voters should not choose representatives to be mere spokesmen for public opinion, who execute existing preferences or judgments. Instead, they should choose a person whom they think will legislate well. The assembly will likely include persons who share and reflect the range of different, credible political groups and views salient in the community. Each legislator forms part of the decision making body and to some extent identifies with and has interests in common with the part of the community he represents. It follows that the assembly is a body that brings the interests and range of views of the community together, in the person of intelligent participants, in a forum that may deliberate and decide.

The legislative assembly reasons in public. The initial selection of legislators frames but does not exhaust the assembly's subsequent argument and action. The way in which legislators reason and choose settles what is enacted. Law-making by assembly enables a microcosm of the community, those selected by other citizens to be competent legislators, to continue to argue about what should be done. An election may result in a party winning a majority of seats in the assembly, so that until the next election the members of this party, if they act together, may settle what the assembly does. Yet even when the party is relatively unified, the parliamentary minority continues to participate in the legislative process, arguing with the majority about what should be done, presenting new facts and questioning proposals. All the legislators, who together represent the community as a whole, participate in an ongoing argument about how best to serve the common good. The majority enjoys an advantage in settling that argument, but cannot dispense with it.

The assembly is a law-maker that is structured to bring forward and to consider the interests of citizens and to permit as many citizens as possible to share in legislating. The large number of legislators makes it possible for a range of perspectives and arguments to inform the legislature's deliberation. Instead of periodically choosing who is to be the king, say, citizens choose representatives whom they think likely to legislate well, perhaps in part because of the candidate's personal record of judgment or achievement, as well as because of the party to which the candidate belongs. When legislators argue for positions that citizens share, as is likely if the electoral process selects a range of persons whom the electors think show sound judgment, then the citizens' case is made in the legislative process. The case will often not be decisive, yet it is still valuable that the arguments that citizens find persuasive have been made. Crucially, the arguments are made in the forum that decides: they inform deliberation and are live, not just symbolic, contributions to the process.[59]

The large number of legislators is relevant to how citizens relate to them. Whereas a monarch is *the* decision maker – the political superior – each legislator is just one person amongst the many who share in decision-making, none of whom have authority to legislate until they persuade the legislature to act as one.[60] It follows that citizens may approach the legislative assembly not as supplicants but as participants once removed, setting out reasons for legislators to argue in this or that way. Kutz argues that the large number of legislators, together with their democratic credentials, makes it possible for citizens to understand themselves as participants in the assembly's deliberation in a way that is not possible where a much smaller group acts.[61] I would add that part of the point of the representative assembly is to make it possible for citizens to identify with the reasoning and action of a group to which they do not formally belong. The group understands its reasoning and action to be for the community and to some extent to be by the community, in the person of those representatives whom the electors have selected to serve. The assembly is thus a forum that is open to the community and authorising an assembly to legislate is consistent with the political equality of all citizens.

Not all reasoning takes place within the assembly, and certainly not in plenary session. Persons outside the assembly, including citizens, interest groups, and officials, often develop proposals fit for enactment. They may put their reasoned proposal to a legislator who may, if he judges it sound, seek to put it before the assembly. The size and diversity of the assembly opens multiple channels for reasoned contributions to the process, and for ongoing community participation in what is to be done. The legislative assembly thinks in public for the community. Its open deliberation is central to that process, not so much because that is where the thinking has to be done as because it is an opportunity to present arguments, raise issues, and request clarification, all as a prelude to a decision by the legislators as to what is to be done.

59 See Waldron, *Law and Disagreement*, 289–91 on the irrelevance of public debate that is unconnected to decision.

60 In practice, this means persuading a majority of legislators to support a bill on its final reading.

61 C Kutz, 'Parliamentary Self-Government: Comment on Waldron' in E Villanueva (ed.), *Legal and Political Philosophy* (New York, Rodopi 2002) 39, 44–8.

The assembly divides legislative power amongst several hundred persons, although its exercise is corporate and the act of the legislature is the act of a single institution, a unified agent. What this means is that the possibility of compromise, of adopting and responding to the views of multiple persons, is built into the decision-making process. A king has reason to take into account the views of his subjects, and sometimes to adopt a position that is a compromise. However, the legislative process by which an assembly acts is structured to permit multiple inputs, thus moving the interests of the community from outside the deliberating body (to whom they are relevant but not constitutive) into the deliberating body. Thus, the person doing the reasoning is now an artificial person, the community personified in the assembly. Or, as Locke put it, 'it is in their legislative [body] that the members of a commonwealth are united and combined together into one coherent living body. This is the soul that gives form, life, and unity to the commonwealth; from hence the several members have their mutual influence, sympathy, and connection'.[62]

4.9 LIMITING LEGISLATIVE AUTHORITY

The design of any particular constitution must respond to the detailed conditions of the community for whom it is intended. Still, general principles exist. The first principle of constitutional order is that those with capacity should exercise authority.[63] The second is that the location of authority should be settled by authority.[64] In that second type of act, one should aim to institute a body capable of holding in view that which is relevant and choosing reasonably, in a way that enables self-government.

It follows that in most political communities those with authority to frame the constitutional order should introduce a representative legislative assembly, structured to respond to the reasons for legal change with coherent, intelligent choices. This assembly need not enjoy plenary legislative power, for legislative authority might reasonably be separated amongst *legislatures*, each charged with responsibility for some aspect of the common good (enumerated powers) and/or the common good of some constituent political community within a (federal) whole. This separation is likely to be instituted in large part by constitutional law (rather than convention) and enforced by courts or some other (special) adjudicative institution. It may be reasonable also for constitution-makers to enact some particular legal propositions that limit the jurisdiction of law-makers, proscribing certain (types of) law-making acts, which there is good reason to foresee will be injurious to the common good. Any such limits should be adopted with caution, lest the legislature lack the capacity to change the law as required for the common good.

62 J Locke, *Two Treatises on Government*, P Laslett (ed.) (Cambridge, Cambridge University Press 1988), II, para. 212.

63 Finnis, *Natural Law and Natural Rights*, 246.

64 Ibid. 249–50.

In the central case of legislative action, the legislature acts for the common good in a way that is consistent with the equality of citizens and enables them to share in government. However, the legislature may of course misuse its capacity to change the law, acting for the private good (which is tyrannical), adopting unsound means and/or acting for ends that do not truly warrant choice (which is incompetent or at best mistaken), or denying citizens any share in government. The legislature might also fail to make reasoned choices, failing to maintain the discipline of responding *qua* legislature to reasons and instead producing statutes as the side-effect of the rational (or self-interested) action of individual legislators. That is, legislative agency might be used to improper ends or it might fracture and fail to be used at all, leaving space instead for the chaotic arbitrary 'action' that, in some scholarly accounts, defines the legislature.

The answer to some standing or likely failure of legislative action in some community may be to reform the structure of the assembly, or to wait on (or introduce and support) changes in the way citizens perceive and engage with legislators. Or it may be to introduce or extend judicial review, which is one way to check legislative power. The practice of judicial review of legislation, in relevant part (I set aside policing the division of authority between federal and state legislatures), is valuable to the extent that it is a reasonable response to the possible misuse of legislative authority. What is reasonable here turns in part on how (or if) the grounds of review are specified by constitution-makers, for judicial review unmoored from past commitments of the political community undercuts the capacity of a free people to rule itself.[65]

The legislature may run amok if legislators come to share the common scholarly view that the institution is a machine that does or should give effect to what the majority wants, or if legislators conform to the public choice stereotype. However, there is no reason to assume or conclude that legislators, any more than other public officials, are likely to fail to do their duty. Legislators are charged with weighty responsibility and are often tempted to misuse their power. Vesting authority in an assembly is itself in part a way to answer the risk of tyranny, incompetence, or alienation. Might judicial review constitute another partial means to avoid the misuse of legislative authority? Framing the question in this way makes clear, I trust, that the point of judicial review should not be to authorise judicial supremacy whenever reasons matter, leaving the legislature to decide other matters. This account of the objects of legislation fundamentally mistakes the capacities of legislature and judiciary but more importantly fundamentally mistakes the nature of the common good for which, in different ways, courts, legislators, officials, and citizens all act. Legislating involves choice, but *reasoned* choice, in which the common good remains always in view.

[65] R Ekins, 'How To Be a Free People' (2013) 58 *American Journal of Jurisprudence* 163.

The need, if any, for judicial review will vary by jurisdiction and over time. The practice might help answer pathologies that may afflict self-government, in which the community acting through its central representative institution, the legislature, fails to permit some group of persons sufficient space in the public argument about what should be done. The legislature may, by virtue of the defects of some political culture and/or the reasoning of many incumbents of legislative office, be likely to overlook or disregard some important class of reason for action or to pay insufficient attention to some side-effect of its actions. It may be rational then to make constitutional provision for this reason for action, such that the court has authority to invalidate legislative acts that fail to take it into account. The difficulty in structuring judicial review is to limit the scope for the misuse of legislative power without licensing the misuse of judicial power and frustrating (by the very potential for misuse of judicial power) the proper exercise of legislative capacity.

Legislation by assembly makes possible self-government, which involves the community adopting a means by which citizens may share in reasoning about and choosing what the law shall be. If this is true, it calls into question some common arguments for judicial review. Consider Harel and Kahana's argument that judicial review should not be justified on the instrumental ground that judges tend to make better decisions than legislators on the relevant class of questions.[66] Rather, they say, judicial review is intrinsically justified because it makes possible the right to participation that is the right to a hearing. This right, Harel and Kahana maintain, is the right to call into question some state act and to have the state explain, to the satisfaction of the court, why the act is justified.

The argument fails – there is no right to such a hearing – because it ignores, but also tacitly fractures and undermines, the assembly's status as the forum in which legislative acts are proposed, defended, and scrutinised at the sharp end of an ongoing public argument, which spans elections and legislative sessions. True, legislative acts should be justified. But this means that the legislature should act for reasons and that the legislative process (like the judicial process in analogous part) should be structured and executed such that the relevant reasons are considered and addressed. Authorising any and every (even if in practice only the well-resourced) citizen to demand an explanation for the legislative act, which explanation the court is to pass judgment on, is to unsettle the legislative act's status as the exercise of a reasonable mode of (reasoning) self-government. The parameters of a judicial dispute – two parties in which one wins while the other loses – make it wholly unsuited to be a central process of self-government.

Consider next the related argument that judicial review avoids the legislature (or the majority?) being judge in its own cause.[67] This argument assumes that some

[66] A Harel and T Kahana, 'The Easy Core Case for Judicial Review' (2010) 2 *Journal of Legal Analysis* 1.

[67] For criticism of this argument, see: J Waldron, 'Legislatures Judging in Their Own Cause' (2009) 3 *Legisprudence* 125.

constitutional provision is relevant to the validity of the legislative act, which the legislature must itself interpret when deciding if it is competent to enact the proposed statute. The argument may extend however to the moral rights of citizens (in short, what should be done for them or should not be done to them), which the legislature must also consider in deciding what should be done. The argument for judicial review on this point is that it would be a failure of natural justice were the legislature's decision to be immune from challenge, for then in the dispute between legislature (or enacting majority) and the citizen who claims a breach of right, the legislature would be judge in its own cause, which is unfair. Thus, the court is needed to determine the dispute as a neutral third party. Schauer defends a similar idea when he says that the virtue of the court is not its superior competence in respect of constitutional law or rights but rather its externality, that it is a body other than the legislature itself.[68]

The problem with this argument is its assumption (made explicit by Schauer, on which more below) that the relevant issue or problem is in some way not before the legislature or is decided by the legislature in its own interest. This misconceives the nature of the assembly, which is a forum for reasoning about what should be done, which course of reasoning includes the relevant issue (to the extent it is relevant). The legislature is not a party to a dispute with some citizen or group about what should be done but is rather the community deliberating about how it should order itself. That is, the argument and decision within the legislature concerns, and is a fair way to arrive at a reasoned decision about, this issue or problem (allowing that legislatures may suffer pathologies such as those discussed above, which are distinct from the 'no judge in his own cause' argument). To repeat, the assembly is not best understood to be a machine to transmit the general will (or collective preference) of the community or some majority of citizens apart from deliberation and choice within the assembly itself. The reasoned choice that the legislative process deliberates about and culminates in is thus not an arbitrary stipulation, which is unfair to the citizen who maintains the choice is wrong, but is instead a reasoned choice fairly made by a body that is structured to make possible collective action, and popular participation, in reasoning and choosing. Authorising judicial review on the ground that the assembly is a machine to transmit the general will is thus to ignore what legislating is.

Schauer argues that the courts have no special competence that makes them superior to legislatures.[69] There is, however, an important reason to authorise them to enforce constitutional rules against the legislature, namely that they are external to the legislature and hence are well placed to enforce rules that limit even well-meaning legislatures.[70] Indeed, Schauer insists that constitutional rules should not be thought

[68] F Schauer, 'Legislatures as Rule-Followers' in R Bauman and T Kahana (eds.) *The Least Examined Branch* (Cambridge, Cambridge University Press 2006).

[69] Ibid. 468, 475; see also Eisgruber, *Constitutional Self-Government*, 19.

[70] Ibid. 475–88.

to be primarily directed at vicious or ill-conceived legislative proposals but to obstruct well-intentioned virtuous legislators.[71] His point is that legislators acting wisely and well are still unlikely to attend to the values that are protected by constitutional rules, for they are under great pressure (perhaps justifiable, given the backstop of judicial review) to act for what appears now to be wise policy or the obvious preference of their constituents.[72]

This argument for judicial review begs the question by presuming that legislators acting jointly do not (and indeed should not) attend to the values that constitutional law affirms. The argument is more attractive to the extent that it takes for granted that the relevant constitutional law should be rule-like and fit for ready enforcement. If constitutional rights were closely specified propositions, clearly ruling out certain courses of action, then the courts would be well placed to apply such propositions to legislation and such application might be consistent with the polity's reasoned self-government over time. This application would call for no legislative reasoning on the part of the court, which is important if judicial review is not to be redundant and to risk imperilling the rule of law and self-government. However, if constitutional rights require extensive further argument before they are fit to settle the validity of legislation, argument which collapses (or should collapse) to the merits of the legislative proposal, then the advantage of being external evaporates. Again, the design and rationale for judicial review must take seriously the nature of the legislature and its capacities if the practice is not simply to introduce arbitrary judicial power and frustrate the legislature acting for the common good.

4.10 CONCLUSION

The legislature should be an agent, not a machine. And the legislature is a type of institution capable of agency, structured to make reasoned choices. The reason to make provision for legislative agency is that the community should be ruled by law, law which is open to being changed deliberately when there is good reason for change. Authority to change the law in this way should be vested in a deliberative, representative assembly, the form of which makes it possible for the community to govern itself reasonably. In reasoning about how to change the law, the well-formed legislature reasons about rights, choosing legal relationships that specify abstract dimensions of human wellbeing or general normative propositions. This is a mode of reasoning and action that characterises much legislation. The common disjuncture between the reasoning, principled court and the wilful, arbitrary legislature is unsound. The reason to authorise an assembly to legislate is precisely that such an institution is capable of choosing well, of securing the common good by promoting and protecting rights, in a way that realises self-government.

[71] Ibid. 472–3.
[72] Ibid. 476–7.

5

From Universal Rights to Legislated Rights

Paul Yowell

5.1 INTRODUCTION

The Universal Declaration of Human Rights, the model for many later human rights treaties and constitutional bill of rights, is itself not a treaty or legal instrument. Proclaimed in 1948, the Declaration is not addressed exclusively or even primarily to courts but to political institutions generally and indeed to every person. Its Preamble calls on 'every individual and every organ of society' to 'strive by teaching and education to promote respect for these rights and freedoms and by progressive measures, national and international, to secure their universal and effective recognition and observance'. In this chapter I argue that human rights are most effectively secured not by looking to courts to be their guardians, but by the painstaking, everyday work of legislatures seeking to craft laws to promote and protect the full range of rights and freedoms in the Universal Declaration.

Human rights need to be implemented through legislation because they are lacking in specific legal content. In the Universal Declaration, the European Convention of Human Rights, and many similar instruments, rights, with few exceptions, are formulated in vague, abstract language that expresses a general value or good but demands no particular action of persons or political authorities in order to meet requirements of justice. It is the task of legislatures to specify what actions are required, forbidden, or permitted in order to attain the values expressed in human rights instruments, in accord with the requirements of justice. Section 5.2 outlines the content of the Universal Declaration and several of the ways in which rights need to be protected and promoted by legislation. Section 5.3 then explains the lack of legal content in human rights through the analysis of rights previously discussed in Chapter 2. I summarise and build upon Grégoire Webber's account of the crucial difference between (1) two-term rights that merely assert that everyone has a right to some substantive value and (2) three-term rights that specify a relationship of justice between a right-holder and another and a specific action (or inaction). This account highlights the need for legislative implementation of rights.

When human rights are implemented in legislation, they receive especially strong protection: legislated rights are not defeasible by arguments about the general welfare. This feature of legislation is explained in Section 5.4, and is contrasted to the treatment of two-term rights in the case law of human rights courts. This case law allows for rights to be interfered with or infringed so long as the interference or infringement is justifiable under a proportionality inquiry. While the technique of proportionality has its place in judicial review, a consequence of taking proportionality to be the standard method of rights adjudication is to weaken the idea of a right. Any right that becomes the object of proportionality review is treated as defeasible so long as a claim about the general welfare (understood in the aggregative sense) is accepted as strong enough to justify interfering with the right. The notion of a right is thereby diminished to the point of vanishing.

The strong protection accorded to legislated rights is next contrasted, in Section 5.5, to Dworkin's theory of 'rights as trumps'. The phrase is often taken as indicating absolute protection of rights, and Dworkin sometimes claimed that rights preclude balancing. On closer inspection, however, we see that Dworkin's concept of rights as trumps is actually built on a balancing or proportionality model, wherein recognising something as a right merely requires a relatively greater weight to justify overriding it. Section 5.6 continues the critique of Dworkin's theory of rights, showing that in addition to the rights as trumps model just described, Dworkin employed a second, distinct model of rights as trumps designed to block ('trump') certain categories of motivations for legislation, such as racist or paternalistic preferences. Common to both models is a conception of rights and the general welfare in which they stand in inherent opposition. This argument runs counter to instruments such as the Universal Declaration – which conceive of human rights as *constituting* the common good – and it has done substantial damage to theoretical understandings of the proper role of legislatures and courts in democracies.

Section 5.7 addresses an objection to the main argument of this chapter, namely that majoritarian legislatures are not institutionally well placed to protect the rights of minorities. I address what is commonly cited as the most compelling historical case for the protection of minority rights through judicial means: the situation of the black minority in the southern United States, especially during the early and middle decades of the twentieth century. Constitutional narratives of this period often attribute the dismantling of segregation to the US Supreme Court, especially its decision in *Brown* v. *Board of Education* (1954). This claim, however, is simplistic and misleading, firstly because it overlooks a long period in which the Court was not only complicit in promoting segregation, but often took a leading role, including by striking down or curtailing important civil rights statutes Congress had enacted in the 1870s. Secondly, with regard to the period of *Brown* and its aftermath, political and legislative action – including the Civil Rights Act 1964 and Voting Rights Act 1968 – advanced racial equality at least as effectively as judicial action.

5.2 IMPLEMENTING HUMAN RIGHTS

In a speech to the UN General Assembly in December 1948, Eleanor Roosevelt, the chair of the drafting committee for the Universal Declaration of Human Rights, stated that the Declaration 'is not and does not purport to be a statement of law or legal obligation', and that it is of 'primary importance that we keep clearly in mind the basic character of the document'.[1] The Declaration was proclaimed as a 'common standard of achievement for all peoples and all nations', and was thus necessarily drafted at a high level of generality. This was first of all practically necessary to achieve agreement among many nations. As Roosevelt observed, some provisions were not fully satisfactory to the US delegation; and other delegations rejected different provisions.[2] This drafting strategy also reflected the views of the members of the drafting committee, particularly of PC Chang, who, alongside Charles Malik, was one of its two most philosophically influential members.[3] Chang, a diplomat, academic, artist, and Confucian philosopher, repeatedly intervened in the Third Committee, which produced the final draft of the Declaration, in support of using language that would be comprehensible by all, because 'the declaration was destined for the vast mass of the world's population'.[4] John Humphrey, who produced the first official draft mainly by collating prior rights declarations, recorded that Chang had a 'gift' for drafting and that his 'towering intellect' was felt by all on the committee,[5] and noted that frequently it was Chang who contributed the formulations that enabled the committee to reach a compromise.[6] On the basis of his rationale that the Declaration should be 'a document for all men everywhere, not merely for lawyers and scholars',[7] Chang had originally submitted a draft on behalf of the Chinese delegation that had only ten articles.[8] Although the final draft included thirty articles, Chang thought that his initial draft had aided in keeping the final draft 'relatively brief' and 'clear' for its purpose of communicating to common

1 Eleanor Roosevelt, 'Bulletin of the State Department 19' (1948) in Josh Gottheimer (ed.), *Ripples of Hope: Great American Civil Rights Speeches* (New York, Basic Civitas Books 2002) 202.

2 Ibid.

3 Mary Ann Glendon, *A World Made New: Eleanor Roosevelt and the Universal Declaration of Human Rights* (New York, Random House 2002) 44.

4 Sumner B Twiss, 'Confucian Contributions to the Universal Declaration of Human Rights: A Historical and Philosophical Perspective' in Arvind Sharma (ed.), *The World's Religions after September 11* (Westport, CA, Praeger 2009) 164.

5 Ibid.

6 See ibid. 164–6 for discussion of the drafting process of particular articles.

7 Ibid. 164.

8 Ibid.

people.[9] The drafting history of the Declaration underscores Roosevelt's statement that it was not intended to be a legal, enforceable document.

The Preamble states the overall goal of the Declaration in a way that stresses the need to lay down specific standards to secure rights: that 'every individual and every organ of society', in addition to promoting rights through education, shall strive through 'progressive measures, national and international, to secure their universal and effective recognition and observance, both among the peoples of Member States themselves and among the peoples of territories under their jurisdiction'.[10] 'Measures' is a key term. It refers to general standards and norms, which ordinarily must be established by political bodies rather than courts.[11] At several points the Declaration calls for legislative enactments or treaties. It provides broad guidelines and general statements of goals to strive for, but not the specific details of a legislative programme or language for deciding individual legal cases. It leaves room for variation and assumes that details will differ from country to country.

Hersch Lauterpacht, another figure who influenced the Universal Declaration with his proposal for an International Bill of the Rights of Man in 1945, embraced the notion that rights need to be specified in legislation.[12] When rights are 'general in character' – such as liberty of the person, equality before the law, and freedom of association – he argued that the details of the substantive law safeguarding such rights 'must be left to the law of the States', noting that national constitutions generally entrust those details to 'ordinary legislation'.[13]

Reading the Universal Declaration with its historical background in mind helps to make sense of a number of individual articles and to understand the document as a whole. Roosevelt, Chang, Malik, and others insisted that the Declaration is not a toolkit for litigating individual cases or advancing special interests, but is meant to sketch a general outline of persons in a political community, the rights and duties that inhere in interpersonal relationships, and the goods that people working together can and must pursue.[14] René Cassin, the principal draftsman for the final stages of the Declaration, pictured it as a temple portico, with Articles 1 and 2 laying out four principles that serve as foundation stones: dignity, equality, liberty, and brotherhood (these were further elaborated in the Preamble). Articles 28–30, referring to reciprocal duties, limits, and order, form the roof or portico. The discrete

[9] Ibid.

[10] Preamble.

[11] See Francisco J. Urbina, Section 6.4 in this book on the need for legal guidance to courts and the special ability of legislatures to provide this.

[12] Hersch Lauterpacht, *An International Rights of the Bill of Man* (Oxford, Oxford University Press, new edn, 2013) 79.

[13] Ibid. Lauterpacht favoured judicial review of human rights at the domestic (though not international) level, but not in a way that excluded or replaced the legislature's responsibility. He stated that a bill of rights 'must to a large extent consist of provisions which are general in character and whose detailed application must be left to the legislature and to the judiciary of each state'. Ibid.

[14] Glendon, *A World Made New* 174–91, 221–3.

rights in the middle articles form four columns or pillars in Cassin's image: (1) Articles 3–11 on life, liberty, and personal security, (2) Articles 12–17 on rights in civil society, (3) Articles 16–21 on rights in the political community, and (4) Articles 22–7 on economic, social and cultural rights.[15]

Article 1 states: 'All human beings are born free and equal in dignity and rights. They are endowed with reason and conscience and should act towards one another in a spirit of brotherhood'. This is the language not of law but of ethics. These are bold claims about the unity of the human race and the nature of persons as rational and capable of brotherly action, and under a duty of conscience so to act.[16] Article 2 continues the theme of human unity, asserting that the rights and freedoms in the Declaration are meant for everyone 'without distinction of any kind'. A legislature that sets out to observe and implement the values expressed in Articles 1 and 2 – as well as all the rest of the Declaration – must understand its role as something very different from aggregating preferences or maximising utility. The legislature should deliberate and decide upon the basis of reasons. In Chapter 4, Richard Ekins explains how legislatures are capable of this and criticises theories that depict the legislative role as preference-aggregation. The Declaration outlines many of the goods and values that constitute reasons for legislating, and thus serves as a guide to the conscientious legislator.

5.2.1 *The First Pillar*

Article 3 states that 'Everyone has the right to life, liberty and security of person'. This is a broad provision that summarises the rest of the first pillar – which deals with different kinds of threats to Article 3 rights – while also articulating the right to life as a distinct matter and establishing the protection of liberty and security as a general principle.

Threats to Article 3 rights emanate both from the state as well as the 'horizontal' dimension of inter-personal relationships. In most societies, there are constant dangers to life and the security of the person – as well as to liberty – from individuals to one another. The protection of these rights depends to a great extent on establishing criminal law and on its effective operation. States have an obligation to enact positive law setting forth prohibitions on harmful actions, accompanied by criminal penalties, in order to protect the right to life. This obligation has been repeatedly affirmed by the European Court of Human Rights, the UK Parliament's Joint Committee on Human Rights, and other bodies.[17] The right to life is thus

[15] Ibid.

[16] Chang had proposed to include in Article 1 a literal translation of the Confucian concept of *jen* ('two-men mindedness'), but eventually was satisfied that 'spirit of brotherhood' captured the idea. Twiss, 'Confucian Contributions to the Universal Declaration of Human Rights' 178.

[17] See, e.g., *Nitecki* v. *Poland*, Appl. No. 65653/01, (ECtHR, 21 March 2002) (Art. 2 'enjoins the State not only to refrain from the intentional and unlawful taking of life, but also to take appropriate steps

protected first and foremost by laws prohibiting murder and other forms of homicide. The right is protected further by the cause of action in tort law for wrongful death, and by various kinds of laws designed to reduce instances of death by negligence or accidental causes (speed limits, industrial safety regulations, pharmaceutical regulations, public health measures etc.). The right to security of the person is protected by criminal laws against rape and assault, and by tort law regarding assault and battery.

The law must simultaneously protect the rights of the accused to a fair trial and to fair procedures more generally, as recognised in Articles 9 to 11. These procedural protections depend of course on judges, but judges and police in turn need a detailed code of criminal procedure in order to administer justice consistently and fairly to everyone.[18]

Article 4 refers to a specific kind of deprivation of liberty of the person in its absolute prohibition of slavery, the slave trade, and forced labour. Slavery is not a thing of the past, but a serious problem worldwide, with human trafficking reaching even into the most stable and affluent cities in Western democracies. The International Labour Organisation estimated twenty-one million victims of forced labour worldwide in 2012.[19] This is an area in need not only of substantial resources for enforcement, for which legislatures must provide, but of legal reform and new legislation, according to numerous domestic and international human rights bodies.[20] Towards this end, the UK has recently enacted the Modern Slavery Act, which among other things increases the maximum penalty for human trafficking from fourteen years to life imprisonment, and for the first time in modern UK law provides definitions of slavery, servitude, and forced or compulsory labour.[21]

Article 5 prohibits torture and 'cruel, inhuman or degrading treatment or punishment'. While this article speaks to courts insofar as they have power to determine punishments or review relevant legislative and executive decisions, it speaks also to legislatures, which are largely responsible for establishing general levels of punishment, and to the executive agencies that oversee the treatment of prisoners and other detainees. Because of the executive's partial insularity from the legislative and judicial branches, the internal reception of human rights within the executive is a

---

to safeguard the lives of those within its jurisdiction'). For further examples see Paul Yowell, 'The Impact of the Joint Committee on Human Rights on Legislative Deliberation', in Mary Hunt, Hayley Hooper, and Paul Yowell (eds.), *Parliaments and Human Rights: Redressing the Democratic Deficit* (Oxford, Hart Publishing 2015) 147.

18 Cf. Maris Köpcke, Section 3.4 in this book.

19 International Labour Organization '21 million people are now victims of forced labour, ILO says' (1 June 2012) www.ilo.org/global/about-the-ilo/newsroom/news/WCMS_181961/lang--en/index.htm, accessed 31 May 2017.

20 See, e.g., Joint Committee on Human Rights, *Human trafficking* (2005–06 HL 245-I, HC 1127-I, 30–1); Human Rights Watch, 'Domestic Plight: How Jordanian Laws, Officials, Employers, and Recruiters Fail Abused Migrant Domestic Workers' (27 September 2011) www.hrw.org/news/2011/10/12/migrant-domestic-workers-jordan, accessed 27 August 2015.

21 Modern Slavery Act 2015, s. 1.

topic of vital importance, though one that is largely beyond the scope of this book. For example, some have argued that torture should be formally illegal but informally practiced and accepted if warranted by extreme circumstances. It is entirely possible that, if such an argument were accepted, a culture of tolerance of torture could arise within the executive, outside not only the purview but even the knowledge of the legislature or judicial system. Once again, we are reminded of the importance of the fact that the Universal Declaration is addressed to 'every individual and every organ of society'.

Articles 6 and 7 return to and expand on the theme of equality. Everyone has the 'right to recognition as a person before the law' (Art. 6), and is entitled to equal protection of the law, without discrimination (Art. 7).[22] Courts play a vital role in protecting the rights of minority groups and ensuring equal protection, but legislatures have historically been at least as important in securing these goals. This theme will be taken up in the context of racial equality in Section 5.7 below.

Article 8 provides that 'Everyone has the right to an effective remedy by the competent national tribunals for acts violating the fundamental rights granted him by the constitution or by law'. Like the rest of the Declaration, this article is not self-executing or directly effective; it does not empower national courts to create their own remedies, nor does it imply that national courts should have such powers of creation. The article is rather a call for legislatures or other law-making bodies to establish not only legal measures that promote fundamental rights but appropriate remedies for their violation. In some legal systems courts have limited law-making powers and might appropriately be motivated by this article in the exercise of such powers. But the weight of responsibility for realising Article 8 falls squarely on the legislature.

5.2.2 *The Second and Third Pillars*

Many of the rights in Articles 12 to 21 are 'negative' rights, according to a standard method of classification that distinguishes them from 'positive' rights that typically have a direct relationship to material resources and legislative decisions about distribution. The negative rights protect various kinds of liberties including freedom of movement and residence (Art. 13(1)), freedom of thought, conscience, and religion (Art. 18), freedom of opinion and expression (Art. 19), and freedom of peaceful assembly and association (Art. 20). As discussed in Section 5.3 below, the legislature's responsibility with regard to these rights may be fulfilled by not acting – by refraining from legislating in a particular area – or by crafting legislation in such a way so as to preserve and not interfere with traditional liberties. Section 5.3 will also show, using the example of freedom of expression, that the area of freedom

[22] Art. Art. 7 reads: 'All are equal before the law and are entitled without any discrimination to equal protection of the law. All are entitled to equal protection against any discrimination in violation of this Declaration and against any incitement to such discrimination.'

can be positively constructed by affirmative legislation. The legislature provides for particular spaces where free speech is given special protection, facilitates expression by enabling forums for it, and adopts remedies against threats to this freedom in the 'horizontal' dimension.

Article 12 has a 'negative' component similar to the liberties discussed above: 'No one shall be subjected to arbitrary interference with his privacy, family, home or correspondence, nor to attacks upon his honour and reputation. Everyone has the right to the protection of the law against such interference or attacks'. Differently from the other negative liberties, however, the Declaration here gives explicit consideration to threats within the horizontal dimension, especially with its mention of attacks on a person's honour and reputation. The call for 'protection of the law' is directed to legislatures, in order to ensure that there is effective law regarding defamation, slander, libel, etc. The vision of privacy in Article 12 is not simply one of being left alone by the state, but one in which the law positively intervenes to protect the sanctity of the home and of family life, as well as personal reputations, from attacks in any dimension of social life. The law of libel and defamation serves to protect reputation. One important area in which positive legislation is needed today is that of data privacy, considering the proliferation of electronic databases holding vast amounts of private and sensitive information.[23] Such laws introduce tension with freedom of expression, but as Webber explains in Chapter 2, this is not best considered as a 'conflict of rights'. In order to realise the value of free expression while also protecting privacy, lines must be drawn and specific standards must be laid down to establish right relations between persons. Much of this task belongs to the legislature.

Legislation can also help to promote other liberties. Freedom of religion can be promoted by laws recognising religious holidays or by Sabbath-closing laws, or by zoning laws requiring distance between religious buildings and other kinds of establishments. Laws forbidding discrimination on grounds of religion, race, and other grounds – in addition to promoting equality – help to protect relevant liberties and the freedom of association.

Other articles in the third pillar obviously require legislative enactment – and sometimes extensive legislation on the subject of the right and related subjects – in order for the rights to be effective. These include the right to marry (Art. 16), which entails *inter alia* appropriate laws regarding duties to spouses and children; and the right to own property 'alone as well as in association with others' (Art. 17), which entails not only systematic regulation of personal and real property ownership but also the law of business associations – the latter subject embracing myriad questions regarding partnership, corporations, shareholding, limitation of liability, and other matters. A related right in the fourth pillar, Article 27(2), provides that 'Everyone has the right to the protection of the moral and material interests resulting from any

[23] For an example of legislative attempt to address this topic, see the UK Data Protection Act 1998.

scientific, literary or artistic production of which he is the author', which requires another extensive system of legislation on intellectual property.[24]

5.2.3 *The Fourth Pillar*

Many rights in the fourth pillar are addressed to individual wellbeing in ways connected to a society's economic resources and social life. The Declaration recognises the right to education (Art. 26) and the 'right freely to participate in the cultural life of the community, to enjoy the arts and to share in scientific advancement and its benefits' (Art. 27). The right to 'social security' is extraordinarily vague (Art. 22), and there are vast implications for public expenditure in a person's 'right to a standard of living adequate for the health and wellbeing of himself and of his family, including food, clothing, housing and medical care and necessary social services, and the right to security in the event of unemployment, sickness, disability, widowhood, old age or other lack of livelihood in circumstances beyond his control' (Art. 25). There is also a right to work (Art. 23), accompanied by a right to 'rest and leisure, including reasonable limitation of working hours and periodic holidays with pay' (Art. 24). Workers have 'the right to form and join trade unions'; 'the right to equal pay for equal work'; and 'the right to just and favourable remuneration ensuring for himself and his family an existence worthy of human dignity, and supplemented, if necessary, by other means of social protection' (Art. 23).

These social and labour rights are implemented and regulated by a vast array of legislative programmes. With regard to social rights concerning welfare, education, and related matters, there are at least fifty-seven pieces of relevant primary legislation in the UK, including the Education Act, Social Security Acts, National Assistance Acts, National Health Service Acts, Housing Acts, the Children Act 1989, and the Mental Health Act – plus more than 1,000 statutory instruments that implement social rights.[25] These figures were compiled by Jeff King, who states:

> These acts provide the basic enabling framework of the welfare state. Their scope, intricate subject-matter, the political compromises they embody, the frequency and necessity of their revision, and the input and participation required to make them workable, make it clear that *only a body with the structure and methods of Parliament, administratively supported by government, could provide the basic framework of a good model.*[26]

While there is a debate over the justiciability of such 'social rights', there is no question that the legislature must be the primary decision-maker in this area because

[24] Other articles that require detailed legislative implementation include Art. 21 (on the right of political participation, and equal access to public services); Arts. 13 and 14 on rights to emigrate and to seek asylum; Art. 14 on the right to seek asylum; and Art. 15 on the right to nationality.

[25] Jeff King, *Judging Social Rights* (Cambridge, Cambridge University Press 2012) 42–3.

[26] Ibid. 43 (italics added).

courts are not in a position to make overall decisions about the national budget, taxation, expenditure, and distribution. Spending on social rights accounts for about 70 per cent of the UK's national budget, and, as King observes, an important principle established by the constitutional (and revolutionary) history of the UK, France, and the US is that 'to preserve social peace and stability, those who pay into the public purse should generally be represented in the key decisions about spending'.[27] As King concludes, the 'main engine for protecting social rights is and always will be primary legislation adopted by a representative legislature'.[28]

5.3 LEGISLATED RIGHTS

As the preceding discussion suggests, the realisation of human rights in legislation is not simply a matter of making a vague right more specific. Legislated rights have important structural features that distinguish them categorically from the usual formulations for human rights in the Universal Declaration and instruments modelled on it. One of these is the quality of not being defeasible by arguments about the general welfare, which is analysed in Section 5.4 below. This non-defeasibility is enabled by another structural feature analysed in this section: that legislated rights have a three-term jural structure, denoting a relationship between two persons, A and B, and an act-description, φ.

Hohfeld identified different kinds of jural structure, which can be illustrated with examples drawn from the context of publication and public expression. A has a *claim-right* not to be defamed by B, correlative to B's *duty* not to utter statements about A that cause substantial harm to A's reputation in the community (where no relevant defence – such as the truth of the statement – applies).[29] Derivatively, A has a *power* to initiate a lawsuit against B, such that B is under a *liability* to a court's authority over the adjudication of defamatory statements. However, if B's statement about A is substantially true, or is reasonably believed by B to be in the public interest, then B has an *immunity* from liability for statements that would otherwise be defamatory (hence A has a *disability* from obtaining damages). These examples illustrate three pairs of Hohfeld's jural correlatives, with the first in each pair naming a distinct type of right: (1) claim-right → duty; (2) power → liability; and (3) immunity → disability.[30]

[27] Ibid. 44.

[28] Ibid. 41.

[29] This example is based on the law of the UK, where the underlying common law cause of action for defamation is decisively framed by the UK Defamation Act 2013, setting forth the requirement of substantial harm and defences. Other jurisdictions create slightly different forms of Hohfeldian rights, for example by defining a defamatory statement as false instead of making the question of truth or falsity part of the defence for which the defendant bears the burden of proof.

[30] Here are the formal definitions: A has a *claim-right* that B should φ (or not φ), if and only if B has a duty to A to φ (or not to φ). A has a *power* relative to B to φ, if and only if B has a liability to have his legal position changed by A's φ-ing. A has an *immunity* relative to B's φ-ing, if and only if B has no power (a disability) to change A's legal position by φ-ing. See Wesley Newcomb Hohfeld, 'Some Fundamental Legal Conceptions As Applied in Judicial Reasoning' (1913) 23 *Yale Law Journal* 16.

A fourth type of Hohfeldian right, liberty, requires a somewhat different analysis from the other three because its correlative is a 'no-claim-right' or 'no-right' rather than a concrete, legally specified duty, liability, or disability. A has a liberty to φ if B does not have a claim-right that A not φ. By the same token, A has a liberty not to φ if B does not have a claim-right for A to φ. While a claim-right, power, or immunity in law is always something that is positively expressed in positive law (which at the same time specifies or implies the correlative duty, liability, or disability), a liberty may exist through the general absence of law. A liberty may exist by virtue of a well-established, recognised custom of law-makers choosing to protect it by choosing not to impose a duty to act (or not act) in relation to some matter. Law-makers often craft legislation so as to preserve a certain liberty, and this can be done either implicitly or expressly by defining terms or creating exemption clauses. The Racial and Religious Hatred Act in the UK, for example, provides an exception for private homes: no offence is committed where words, behaviour, or written material are used by a person 'inside a dwelling and are not heard or seen except by other persons in that or another dwelling'. This is not affirmative license to engage in racist speech in a home, but rather an explicit preservation of the traditional, general liberty to speak freely and on any topic in one's home.

Preservation of a liberty can also be accomplished by silence.[31] Consider the ancient liberty to make a speech to passers-by in a public place. Although this liberty is generally not specified as such in legislation, it is sufficiently established by custom and specific enough to be asserted as a three-term right (viz., A's liberty to make a speech to a passerby, B, is correlative to B's no-claim-right that A not make a speech). This liberty is recognised by other laws and shaped and supported by them, such as legal duties on the police not to arrest A merely for making a speech that others consider offensive,[32] as well as laws that limit speech so that A is prohibited from provoking violence against B or using threatening words that cause B to believe violence is imminent.[33] A more general form of this liberty is to organise an assembly or march in public places. The UK Public Order Act 1986 implies such a Hohfeldian liberty. The Act imposes no requirement to obtain a permit to hold a public assembly or procession; however, those who plan a procession are required to notify the police in advance (the notification requirement does not apply to assemblies that remain in one location). The police in turn have power under section 12 of the Act to impose conditions on the procession for the sake of public order; and if those powers are not sufficient to prevent the procession from resulting in 'serious public disorder', then the police can apply to the district or council for an order prohibiting

[31] See, e.g., the UK Health Care Act 2006, wherein Parliament chose to maintain the liberty to smoke outdoors and in private homes, not by express exemption but by the way it defined the public spaces in which smoking is banned.

[32] See *Redmond-Bate* v. *Director of Public Prosecutions* [1999] EWHC Admin 732.

[33] UK Public Order Act 1986 s. 4(1).

the procession. Other jurisdictions recognise this liberty through different regulatory schemes that require organisers of assemblies or marches to apply for permits.

One reason that the Hohfeldian schema is important and repays the attempt to master it is that it shows that our notion of legal right is not univocal: there is no single definition that applies to all that we call rights. Each Hohfeldian right refers, in his words, to a 'fundamental legal conception';[34] the different types cannot be reduced to each other or to a lower common denominator. Another benefit of Hohfeld's schema is that it shows that many of the 'rights' in human rights instruments lack the specified jural structure of ordinary legal rights. There are a few rights in the Universal Declaration that do have jural structure. They are Hohfeldian claim-rights that typically have the following form: 'No one shall be ... [held in slavery, subjected to torture, deprived of his nationality ...]'. Notably, these formulations do not use the term 'right'; they set forth the concept of the right in question by direct reference to duties, that is, actions B is under a duty not to perform in relation to the right-holder A.[35]

It might be thought that human rights such as the freedom of expression, assembly, and religion are Hohfeldian liberties. The problem with classifying them as such, however, is that their two-term structure does not describe any particular relationship between persons. The specific liberties discussed in the previous paragraph describe a three-term relationship with more or less specificity. A has a liberty to make a speech to B even if the speech is offensive; but A is prohibited from using threatening words that induce a fear of violence. Interpretation is still required to determine the line between what is offensive and what is threatening. But these are intelligible categories, and applying them to the facts of particular cases falls squarely within what we expect judges carrying out their responsibility to do: interpret legal texts. Contrast the operative sentence of Article 10 of the European Convention on Human Rights: 'Everyone has the right to freedom of expression'. This leaves all the salient detail to be filled in later, typically through application of the clause providing that the exercise of the right may be limited for certain purposes as 'necessary in a democratic society'. It is possible for courts to provide specification, but the standard technique of proportionality does not lend itself to this.[36] In any event, whatever role is envisioned for courts in protecting freedom of expression, legislatures have a large and important task ranging over a wide area.

An important part of that task is to set reasonable limits on the freedom of expression. Such limits need not be understood as deprivations or as the loss of some good or benefit. The legislature helps to shape a realm of social interaction, to form a shared space in which you and I treat one another with respect and justice – in which the

34 Hohfeld, 'Some Fundamental Legal Conceptions as Applied in Judicial Reasoning'.

35 See Grégoire Webber, Section 2.2 in this book.

36 See Grégoire Webber, 'Rights and the Rule of Law in the Balance' (2013) 129 *Law Quarterly Review* 399, 417.

question 'how should I act' is answered in part by specified legal rights and duties.[37] In addition to the examples above drawn from the law of libel and of public assemblies and processions, the law imposes civil liability or criminal punishment on fraudulent and some deceptive speech. The law generally prohibits obscene publications (narrowly defined) but distinguishes obscenity from indecency, which is restricted in some contexts but not others. The law prohibits or makes actionable, in some contexts, speech that disparages someone on account of sex, race, religion, and similar characteristics. The law forbids certain misleading statements that affect the value of shares in publicly traded companies, as well as accurate statements about such shares if they are based on insider information; it restricts commercial advertising not only with regard to misleading claims but also to uphold public policy. The law penalises all of the following: treason; revealing classified secrets or other material relevant to national security concerns; advocacy or glorification of terrorism; inciting people to violence, making threats of violence, and disturbing the peace; perjury; lying to the police or government investigators; and making false statements in certain official forms.

As will be discussed in Section 5.4 below, it is best not to think of all these laws as so many infringements on the right to freedom of expression. There is no right, properly understood, to threaten violence or to defame one's neighbour. Rather, these laws are part of a general project of specifying many Hohfeldian rights that can be considered as falling under the overall umbrella of the right to freedom of expression. Some laws create claim-rights, powers, or immunities. Others set forth liberties explicitly, and many help to shape liberties implicitly when legislators choose where to draw lines in restraining various kinds of harmful or potentially harmful speech. The specification of human rights is a complex endeavour, and it allows for different results in different places and times. In the UK, for example, political parties are not permitted to place paid advertisements on radio or television.[38] However, parties have a claim-right to broadcast political messages on the BBC without cost, arising from a specific statutory scheme.[39] Other laws regulate the conditions under which a group can qualify as a political party and lose that status. The BBC's duty to broadcast such messages is subject to a general statutory requirement to uphold standards of taste and decency, as seen in the *ProLife Alliance* case.[40] The ProLife Alliance has a general liberty to disseminate its message against abortion (in, say, print literature or on its own website), even through images that are disturbing or gruesome; the liberty is correlative to the no-claim-right of others, including those that might be disturbed or shocked by the images. But this liberty is not co-extensive with its claim-right to public broadcasts; the claim-right was held by the House of Lords not to require the BBC to broadcast an advertisement containing images of aborted foetuses that the BBC deemed to violate its requirement to observe standards of taste and decency.[41]

37 See Webber, Section 2.2 in this book.

38 UK Communications Act 2003, s. 319(2)(g).

39 Ibid. s. 333.

40 *ProLife Alliance* v. *British Broadcasting Corporation* [2003] UKHL 23.

41 Ibid.

It is important to note that although this book speaks mainly of primary legislation, the elected legislature is not the only law-maker of interest for the concept of 'legislated rights'. Maris Köpcke's account in Chapter 3 of the progressively detailed process of specification of rights recognises that some of the important steps in working out a scheme of convergence or coordination will be at a level of detail beyond that of primary legislation. The relationship between a legislature and delegated law-makers deserves further study that can be illuminated by the argument of this book. Administrative agencies and other delegated law-makers share some of the characteristics and capacities of an elected legislature but lack others, and an analysis of their strengths and weaknesses is an important part of arriving at a full understanding of how human rights are specified by institutions, and of the proper lines of delegation and accountability between those institutions.

A further area of complexity arises specifically in common law systems. In many areas legislation was enacted so as to embody a prior set of common law rules, and in some instances core rules were left intact as common law while legislation was adopted to shape and frame surrounding rules and exceptions. This process can be seen, for example, in the UK law of libel and defamation discussed above. In a few areas of law, the common law still predominates over statutory supplements. Our use of the term 'legislated rights' is meant to extend to Hohfeldian rights embodied partially (or even mainly) in common law. That does not mean we are indifferent to the choice between legislation and common law as a method of law-making. I have argued that legislation is intrinsically better suited than common law to comply with Rule of Law values, especially the important virtue of clarity.[42] One of the problems of common law, which will be analysed by Francisco Urbina in Chapter 6, is that it can be changed only by a decision in which the judge applies that change in the case *sub judice* – a change that the parties to the case may not have foreseen.[43] The judge in a case under the common law has a dual role of law-applier and (potentially) law-maker. This means that the relevant law-maker is severely restricted in how he can change the law; simultaneously, any change in the law is problematic with regard to the Rule of Law virtues of clarity and certainty.[44]

5.4 LEGISLATED RIGHTS AS NON-DEFEASIBLE

Rights that exist in legislated form – legislated rights – are not defeasible by arguments about the general welfare. Courts do not apply a balancing test to determine whether awarding a claimant his right under a particular statute is outweighed by the public interest. A few human rights are formulated in a similarly non-defeasible way, such as the right not to be enslaved or tortured; indeed these rights are treated

[42] See Paul Yowell, 'Legislation, Common Law, and the Virtue of Clarity' in Richard Ekins (ed.), *Modern Challenges to the Rule of Law* (Wellington, LexisNexis 2011).

[43] Ibid.

[44] Ibid.

as absolute and unconditional. But under what Webber calls the received approach, most human rights are effectively treated as prima facie rights. Their role is to invoke the application of a proportionality test, which is triggered by a court's finding that a state measure (legislation or executive action) has interfered with or infringed a human right. The court then considers whether, in accord with the principle of proportionality, such interference with the right is justified. This two-stage process of the received approach – a finding of interference with the right followed by the proportionality inquiry – is based on the premise that a human right may be justifiably infringed.[45] This is a flawed notion that distorts our basic understanding of legal rights. Instead of presupposing that human rights must be vindicated or protected, the received approach and proportionality inquiry have as their central concern the determination of when interference with a human right is justified.[46] Courts frequently conclude that a human right has been justifiably infringed for the sake of the general welfare or 'state interest'. The received approach thus reflects the idea that sufficiently strong general or 'state' interests can override human rights.[47]

This analysis can be illustrated by an example. Suppose that contractual rights were treated as prima facie rights. If a company refused to pay an employee a month's salary, the employee could bring a case alleging that the company had interfered with her contractual right to be paid his salary. The company could then argue that the interference with the right is justified because the company is facing severe cash flow problems, and unless it temporarily suspends salary payments it will be unable to post a bond to qualify for a lucrative government contract thought to be necessary for the company's future financial viability. In the terms of the proportionality inquiry, the company could prove it had a legitimate aim (a lucrative contract) and that the means (temporarily suspending salary payments) are suitable and necessary. The case would fall to be decided on an all-things-considered balancing test that weighed the employee's 'right' to be paid under the contract (scare quotes here signify a prima facie right) against the interests of the company (and perhaps the 'rights' of other employees who will benefit from the lucrative contract, as well as perhaps the wider interests of the employees' families and the surrounding community).

[45] See, e.g., *Mayeka* v. *Belgium* App no 13178/03 (ECtHR, 12 October 2006) ('The Court reiterates that an *infringement of an individual's right* to respect for his or her private and family life will *violate* Art. 8 *unless* it is "in accordance with the law", pursues one or more [legitimate aims] and is "necessary in a democratic society", in other words, proportionate to the pursued objectives. The question before the Court is whether the *interference* was justified under para. 2 of Art. 8 of the Convention'.) (italics added).

[46] When courts reason in this way, proportionality is doing all the work. The standard for judgment is not set by the right itself, but by the proportionality test. In the received approach, once the court moves from the first stage of finding an interference with the right to the second stage, the right drops out of the analysis. The mode of judgment would be essentially the same under a stand-alone proportionality test that is generally available as a ground to challenge state measures.

[47] In the received approach, two-term human rights can also be overridden by other two-term right See Webber, Section 2.3 in this book.

An employee who possessed only such a prima facie right would think that what she has is not really a legal *right* to be paid but rather an *interest* in being paid. Fortunately, contractual rights are not treated as prima facie rights but as non-defeasible rights.

It should be noted, however, that this does not entail that contractual rights are immune from specific and legislatively determined ways of altering them. For example, if a company is insolvent, bankruptcy legislation gives the company the Hohfeldian power to declare bankruptcy, which can result in a change in the claim-rights of creditors, including employees. The aim of bankruptcy legislation is fair treatment of various holders of claim-rights against the debtor, when it is not feasible for all of them to be satisfied fully. There are other examples in which legislated rights can mutually affect other legislated rights, sometimes by way of cancelling. Nonetheless, the characterisation of legislated rights as generally non-defeasible holds true. When individuals have a legislated right, courts cannot treat is as defeasible when necessary to advance the general welfare. Rather, the overall scheme of legislative rights, liberties, powers, and immunities must be read holistically, such that the employee's legislated claim-right will be bounded by the power of the employer to declare bankruptcy. In such circumstances, the right is not defeasible *tout court*; it is subject to a specified legal power, which by definition changes the nature of the right-duty relationship between employee and employer. The thought that the right is defeasible against the general welfare is nowhere present.

But that is precisely how human rights are treated in the received approach. Although human rights are often thought to have a more elevated status than ordinary legal rights, in part because they are thought to concern the most basic and important interests that all persons share in common, the way in which courts treat them suggests something different. Despite lofty sentiments, in legal practice human rights are treated as interests that are defeasible by the general welfare. When there is a need to guarantee protection of a particular interest fully, law-makers create not a prima facie, defeasible right but a full legal right in legislated form.[48]

It might be thought that this criticism of the defeasibility of human rights reaches only the semantics of rights discourse. We have no difficulty in accepting that 'liberties' or 'freedoms' are limited, and I have described in Section 5.3 the need for the legislature to set reasonable limits to freedoms. What then is the problem with affirming, for example, a defeasible human right to freedom of expression that can justifiably be interfered with? In the aspirational language of a non-justiciable document like the Universal Declaration, the problem is not so acute. There is some potential for confusion in the Declaration's statement that the exercise of a right is

[48] Cf. the discussion by Francisco J. Urbina, Section 6.3 in this book, of Etienne Mureinik's criticism of the South African bill of rights for not including absolute rights, especially against non-emergency detention without trial.

limited by the needs of the general welfare,[49] when those rights are precisely what make up the general welfare.[50] However, so long as such a 'right' remains non-legal and non-justiciable, the language of 'rights' in a context such as the Declaration is understandable and the choice to use it can express a certain urgency for protecting the value in question.[51] But a problem arises when this language of defeasible rights is transferred to the judicial realm, as in the adoption of the European Convention and later establishment of an extensive system of enforcement through the Strasbourg Court. The European Convention formulates rights similarly to the Universal Declaration, and the received approach typified in the case law of the Strasbourg Court gives a juridical cast to the notion of a justified infringement of a right. This leads us to think of rights not as law that must be enforced (in the manner that legislated rights are enforced) but simply as values or interests to be weighed up by a court in an overall assessment of legislation.

This weakening of the notion of a legal right has further consequences. If it is accepted that legal rights simply set forth a value to be considered and weighed up, then it seems obvious to extend the language of rights across a whole range of values that are important for a political community. This is sometimes done in a context where rights are judicially enforceable, and sometimes where it is unclear to what extent rights are judicially enforceable, as with the EU Charter of Fundamental Rights.[52] It is common to our Western legal heritage and legal language that courts have the function of enforcing legal rights; the fact that something is a legal right entails that it is a court's task to apply it and interpret its meaning authoritatively. Thus when something is labelled as a 'right' – including in modern human rights instruments – this trades on that legal and linguistic heritage and implies that the 'right' is the proper subject of judicial disposition (unless an effort is made to exclude this conclusion, as with Eleanor Roosevelt's framing of the Universal Declaration). Hence many are prepared to accept that judges properly have authority over anything labelled as a 'human right', extending even to areas such as national health expenditure, provision of public housing, and climate change. Many such 'rights', however, lack the jural structure that has historically grounded the willingness to

[49] UDHR Art. 29(2): 'In the exercise of his rights and freedoms, everyone shall be subject only to such limitations as are determined by law solely for the purpose of securing due recognition and respect for the rights and freedoms of others and of meeting the just requirements of morality, public order and the general welfare in a democratic society'.

[50] See John Finnis, *Natural Law and Natural Rights* (2nd edn, Oxford, Oxford University Press 2011) 214–15.

[51] For a discussion of which kinds of human needs are appropriate to express as claim-rights see David Wiggins, *Needs, Values, Truth: Essays in the Philosophy of Value* (Oxford, Oxford University Press 1998) 32ff.

[52] On the difficulty of determining which parts of the EU Charter are justiciable in which contexts, see Paul Yowell, 'The Justiciability of the EU Charter of Fundamental Rights in the Domestic Law of Member States' in PM Huber and K Ziegler (eds.), *The EU and National Constitutional Law* (Munich, Richard Boorberg Verlag 2012).

accept something to be the proper object of judicial disposition. The breadth of modern human rights language thus vastly expands the range of areas over which we accept judicial authority. Simultaneously, it conditions us to look to courts rather than legislatures for solutions, and to forget that legislative action is necessary in many important areas of human rights, and that legislatures are capable of providing strong, non-defeasible protection to rights.

5.5 LEGISLATED RIGHTS AND RIGHTS AS TRUMPS

I have argued that legislated rights are not defeasible by arguments regarding the general welfare. This sounds similar to Dworkin's theory of rights as trumps, but it is a different and stronger claim. In the Introduction to *Taking Rights Seriously*, Dworkin calls individual rights 'political trumps held by individuals'[53] and gives this general definition:

> Individuals have rights when, for some reason, a collective goal is not a sufficient justification for denying them what they wish, as individuals, to have or to do, or not a sufficient justification for imposing some loss or injury on them.[54]

Though Dworkin has said that rights function as trumps against any type of collective goal, the arguments in *Taking Rights Seriously* discuss collective justifications for laws almost entirely in terms of utilitarianism. The idea of rights defended there is, he says, 'parasitic on the dominant idea of utilitarianism, which is the idea of a collective goal of the community as a whole'.[55]

Thus Dworkin begins by accepting as a working postulate Bentham's definition of the general welfare in utilitarian terms. Although Dworkin calls his theory of rights 'anti-utilitarian', it accommodates and privileges basic utilitarian principles by conceiving of the general welfare as an aggregation of interests or preferences to be satisfied, and by assuming that it is possible to advance the general welfare of the whole by imposing loss or injuries on some. Rights 'trump' utilitarian justifications for laws in two different ways in Dworkin's work. In the first, which I call the shielded-interest theory, rights form a protective barrier around certain important individual interests and shield them against utilitarian arguments. I consider the second, the filtered-preference theory, in Section 5.6 below. When expounding the shielded-interest theory, Dworkin frequently casts rights claims in the following form: to say that A has a right to X, is to assert that A is entitled to X even if the general welfare could be promoted by denying X to A. It is the hypothetical conflict with the general welfare that gives intelligibility to a claim of right. This definition sets up an

53 Ronald Dworkin, *Taking Rights Seriously* (Cambridge, MA, Harvard University Press 1978) xi.
54 Ibid.
55 Ibid.

intrinsic opposition between rights and the general welfare. Rights are vindicated or protected when some measure that would promote the general welfare is defeated.

The authors of this book reject Dworkin's approach. We contend that individual rights and a sound understanding of the general welfare should be understood in a complementary way, so that each is continuous with the other. Harm done to individual rights is also harm to the general welfare, understood as the common good. Human rights instruments sketch the common good in outline form. However, human rights stand in need of specification, and very often this specification needs to be done by the legislature. Once that specification has been made in legislation, no appeal to the general welfare may be made to defeat a legislated right.

The concept of a non-defeasible legal right defended in the previous section is not that of a trump – which overpowers other things – but rather a rule about what kinds of arguments and claims are permissible in a legal forum. The trumping metaphor envisions someone playing, say, a king of diamonds, and another player overpowering it with a two of spades (the trumping suit). In Dworkin's view of constitutional rights adjudication, the state plays a card from the suit of general welfare, but this is overcome by the individual playing a card from the suit of rights. A legislated right, in our view, does not trump the general welfare but rather renders impermissible the argument that the right can be overcome by other needs of the general welfare – given that the right itself expresses requirements of the general welfare.

In Dworkin's claims about the trumping power of rights, the bark is stronger than the bite. He says that he rejects the balancing model of rights, which 'recommends striking a balance between the rights of the individual and the demands of society at large'.[56] Though that model is 'established in our political and judicial rhetoric', Dworkin contends it is 'false' and that the 'heart of the error' is the balancing metaphor.[57] But in fact the shielded-interest theory is similar to the balancing and proportionality tests used under the received approach to human rights.

Dworkin acknowledges that the state can legitimately curtail the exercise of even a fundamental right in order to prevent substantial harm to others or society. The shielded-interest theory rejects only *sheer* balancing: the proposition that a right is overcome whenever the considerations that support a proposed law tip the balance toward the general welfare, however slightly. In his review of *Taking Rights Seriously*, Joseph Raz said that Dworkin's arguments amount to two truisms: that rights matter and that they may defeat other considerations. He observed that 'almost always Dworkin sounds as if he meant to say something much more far-reaching'; however, '[n]owhere does he say clearly and unambiguously anything more than that rights have some weight however little and may override considerations which aren't themselves rights'.[58] Responding to Raz's critique, Dworkin offers only a minor

[56] Ibid. 197–8.

[57] Ibid. 198–9.

[58] Joseph Raz, 'Professor Dworkin's Theory of Rights' (1978) 26 *Political Studies* 123, 126.

adjustment. He states: 'No alleged right is a right (on my account) unless it overrides at least a marginal case of collective justification'.[59] But Dworkin makes no detailed attempt to describe the strength or weight that rights have in withstanding collective justifications and acknowledges that 'some rights are more important than others', meaning that they resist some collective justifications more forcefully than others.[60]

The logic of Dworkin's definition of rights under the shielded-interest theory can be clarified by exploring what its converse formulation would be. The original form of Dworkin's definition is:

> A has a right to X even if denying X to A would promote the general welfare.

Dworkin conceded, in his response to Raz quoted above, that this definition does not hold when denying X to A would promote the general welfare to a marginal degree. With this clarification, Dworkin's basic definition is:

> A has a right to X if denying X to A would promote the general welfare to more than a merely *marginal* degree.

Therefore, the converse of Dworkin's definition is this:

> If there is a *sufficiently strong* collective justification for denying X to A (to promote the general welfare), then A has no right to X.

Thus the logic of Dworkin's shielded-interest theory is fully consistent with balancing tests. In a sense, the theory of rights as trumps is a balancing test. The invocation of 'A's right to X' is simply a rhetorical tool for indicating (in an indeterminate way) that there must be a *weighty* justification for denying X to A.

To have a generally non-defeasible right, we do not need any special theory about the weight of rights in the abstract. What we need is a legal right with a specified, three-term jural structure. The way we treat such ordinary legal rights excludes arguments to defeat the right on grounds of the general welfare. Similarly, the absolute rights in human rights instruments, such as the right against torture, have such a three-term jural structure. Instead of a two-term relationship between A and an abstract value, the Universal Declaration provides that 'No one shall be subjected to torture or to cruel, inhuman or degrading treatment or punishment'. In other words, A has a claim-right not to be tortured correlative to B's duty not to torture A (where A is every person, and B is every person – in particular government officials with the means and motive to engage in torture). The act-description of torture is, like all natural and legal language, vague to some degree. The authorities responsible

59 Dworkin, *Taking Rights Seriously* 366.
60 Ibid.

for applying and interpreting torture will need to decide marginal cases.[61] But this will leave a core set of cases as clearly falling within the definition of torture. The specified jural structure of the right excludes arguments that torture is justified for the sake of the general welfare.[62]

5.6 RIGHTS AND THE COMMON GOOD

Human rights should be understood as integral to and constitutive of the general welfare or common good. Human rights instruments sketch an outline of the common good across a range of human values and goods, and much legislation can be understood as an attempt to specify human rights into legislated rights. However, there are theories and practices regarding rights that suppose (or construct) an intrinsic opposition between rights and the general welfare. The received approach to rights adjudication discussed in Section 5.4 is one such practice. It reduces human rights to prima facie rights – or mere individual interests – which are in constant tension with, and can be outweighed by, the general welfare, sometimes labelled the 'state interest', 'collective interest', 'public interest', 'government interest', etc.

The assumption of an inherent conflict between rights and the general welfare can lead to dual-forum theories of political justification. Such theories explicitly or implicitly hold that the function of legislatures is to promote collective or aggregate interests – either as a postulate about how legislatures are expected to act, or a normative claim about how they should act – while courts have a special responsibility to protect individual rights. The most sophisticated and influential dual-form theory was propounded by Dworkin. It is contained in his second theory of rights as trumps, which I call the filtered-preference theory. In this section, I provide an account of that theory and an argument that it should be rejected in favour of an approach that accepts the essential unity of human rights and the general welfare, and that the role of the legislature is to promote both.

Like the shielded-interest theory, Dworkin's second theory assumes utilitarianism as the background justification for laws. He argues that utilitarianism has an underlying 'egalitarian cast' reflected in Bentham's dictum that 'Each man [and woman] to count for one and none for more than one'.[63] The political process, he says, 'is meant to translate that requirement into legislation through the institutions of representative democracy'.[64] People reveal their preferences by voting and other political activity,

[61] See, e.g., *Gäfgen* v. *Germany* (2010) ECHR 759, where the European Court of Human Rights held that German police officers engaged in torture when threatening to torture a suspect unless he revealed to them the location of a boy that he had abducted and claimed (falsely, as it turned out) was still alive.

[62] See ibid., for a discussion of the absolute character of the right against torture.

[63] Ronald Dworkin, 'Social Sciences and Constitutional Rights – the Consequences of Uncertainty' (1977) 6 *Journal of Law and Education* 3, 10.

[64] Ibid.

thereby contributing to 'a machine which is calculated, though imperfectly, to reach decisions such that, though some individuals suffer and others gain, the overall preferences of all the people, considered neutrally with the same consideration for the preferences of each, is improved'.[65] Although Dworkin does not explicitly argue that legislatures should attempt to translate every preference into law as a general rule, he accepts that they generally do and builds that function into the normative framework of his utility machine.[66] The legislature is not expected to engage in rights-based, principled deliberation; it simply tallies preferences and shapes laws to match.

Dworkin argues that utilitarianism is legitimate when based on the personal preferences that people have but is corrupted by their external preferences for how goods and opportunities should be distributed to others.[67] Dworkin is especially concerned to exclude from the utilitarian calculation (i) racist and similar prejudices that would deny opportunities to certain classes of people, and (ii) 'moralistic' preferences that would assign or withhold goods on the basis of moral judgment regarding someone else's choice of lifestyle.[68] It is not the *content* of external preferences, however, but their *externality* that causes them to corrupt utilitarian justifications for laws. Thus, Dworkin acknowledges, even altruistic external preferences for how goods should be distributed to others corrupt utilitarian justifications for law.[69] The formal device Dworkin relies on to argue that external preferences have this effect is 'double-counting': if Sarah has preferences for certain goods, and the preferences of Sarah-lovers for goods to be given to her are then added to her own, then the resulting distribution is unfair and contrary to utilitarianism's basic egalitarian impulse.[70]

Bringing together the different strands in the argument, Dworkin proposes a 'general theory of rights':

> The concept of an individual political right … is a response to the philosophical defects of a utilitarianism that counts external preferences and the practical impossibility of a utilitarianism that does not. It allows us to enjoy the institutions of political democracy, which enforce overall or unrefined utilitarianism, and yet protect the fundamental right of citizens to equal concern and respect by prohibiting decisions that seem, antecedently, likely to have been reached by virtue of the external components of the preferences democracy reveals.[71]

By the words 'prohibiting decisions', Dworkin refers to judicial review of legislation to enforce rights. Independent courts, Dworkin argues, should have the power

[65] Ibid.
[66] Ibid.
[67] Dworkin, *Taking Rights Seriously* 276–77.
[68] Ibid. 276.
[69] Ibid. 235, 238.
[70] Ibid. 231–8.
[71] Ibid. 277.

to overturn decisions based on corrupted utilitarian justifications, because judges are insulated from society's external preferences expressed through electoral politics.[72] He contends that there is a 'high antecedent probability that the political judgment reached about a particular matter will not fairly reflect the kind of preferences that rightly make up the general welfare, but will give influential expression to preferences based on prejudice'.[73] Therefore, Dworkin concludes, '[t]he key point of this explanation of constitutional rights is that rights are based on antecedent probabilities'.[74]

Rights, on this view, are needed to exclude or to filter out certain kinds of preferences that would otherwise corrupt the utilitarian justification for laws. Though Dworkin is uneasy with utilitarianism, he accepts it as the prevailing background justification and proposes that it can be refined, thereby realising its inherent egalitarian potential. But it is not for the legislature itself to apply the filter. The refining process requires courts empowered to strike down laws based on corrupted utilitarian justifications. What will then remain is a legitimate body of law justified through an egalitarian utilitarianism. Like the shielded-interest theory, the filtered-preference theory involves a symbiotic relationship between rights and utilitarianism. In the shielded-interest theory, rights are defined as personal interests important enough to withstand (some) utilitarian justifications for law. In the filtered-preference theory, rights do not have their own independent existence; they are the by-product of filtering out or trumping external preferences. The trumping of moralist preferences yields a 'right of moral independence', and the trumping of racist and similar prejudices yields a 'right of political independence'.[75]

Dworkin abandoned the filtered-preference theory following an exchange with HLA Hart, in which he initially defended a refined version of theory. But what Dworkin abandoned was only the formal structure of the theory. Some of the underlying ideas of the filtered-preference theory, as well as its core strategy of opposing rights to the general welfare, survive into his later work. It is worth re-tracing Dworkin's exchange with Hart because both his early rhetoric of rights as trumps as well as argumentative moves he made in response to Hart have informed his influential rhetoric of rights as trumps.

Hart argued that double-counting was not inimical to utilitarianism but entailed by its basic premises, and he suspected that Dworkin's true concern was the prejudicial content of external preferences, not their externality or tendency to double-counting. In response, Dworkin employed a new conception of external preferences. He attacked 'political' preferences in which someone takes the mere popularity of a

[72] See Ronald Dworkin, *A Matter of Principle* (Cambridge, MA, Harvard University Press 1985) 70.

[73] Dworkin, 'Social Sciences and Constitutional Rights' 10.

[74] Ibid.

[75] Dworkin, *A Matter of Principle* 364.

proposal as itself a reason for adopting it.[76] Dworkin sometimes depicts this bootstrapping as something individuals do (a circular logic in which someone thinks: I support this proposal because it reflects my opinion). More often, Dworkin locates this thought in the political process, depicting legislatures as deciding to enact a proposal simply because the majority favours it instead of on the basis that the proposal promotes justice or is otherwise worthy of choice.[77] Despite his attempt to deflect Hart's criticisms, Dworkin struck a concessionary note by stating that the double-counting device was 'meant to summarize the argument, not to make it, and I will not press that particular characterization'.[78] In fact, Dworkin never returned to the double-counting approach and ceased depicting rights in the formalistic terms of his early work.

What Dworkin abandoned were the formal structures of refined utilitarianism and the filtered-preference theory: the fixation on utilitarianism as the background justification, and the exclusion of 'external' preferences – first defined to include even altruistic preferences, and later re-defined as supporting a proposal on the basis of its popularity. Dworkin continued to argue that rights exclude political motivations based on racist, moralistic, or similar prejudice, but in his later work he normally directs his arguments against the content of those prejudices rather than their externality (in line with Hart's contention that this was his true concern all along).[79] At key points, however, Dworkin has re-deployed the strategy of depicting legislatures as voting for proposals because the majority favours it. In his later work Dworkin sometimes rejects legislation on the grounds that it is based upon 'official or majority disapproval'[80] or is directed against behaviour or opinions that offend 'shared or conventional morality';[81] and he defines the 'majoritarian' or 'statistical' conception of democracy as one 'in which anything a majority or plurality wants is legitimate for that reason',[82] treating this view as if it were a widely held theory of democracy.

This cynical view of political and legislative processes resonates with the principle-policy distinction of Dworkin's early work. Courts, Dworkin had argued, are a forum of principle, while legislatures are a forum of policy. Rights are a matter of principle, and thus the special responsibility of courts.[83] Legislatures are responsible for

[76] Ibid. 368.

[77] Ibid. Finnis describes Dworkin's attempt to defend his theory against Hart 'a plain fallacy or sophism, and its cultural success is a deplorable testimony to decay in standards of public argumentation. Indeed, it is a form of refined incivility'. John Finnis, *Intention and Identity: Collected Essays, Vol. II* (Oxford, Oxford University Press 2011) 112.

[78] Dworkin, *A Matter of Principle* 366.

[79] See HLA Hart, 'Between Utility and Rights' (1979) 29 *Columbia Law Review* 843.

[80] Ronald Dworkin, *Freedom's Law: The Moral Reading of the American Constitution* (New York, Oxford University Press 1999) 218.

[81] Ronald Dworkin, *Sovereign Virtue: The Theory and Practice of Equality* (Cambridge, Harvard University Press 2002)158.

[82] Dworkin, *Freedom's Law* 209, 364. See also Dworkin, *Sovereign Virtue* 16.

[83] Dworkin, *Taking Rights Seriously* 90–1; Dworkin, *A Matter of Principle* 70.

promoting the general welfare and need not take account of rights.[84] Indeed according to Dworkin's definition of rights as trumps against the general welfare, a legislature would have to choose between either promoting the general welfare or protecting individual rights. While this presents a tragic dilemma for legislatures, the capacity of courts to refine the legislature's actions allows for happy solutions. But rights, on this view, are vindicated only when courts uphold a claim of right against a countervailing consideration regarding the general welfare. After Dworkin abandoned the filtered-preference theory, he also collapsed the distinction between policy and principle, such that the responsibilities of courts and legislatures were not sharply separated as before.[85] But by this time, the language of rights as trumps had taken on a life of its own, and his dual-forum theory of political justification had bored deep in the consciousness of many legal and political theorists.

Dworkin's exchange with Hart also served to draw out the conclusion of Dworkin's fundamental strategy of defining rights as being inherently opposed to the general welfare. Hart criticised Dworkin's attempt to find rights in the 'shadow of utilitarianism', pointing out that if the content of rights is logically dependent on the background justification of utilitarianism, then people would hold no rights against a tyrant who did not seek to promote the general welfare. Dworkin conceded Hart's claim. Taking Hart's example of a ruler who bans all religious practice in a community of devout believers, Dworkin says this would be 'insane or wicked' but that the ban is not properly described as a violation of rights.[86] 'We need rights', he says, 'as a distinct element in a political theory, only when some decision that injures some people nevertheless finds prima facie support in the claim that it will make the community as a whole better off on some plausible account of where the community's general welfare lies'.[87] We do not need the idea of rights to condemn the wicked acts of a Nero or Hitler, Dworkin argues, because such tyrants do not even purport to promote the general welfare.[88]

The framers of the Universal Declaration took a different view. In their language, the 'barbarous acts which have outraged the conscience of mankind' of recent regimes violated the human rights that belonged to all persons everywhere.[89] For many years Dworkin resisted speaking of human rights,[90] and the reason for this is

[84] See Dworkin, *Taking Rights Seriously* ix, 115.

[85] See Ronald Dworkin, *Law's Empire* (Cambridge, Harvard University Press 1986) 311–12. For discussion of the changes in Dworkin's theory over the years, see Paul Yowell, 'A Critical Examination of Dworkin's Theory of Rights' (2007) 52 *American Journal of Jurisprudence* 93.

[86] Dworkin, *A Matter of Principle* 370–1.

[87] Ibid. 371.

[88] Ibid. 370.

[89] UDHR, Preamble ('Whereas disregard and contempt for human rights have resulted in barbarous acts which have outraged the conscience of mankind ...').

[90] Dworkin finally endorsed the language of human rights in 2006, but, relying on the same fundamental strategy as before, he defined human rights not as basic aspects of human wellbeing but the consequence of excluding certain especially vicious motivations for state action. Ronald Dworkin,

apparent in his reply to Hart. Hart had argued that the 'core notion' of constitutional rights and extra-legal, moral rights is 'basic or fundamental individual needs'.[91] Discourse at this level of rights treats 'certain freedoms as ... essential for the maintenance of the life, the security, the development, and the dignity of the individual'.[92] Dworkin may have had these statements in mind in this response:

> [Hart's] objections ... suppose that whatever rights people have are at least in large part timeless rights necessary to protect enduring and important interests fixed by human nature and fundamental to human development, like interests in the choice of sexual partners and acts and choice of religious conviction. That is a familiar theory of what rights are and what they are for, and I said that I would not give my reasons, in this essay, for thinking that it is in the end an inadequate theory of rights.[93]

Dworkin insists that rights are not 'timeless' or 'fixed by human nature' but are 'relative to the other elements of a political theory'; rights come in 'complex packages of political theory' which include the background justification and some description of the way rights trump that theory's conception of the general welfare.[94] The persistent strategy of Dworkin's work on rights has been to locate the essence of rights not in individuals and their needs but in the exclusion of arguments or political justifications opposed to equality. As he has said, 'rights cannot be identified independently of the overall political morality in which they are meant to figure'.[95]

This conception of rights should be rejected in favour of that reflected in the Universal Declaration, which is proclaimed as a 'common standard of achievement for all peoples and all nations'. As Finnis has pointed out, the Declaration (and like instruments) sketch the outlines of the common good and assert the responsibility of those responsible for co-ordinating the common life to consider and favour, at all times, 'each and everyone's wellbeing, in each of its basic aspects'.[96] The Declaration implicitly rejects a conception of the general welfare that can be furthered by sacrificing individual rights, as well as the notion that the proper or presumptive role of the legislature is to promote some collective goal such as calculating overall preference satisfaction, while rights are the special responsibility of courts. Its Preamble calls on 'every organ of society' to promote rights, not just courts as in Dworkin's account. In order to see legislatures as having full responsibility for protecting and

Is Democracy Possible Here?: Principles for a New Political Debate (Princeton, NJ, Princeton University Press 2006) 33–5.

91 HLA Hart, 'Bentham on Legal Rights' in AWB Simpson (ed.), *Oxford Essays in Jurisprudence, Second Series* (Oxford, Oxford University Press 1973) 201.

92 Ibid. 197. At the level of rights in the 'ordinary' law, Hart endorsed the 'choice' theory of rights.

93 Dworkin, *A Matter of Principle* 369.

94 Ibid. 370.

95 Dworkin, *Sovereign Virtue* 481 n. 9.

96 Finnis, *Natural Law and Natural Rights* 214.

promoting human rights, one must see rights as integral, constitutive aspects of the general welfare, and not as trumps against it.

5.7 THE LEGISLATURE AND MINORITY RIGHTS

One might agree that legislation is needed to protect and promote the range of human rights discussed in Section 5.2 and reject the preference-aggregation account of legislative action criticised in Section 5.6, and yet remain sceptical of the actual ability of legislatures to escape majoritarian biases or prejudices. Many have concluded that legislatures are not well positioned to protect the rights of minorities, because their responsiveness to demands of the electorate and majority voting leads them to be indifferent to minority interests or even biased against them. This line of thought has often led human rights lawyers to draw a further practical conclusion: that, especially with regard to minority rights, we should look to courts as the only or at least primary source for social reform and human rights litigation as the means to prompt it.

The question of whether judges or legislators are more likely to protect minority interests is largely a question of fact, though one's conclusion on this matter may well be influenced by one's theoretical view of appropriate institutional roles. Here is Dworkin's prediction on the factual question:

> Legislators who have been elected, and must be reelected, by a political majority are more likely to take that majority's side in any serious argument about the rights of the minority against it; if they oppose the majority's wishes too firmly, it will replace them with those who do not. For that reason legislators seem less likely to reach sound decisions about minority rights than officials who are less vulnerable in that way.[97]

When considering whether judges should take a passive approach to constitutional interpretation and defer to the legislature, or take the more robust interpretive approach he favours, Dworkin claims that 'we would have more to regret if the Court had accepted passivism wholeheartedly: southern schools might still be segregated, for example'.[98] He is referring, of course, to *Brown* v. *Board of Education* (1954), and attributes an extraordinary significance to the case in supposing that, in its absence, legal segregation in the United States might have endured into the late twentieth century. Dworkin's argument is indicative of how large that case looms in the historical narratives of constitutional and legal theorists, even if few would go so far in their estimation of *Brown*'s effect on history.

[97] Dworkin, *Law's Empire* 375.

[98] Ibid.

Examining Dworkin's claim provides an example by which to consider the central case account of legislatures presented in this book and defended in the Introduction. Whatever their theoretical capacity to act reasonably, do legislatures fail when put to the test of a real, historical situation? It is, moreover, useful to consider *Brown* as a test case for the question of whether we need counter-majoritarian courts to effect social reform that benefits minorities. In the first place, the black minority in the United States has often been the prime example of a 'discrete and insular'[99] minority, that is, one that is unable to influence the political process and hence in need of judicial protection. And *Brown* has widely been considered as the paradigm case of courts' ability to produce reform – the 'principal inspiration to others who seek change through legislation'.[100]

Historical and empirical studies of the mid-century civil rights movement have forcefully countered this view of *Brown* and reached conclusions that are nearly opposite Dworkin's with regard to its historical impact.[101] In 1964, a decade after *Brown* was decided, schools remained almost completely segregated in the seventeen southern states whose laws mandated segregation in 1954.[102] Only 1.2 per cent of black school children in those states attended schools with white school children.[103] Throughout that decade the US Congress was mostly inactive with regard to racial equality. Then Congress enacted the 1964 Civil Rights Act, the 1965 Voting Rights Act, and the 1965 Elementary and Secondary Education Act (ESEA), which provided funding for schools with a high percentage of low-income children. It was at this point that the number of black children attending integrated schools finally began to increase substantially, rising steadily over the next decade. By 1973, over 90 per cent of black children in the South attended integrated schools.[104]

Gerald Rosenberg attributes this change squarely to Congress and other political actors, and provides data for the view that a similar pattern obtained across other areas regarding racial equality.[105] His conclusion is stark:

> The use of the courts in the civil rights movement is considered the paradigm of a successful strategy for social change. ... Yet a closer examination reveals that before Congress and the executive branch acted, courts had virtually no direct effect on ending discrimination in the key fields of education, voting, transportation,

99 *US* v. *Carolene Products Company*, 304 US 144, 152 n. 4 (1938).

100 Jack Greenberg, 'Litigation for Social Change: Methods, Limits, and Role in Democracy' (Association of the Bar of the City of New York, 1974) 331.

101 See especially Gerald N Rosenberg, *The Hollow Hope: Can Courts Bring About Social Change?* (2nd edn, Chicago, IL, University of Chicago Press 2008); Michael J Klarman, *From Jim Crow to Civil Rights: The Supreme Court and the Struggle for Racial Equality* (Oxford, Oxford University Press 2004).

102 Rosenberg, *The Hollow Hope* 52.

103 Ibid.

104 Ibid. 52–3.

105 Ibid. Ch. 2.

> accommodations and public places, and housing. Only when Congress and the executive branch acted in tandem with the courts did change occur in these fields. ... *Brown* and its progeny stand for the proposition that courts are impotent to produce significant social reform.[106]

Michael Klarman, who has produced the most detailed study of the legal developments from the post-Civil War era through to *Brown*, reinforces Rosenberg's conclusions about *Brown*'s lack of direct, causal effect in ending segregation.[107] Klarman's research shows that US Supreme Court decisions involving racial equality consistently reflected the clear national consensus, both in several cases that upheld segregation such as *Plessy* v. *Ferguson* (1896) and in the few pre-*Brown* cases that struck down isolated state laws.[108] Where public opinion is fairly evenly divided, Klarman says the Court is apt to move in the direction of the opinion of the elite class from which the Justices are drawn. *Brown*, he argues, was such a case. National opinion polls following the decision found that half of Americans accepted it.[109] What swayed the Court, Klarman argues, is that the justices unanimously believed that racial segregation was an immoral institution that should eventually be eliminated throughout the US.[110] This viewpoint was strengthening – particularly among educated elites and the governing class[111] – following World War II, where blacks had fought alongside whites to defend democracy. To deny full equality to blacks was increasingly seen as not only intrinsically unjust, but as harmful to US interests in countering the rise of communist regimes, who highlighted racial segregation in the US to characterise its commitment to democratic equality as a pretence.[112]

[106] Ibid. 70–1.

[107] Klarman, *From Jim Crow to Civil Rights*.

[108] See ibid. 448–50.

[109] Ibid. 450.

[110] Ibid. 447–8.

[111] Reflecting the attitude of this class, the US Government filed an amicus brief in *Brown*, which stated:

> The problem of racial discrimination is particularly acute in the District of Columbia, [the] window through which the world looks into our house. ... Foreign officials and visitors naturally judge this country and our people by their experiences and observations in the nation's capital; and the treatment of colored persons here is taken as the measure of our attitude toward minorities generally.

See Peter H Irons, *Jim Crow's Children: The Broken Promise of the Brown Decision* (New York, Penguin 2004) 135.

[112] Klarman, *From Jim Crow to Civil Rights* 443–5. The US Government's *amicus* brief (see Irons, *Jim Crow's Children* 136) stated: 'Racial discrimination furnishes grist for the Communist propaganda mills, and it raises doubts even among friendly nations as to the intensity of our devotion to the democratic faith'. The brief attached a letter from Secretary of State Dean Acheson to the US Attorney General stating:

> As might be expected Soviet spokesmen regularly exploit this situation in propaganda against the United States, both within the United Nations and through radio broadcasts and the press,

What often gives the Supreme Court's decisions the appearance of being a counter-majoritarian force is that many of the Court's most noteworthy or controversial decisions impose a national consensus on outlying states.[113] This was partially true of *Brown* in that a minority of states legally mandated segregation in schools; however, the Court's previous rulings in favour of racial equality had been directed against state laws representing a much smaller minority position in comparison to the strong support for segregation in the South.[114] *Brown* had the effect of producing a backlash in southern states, several of which refused to implement the decision.[115] Indeed, an unintended, and to some extent unexpected, consequence of *Brown* was to radicalise southern politics. Moderate supporters of segregation were pushed to more extreme positions, or voted out and replaced by stauncher segregation proponents.[116] Attempts to enforce *Brown* sometimes resulted in violent events publicised nationwide. Klarman argues that *Brown*'s main causal contribution to ending segregation came in a round-about way: by producing a backlash in the southern states, it made the rest of the nation more aware of the need for political action and thus gave impetus to passing civil rights legislation.[117] Although Klarman therefore supports Rosenberg's argument about *Brown*'s lack of direct effect on segregation in schools, he is less sceptical than Rosenberg about the courts' capacity to produce social change in general.[118]

Klarman's and Rosenberg's arguments about the inefficacy of *Brown* have of course been challenged, as has Rosenberg's more general argument about the inability of courts to produce social reform.[119] I do not here defend either the narrow thesis about *Brown*'s lack of direct causal effect on segregation or Rosenberg's more general argument about courts; my argument is, in one respect, narrower. My claim is not that courts are powerless to effect social reform on their own, but rather that legislatures are capable of producing social change that benefits minorities and are often indispensable to that goal. Whatever else Klarman's and Rosenberg's arguments show, they at least demonstrate that Congress played a vitally important role

---

> which reaches all corners of the world. ... The segregation of school children on a racial basis is one of the practices in the United States that has been singled out for hostile foreign comment in the United Nations and elsewhere.

Acheson concluded that racial discrimination 'remains a source of constant embarrassment to this Government in the day-to-day conduct of its foreign relations; and it jeopardizes the effective maintenance of our moral leadership of the free and democratic nations of the world'.

113 Ibid. 452.

114 Ibid. 452–3.

115 Ibid. 440–2.

116 Ibid. 440.

117 Ibid. 451, 467.

118 Ibid. 453, 461.

119 But see TM Keck's observation that 'Klarman's insistence on the limited relevance of *Brown* is now approaching scholarly consensus'. 'Does the Court Follow the Election Returns?' (2004) 32 *Reviews in American History* 602, 608.

in advancing racial equality. The counter-arguments to Rosenberg and Klarman do not challenge that point but rather attempt to buttress the contribution that courts made to that process. It might be thought that, despite Congress's enactment of civil rights legislation, the hostility of many legislatures in southern states is a dramatic example of legislatures being captured by majoritarian bias, to the detriment of minority groups. And so it is,[120] and again nothing in the argument of the book denies that this is possible. Rather, we argue that there is no inevitable propensity to such majoritarian bias. Congress's own action is an equally dramatic example of the opposite possibility.

The simplistic view of legislatures being inevitably biased in majority-minority disputes is usually accompanied by an optimistic view of the judiciary's capacity to resist this. But this optimism needs to be tempered by an awareness that the courts can likewise be subject to majoritarian bias: looking to state courts in the South to resist segregation would have been fruitless. Moreover, the historical record shows that courts can block beneficial social reforms initiated by the legislature. This should be borne in mind with regard to the overall question of judicial power and social reform that Rosenberg addresses. Looking to the other side of the coin from Rosenberg, I would call attention to cases in which decisions by the Court had a negative effect on racial equality, producing effective social change but in the wrong direction. It is important to consider this comparative dimension because the question raised at the outset of this section is whether courts are more likely than legislatures to protect minority rights, and because Dworkin has influentially defended a strong version of the thesis that they are. As we saw in Section 5.6, this institutional theory is built into his concept of rights as trumps.

The most infamous anti-minority decision of the Supreme Court is *Dred Scott* v. *Sandford* (1857),[121] in which the Court attempted to provide a legal, constitutional settlement to the political question that had inflamed passions throughout the nation: whether slavery would be allowed to expand westward as US settlers entered territories that were to become new states. On this question depended not only the balance of power in the Senate (which was evenly divided between free and slave states) but the character of the growing nation. Dred Scott was a slave in Missouri,

[120] However, as Klarman observes, Southern legislatures at the time were far from being representative of the actual population, because about 80 per cent of blacks were disenfranchised and state legislatures were 'badly malapportioned in favor of rural whites, who were the most committed to maintaining white supremacy'. Klarman, *From Jim Crow to Civil Rights* 451. Klarman says this 'raises the interesting question of whether *Brown* might have been unnecessary if blacks had been fully enfranchised and one-person, one-vote principles had been in operation'. Ibid. He thinks it is likely – though uncertain – that school segregation would have been maintained in southern states for some time, ibid., but this nonetheless helps to explain why blacks fought much harder to gain voting rights than for school integration. See ibid. 453–4. As Klarman states: 'Voting protects other rights, and in the postwar period many black leaders insisted that if southern blacks could win genuine protection for their voting rights, they could secure other rights for themselves through politics'. Ibid. 454.

[121] 60 US 393 (1857).

a slave state, who sued for his freedom on the ground that he had once been held in a territory where slavery was forbidden. The Court denied his claim and issued a wide-ranging opinion on the federal government's power to regulate slavery and on the legal status of black slaves. The Court held that black slaves could not be citizens under the Constitution because, *inter alia*, the Founders had considered blacks as 'beings of an inferior order, and altogether unfit to associate with the white race, either in social or political relations, and so far inferior that they had no rights which the white man was bound to respect'.[122] Instead, slaves had the legal status of property. In a novel interpretation of the Fifth Amendment, the Court held that slaveholders in western territories held property rights in slaves, which would be deprived without due process of law if a territory banned slavery.[123] This had the effect of overturning the 1954 Kansas-Nebraska Act, which Congress had enacted to allow settlers in the territories to vote on whether the territory would become a free state or slave state. The Court effectively ruled that, as a matter of constitutional law, new states admitted to the union must be slave states. This prevented political compromise, and the Court's opinion thus took its place among several historical causes driving the United States towards civil war.

After the Civil War, which lasted from 1861 to 1865, Congress proposed the Thirteenth Amendment, which abolished slavery; the Fourteenth Amendment, which provided for equal protection of the law and established civil and political rights on a national basis, prohibiting individual states from denying 'the privileges or immunities of citizens of the United States'; and the Fifteenth Amendment, which provided that the right to vote could not be denied on account of race. The three Reconstruction Amendments were ratified by the states. Each amendment specifically empowered Congress to enact further appropriate legislation for the enforcement of its provisions, thus adding to the original list of enumerated federal powers in the Constitution.

In pursuance of the new powers granted to it, Congress passed a series of Civil Rights Acts in 1866, 1870, 1871, and 1875.[124] These Acts sought to go beyond the mere abolition of slavery and to establish the full protection of civil and political rights for former slaves.[125] The 1866 Act granted to citizens of 'every race and color' the right 'to make and enforce contracts, to sue, be parties, and give evidence, to inherit, purchase, lease, sell, hold, and convey real and personal property, and to full and equal benefit of all laws and proceedings for the security of person and property, as is enjoyed by white citizens, and shall be subject to like punishment, pains, and penalties, and to none other, any law, statute, ordinance, regulation, or custom, to

[122] Ibid. 407.

[123] Ibid. 450.

[124] 14 Stat. L. 27 (1866); 16 Stat. L. 140 (1870); 17 Stat. L. 13 (1871); 18 Stat. L. 335 (1875).

[125] See Eugene Gressman, 'Unhappy History of Civil Rights Legislation' (1951) 50 *Michigan Law Review* 1323.

the contrary notwithstanding'. The 1870 Act sought to implement the Fifteenth Amendment not only by prohibiting state officials from denying citizens the right to vote on account of race, but also by prohibiting private individuals from preventing or impeding citizens to exercise their right to vote, and conspiring to do so. The 1875 Act provided that 'all persons within the jurisdiction of the United States shall be entitled to the full and equal enjoyment accommodations, advantages, facilities, and privileges of inns, public conveyances on land or water, theatres, and other places of public amusement'; and it provided for criminal penalties against individuals denied such rights. The Act also provided that citizens could not be precluded from serving on juries on grounds of race or colour.

The US Supreme Court struck down the 1875 Civil Rights Act in the *Civil Rights Cases* (1883),[126] and in other cases it adopted a narrow reading of the Reconstruction Amendments – in particular the 'privileges and immunities clause' – that denied Congress the power to enforce against private individuals the full range of rights that the various Acts had sought to protect.[127] The Court held that the Amendments empowered the federal government only to counteract action taken specifically by the state. The larger threat to the rights of former slaves, however, came from private individuals.[128] When the Reconstruction Amendments were being debated, they were understood both by proponents and opponents to grant Congress legislative power to address the subject matter in the manner that it did in the series of Civil Rights Acts between 1866 and 1875, and to make laws applicable to individuals.[129] Much later, the Supreme Court would expand the range of rights protected under the Fourteenth Amendment; but it was through the 'due process' rather than the 'privileges and immunities' clause, and the Court retained its understanding of the Reconstruction Amendments as applying only to state action. This narrow construction and the Court's decision to strike down the 1875 Act effectively ended the promise of the Reconstruction Amendments to empower Congress to provide full national protection for the civil and political rights of blacks and former slaves. When Congress later enacted the Civil Rights Act in 1964, it was still hampered by the Court's earlier rulings on the Reconstruction Amendments and thus enacted the 1964 Act under its power to regulate interstate commerce.[130]

[126] 109 US 3 (1883).

[127] See especially *The Slaughter-house Cases*, 83 US 36 (1873), and discussion in Gressman, 'Unhappy History of Civil Rights Legislation' 1336–8.

[128] Ibid. 1330.

[129] Ibid. 1332–6.

[130] In the *Civil Rights Cases*, 109 US 3 (1883), the Court had raised interstate commerce as a potential ground of jurisdiction for the Civil Rights Act 1875 but dismissed it because the government had not argued for this and had instead argued under the Thirteenth and Fourteenth Amendments. It is arguable that the commerce power, as construed by the Court at that time, could have supported the Civil Rights Act 1875 if the Court had reached the issue. By the 1960s, the Court's understanding of the commerce power had extended further, and it upheld the Civil Rights Act 1964 on this jurisdictional ground in *Heart of Atlanta, Inc.* v. *United States*, 379 US 241 (1964).

In 1890, seven years after the Court struck down the Civil Rights Act 1875, Louisiana enacted a law requiring separation of blacks and whites on railroads – which would have been forbidden under the 1875 Act. The Supreme Court upheld the Louisiana law in *Plessy* v. *Ferguson* (1896),[131] which established the 'separate but equal' doctrine that endured until *Brown*. While some historians have argued that *Plessy* led to the expansion of segregation, Klarman argues that there is no direct evidence of this.[132] Rather, *Plessy* reflected the new national consensus and was part of a trend during the 1880s and 1890s departing from the efforts at integration that marked the Reconstruction era.[133] In all of these examples – *Dred Scott*, the *Civil Rights Cases*, *Plessy* – my point is not to try to prove what would have happened in a counter-factual history in which the Supreme Court had ruled differently. Rather, it is to show that in many key cases involving minorities, the Court has (contrary to the role envisioned for it by Dworkin) failed to take a counter-majoritarian position. As Klarman remarks: '[D]uring the time period covered by this book [i.e., from the *Plessy* era to *Brown* and its aftermath], not a single Court decision involving race clearly contravened national public opinion'.[134] The *Civil Rights Cases* (1883) did clearly contravene the will of the Congresses that had enacted the Civil Rights Act 1875 and related Reconstruction era acts; but the political will to enforce and maintain them was waning in the 1880s.[135]

Moving forward to the modern era, the main flash point between the Court and legislatures on racial equality in recent decades has been over the constitutionality of affirmative action legislation. These cases have repeatedly involved Congress and state governments attempting to promote the interests of minorities through various kinds of affirmative action laws and programmes, and the Supreme Court and other federal courts using the Equal Protection Clause to curtail or strike down those efforts.[136]

When the historical record is thus expanded to take account of the century before *Brown* (beginning with *Dred Scott*) and the decades following it, the argument that the Supreme Court was the key institution in bringing about racial equality looks hollow. Cass Sunstein, in an article reviewing scholarship on *Brown*, concisely summarises that historical record:

> Fifty years later, *Brown* does seem increasingly anomalous. Before the Warren Court, the justices were almost never a force for social reform, and they have rarely assumed that role in the past two decades. Most of the time, the judiciary has been

[131] 163 US 537 (1896).
[132] Klarman, *From Jim Crow to Civil Rights* 47.
[133] Ibid. Ch. 1.
[134] Ibid. 450.
[135] Ibid. 48.
[136] See Kevin R Johnson, 'The Last Twenty Five Years of Affirmative Action?' (2004) 21 *Constitutional Commentary* 171.

> an obstacle to racial equality. Before the Civil War, the Supreme Court, in the *Dred Scott* case, interpreted the Constitution so as to entrench slavery. After the Civil War, the Court sharply limited Congress's power to protect the newly freed slaves. During the first half of the twentieth century, the Court did little to promote racial justice (and for much of that time, as Frankfurter and Jackson were painfully aware, it was hostile to legislative attempts to reduce economic inequality); in the last quarter of the century, the Court's most important racial-discrimination decisions struck down affirmative-action programs.[137]

If Sunstein's general claim is correct, – 'Most of time, the judiciary has been an obstacle to racial equality' – then Dworkin's theory of institutional capabilities must be rejected as applied to the US Congress and the US Supreme Court; and his general theory of rights should be evaluated in light of its reliance on his historical reading of the actions of Congress and the Court in this subject area.

The tragic history of the US with regard to racial equality – in which Supreme Court decisions often played a crucial role in furthering inequality – can be contrasted to the record of the UK. In 1833, twenty-four years before the *Dred Scott* decision, the UK Parliament ended slavery throughout the Empire. Parliament had abolished the slave trade in 1807, but not slavery itself. As in the US, slavery had played a large role in economic activity in the UK. Before 1807, British ships transported around 3.4 million slaves to the Americas (only a small portion of whom were taken to North America).[138] When the Slavery Abolition Act 1833 was enacted, there were 800,000 recognised slaves in the British Empire, most in the West Indies.[139] Slavery was backed by powerful financial interests in Parliament and tolerated by the majority of people, many of whom directly or indirectly benefited from it economically.[140] Nonetheless, a long, persistent political campaign for abolition, led by William Wilberforce and Thomas Clarkson,[141] eventually persuaded Parliament to adopt the 1807 and 1833 Acts. All this took place without judicial review of legislation.

The argument that we must look to courts to protect minority rights because legislatures are institutionally incapable of doing so has little grounding in the historical record on the issue of racial equality just reviewed – which is often taken to be the case that presents the most compelling need for counter-majoritarian judicial power.

[137] Cass R Sunstein, 'Did Brown Matter?' *The New Yorker* (3 May 2004) www.newyorker.com/magazine/2004/05/03/did-brown-matter.

[138] David Richardson, 'The British Empire and the Atlantic Slave Trade, 1660–1807' in PJ Marshall and others (eds.), *The Oxford History of the British Empire: The Eighteenth Century* (Oxford, Oxford University Press 1998) 441.

[139] Philippa Levine, *The British Empire: Sunrise to Sunset* (Harlow, Pearson Education 2013) 27.

[140] Catherine Hall, *Legacies of British Slave-ownership: Colonial Slavery and the Formation of Victorian Britain* (Cambridge, Cambridge University Press 2014).

[141] Wilberforce made his first speech on the subject in the House of Commons in 1789.

5.8 CONCLUSION

This chapter has argued that legislatures have a vital and indispensable role to play in protecting and promoting human rights. This argument runs counter to much modern human rights discourse, which looks mainly to courts to fulfil the promise of human rights, but it reflects the approach taken by the drafters of the Universal Declaration of Human Rights. The broad, abstract language they used to express human rights is consistent with their intention not to create a judicially enforceable instrument but a document that could be read and understood by everyone, and that could serve as a guide for legislating, for governing, and promoting the welfare of political communities and all their members. It was precisely to everyone – 'every individual and every organ of society' – that the drafters looked to do the work of ensuring human rights.

It is common to think of human rights as liberties preserved from state interference, or claim-rights one can assert against the state. Dworkin gives shape and structure to this thought in his theory of rights as trumps, but its end result is to draw a division between rights and the common good, so that rights are defined as something individuals hold *in opposition to* the common good. This, in turn, entails institutional opposition between legislatures and courts: legislatures act mechanically to aggregate preferences and translate them into laws (the general welfare is conceived in utilitarian terms), while courts act for the sake of principle by upholding an individual's claim against the general welfare (and hence against the legislature).

As soon as we reject Dworkin's dichotomy between rights and the general welfare – as indeed the Universal Declaration does – we see that rights *are what constitute* the general welfare. The Declaration calls on those responsible for co-ordinating the common life to consider and favour, at all times, 'each and everyone's wellbeing, in each of its basic aspects'.[142] The protection and promotion of human rights involves, among other things, choosing those specifications of relationships between individuals, and between individuals and the state, that meet this goal, in accordance with the requirements of justice.

In order to implement the rights found in the Universal Declaration and many similar instruments, which are usually vaguely formulated as two-term rights between a person and a subject-matter, legislatures set out laws with three-term rights. These rights define a relationship between two persons, such as the holder of a claim-right and the bearer of a correlative duty, and specify the action or forbearance required to promote the wellbeing of persons and to realise justice. Many of the rights in the Universal Declaration – rights to marry, to health, to own property, and to a fair trial, to take a few examples – can be effectively realised in full only by extensive, detailed schemes of legislation. The legislated rights contained therein consist in claim-rights, powers, immunities, and liberties, and sometimes complex combinations of these.

[142] Finnis, *Natural Law and Natural Rights* 214.

Once the legislature chooses a legislated, three-term right as a specification of what the general welfare requires, no further appeal to general welfare can be made to defeat the right. The strong protection accorded to a legislated right is similar to that accorded to the few absolute human rights, such as the right not to be tortured (which has a three-term jural structure), but it stands in contrast to the way that two-term human rights are treated when they are made directly judicially enforceable. Such rights are effectively treated as prima facie rights, which can be infringed so long as the argument in favour of doing so is supported by sufficiently strong considerations based on the general welfare. This observation does not, in itself, amount to an argument that courts should not have power to enforce such rights against the state, or to use proportionality analysis to control legislation or state measures. But modern human rights discourse, in focussing on this kind of rights litigation as the main vehicle for protecting human rights, overlooks the positive role for the legislature and legislative measures reflected in the Universal Declaration.

Just as the day-to-day work of legislating is indispensable for protecting human rights, so is the day-to-day enforcement of legislated rights in courts. Francisco Urbina takes up this argument in the next chapter, and explains that a benefit of legally directed adjudication is that it helps judges in resisting outside, popular pressure to reach certain results, by enabling them to attribute their decisions to legal standards already laid down. Urbina's analysis shows that there is a flip side to Dworkin's claim that judges are better able than legislators to protect minority interests because judges don't face elections. When constitutional norms are unclear, judges are forced to rely on their own moral reasoning; and as the history of US cases on race shows, judges do not conduct moral reasoning in a vacuum. Klarman makes two related points, which connect the discussion of US cases on race in Section 5.7 to Urbina's account of the problems facing a judge who lacks legal guidance and must rely on unconstrained moral reasoning. Firstly, Klarman notes that 'when the law is clear, judges will generally follow it, unless they have strong personal preferences to the contrary'.[143] Secondly, however, he concludes (drawing on his historical research) that 'because constitutional law is generally quite indeterminate, constitutional interpretation almost inevitably reflects the broader social and political context of the times'.[144] As we have seen in Section 5.7, that interpretation sometimes works to the detriment of minority interests. Neither Urbina's arguments nor those of the book as whole deny that the work of protecting human rights can sometimes be done by judges exercising the power of judicial review. But whatever view one takes on this question, it should not be overlooked that judges can also protect and promote human rights by enforcing the specified terms of legislation that aims to realise human rights.

[143] Klarman, *From Jim Crow to Civil Rights* 5.

[144] Ibid.

6

How Legislation Aids Human Rights Adjudication

Francisco J. Urbina

6.1 INTRODUCTION

The central aim of this book is to show the importance of legislation for the protection and promotion of human rights. This is crucial for evaluating the practice of judicial review of legislation, an evaluation that cannot succeed without first understanding the value and point of legislative activity. A widespread view conceives of courts as the institution central to the fulfilment of rights and of legislatures as concerned especially with the satisfaction of collective interests or preferences. This dual-forum thesis, challenged in preceding chapters, opposes the book's thesis that the legislature has rights as its primary object and concern, and that legislation is needed to protect and promote human rights.

This need is explained in part by the law's desideratum of precision and detail, a desideratum informed by the need to provide guidance to subjects by expressing clearly and precisely what is legally required.[1] To provide such guidance, the law matches the complexity and diversity of human affairs with a complex and differentiated system of rules and standards. The guidance required of human rights law goes beyond what is offered by bills of rights and recommended by many human rights scholars. There is a need for a developed and sophisticated body of law in the

[1] True, the law cannot provide full guidance for all cases. Our languages cannot express with full precision all the legal requirements: some ambiguity will always remain. Vagueness is not always a deficiency. Some vagueness may be needed so as to accommodate new facts that the lawmaker might not be able to foresee, or some other valuable aims that might be involved in the situation. See HLA Hart, *The Concept of Law* (3rd edn, Oxford, Oxford University Press 2012) 128ff. Relatively vague and general language might also be necessary for the law to guide effectively and realise the virtue of clarity (since too detailed a regulation might be difficult, if not impossible, to apprehend and apply by those subject to it). See Timothy Endicott, *Vagueness in Law* (Oxford, Oxford University Press 2000) 190. Nothing in this denies that the law can provide a substantial amount of guidance. See Paul Yowell, 'Legislation, Common Law, and the Virtue of Clarity' in Richard Ekins (ed.), *Modern Challenges to the Rule of Law* (New York, LexisNexis 2011) 101 (arguing for the strategic role of the rule of law *desiderata* of clarity, understood as a virtuous mean between specificity and generality).

field of human rights, both to guide persons in their affairs and to guide courts in the adjudication of these affairs.

This chapter explores the potential for legislation to aid adjudication in its task of enforcing human rights. It is not disputed that there can be situations where adjudication in the form of judicial review of legislation can improve the overall quality of legislation, in part by identifying legislation that contravenes human rights.[2] This possibility is, of course, ever-present in debates on the merits of judicial review and human rights. Largely absent, however, is another equally powerful idea: that legislation can *improve human rights adjudication*. This chapter explores this potential for legislation. It offers an account of legislation and of legal authority generally as critically important for rights adjudication. My account is best explained by drawing a contrast with an opposing account of human rights adjudication, one that espouses a particularly negative view of the role of legislation and of legal authority, coupled with a positive evaluation of vague human rights standards and unconstrained moral reasoning by judges. This latter account has gained prominence in academic human rights debates and provides a lucid articulation of mainstream human rights thought and practice. My aim is not to compare courts with legislatures in order to establish which is better suited for deciding human rights issues, but rather to bring to light a consideration that is easily unnoticed in such comparisons. That consideration is this: some characteristic institutional advantages of courts and their adjudicative function depend on judges applying, following, and being constrained by the law and, specifically, legislation. In this sense, my aim is to show the potential of a specific form of institutional interaction for the promotion and protection of human rights, one in which courts benefit from legislative direction.

6.2 AUTHORITY AND DISCRETION

It is a moral presupposition of legal practice that there are some things that justice requires that we do in relation to some other person or persons. Requirements of justice ground rights and duties that we – each one of us – are under a moral duty to respect. It is perhaps the most important aim of legal practice that legal adjudication respects these rights and duties, and rules in accordance with them.

Achieving this is no easy task. Reason can guide us in understanding the specific requirements of justice and their implications. Reason can also fail. Sometimes

[2] Of course, the merits of judicial review cannot be intelligently assessed by thinking only about such cases (cases where judicial review would, say, remove an unjust law from the legal system at a reasonable cost and without producing a backlash or other important negative consequences). One should think as well about the possibility of undesired outcomes that become possible when judicial review is adopted, such as when important and just legislation is declared unconstitutional. 'The idea is that judicial review always produces a set or package of outcomes over an array of cases, that some of those outcomes will be good and others bad. ... [J]udicial review must be evaluated by reference to its worst possible outcomes as well as its best'. Adrian Vermeule, *Judging Under Uncertainty: An Institutional Theory of Legal Interpretation* (Cambridge, MA, Harvard University Press 2006) 12.

there is not only one course of action for realising the requirements of justice, but any number of unranked options that would realise those requirements. Even here, reason may direct that *a* choice must be made, even if there is no *one* choice that is rationally preferable to all others.[3]

This brings us to the following question: Who is to identify the requirements of justice and to make the choices identified but unresolved by those requirements? The question is pressing in thinking about legal adjudication. For here a choice may be made prospectively for a range of situations by adopting a general rule. Those deciding individual cases that fall under the general rule will be called upon to decide in accordance with the rule. An alternative is to leave the responsibility for identifying and applying the requirements of reason with each individual decision-maker on a case-by-case basis. Taking these two opposite possibilities, there are two orientating variables: *authority* and *discretion*. The variables designate properties that can be present to different degrees in different schemes and yet, at some level, they identify mutually exclusive options: a judge cannot have discretion to decide and at the same time be bound to decide in a certain way.[4]

There are risks associated with both pathways for legal adjudication. Where the judge is bound by a scheme of authoritative directives that largely determine the decision of a case, that scheme may be unjust in general or unjust as applied to the case at hand. In such cases, judges will be unable to do justice because they will be unduly constrained. There is no risk of this kind when there is discretion in adjudication. For when judges are empowered by such discretion, they are free to make a decision of their own making, guided by their own moral judgment and thus are never or almost never constrained in a way that makes a just decision impossible to achieve. But, as it will be explained below, discretion in adjudication has its own risks. It is emphatically not the case that the only risk confronting the adjudicative function is the risk of injustice in the application of authoritative directives.

By and large, developed legal systems have chosen a model of authority. Legal adjudication is constrained by legislation, precedent (especially in common law systems), government regulations, and epistemic authorities (especially in civil law systems). There is little legal adjudication in developed legal systems that takes the form of what Max Weber called 'khadi-justice' – adjudication unconstrained by formal authorities and governed exclusively by the judge's own 'ethical or other practical valuations'.[5]

3 See John Finnis, *Natural Law and Natural Rights* (2nd edn, Oxford, Oxford University Press 2011) 284–90.

4 This does not deny that in a given situation there may be a mixture of authority and discretion, in that there may be discretion to decide some aspects of a situation, and the decision-maker may be bound in deciding some other aspects of the situation (this is the case when, for example, the decision-maker has discretion to decide within certain limits or constraints that are authoritatively settled, as in criminal sentencing).

5 Max Weber, *Economy and Society* (Guenther Roth and Claus Wittich (eds.), Berkeley, CA, University of California Press 1978) 976. See also ibid. 806.

And yet, the attraction of allowing judges to have unconstrained access to the requirements of justice is considerable. Some of this is manifest in adjudicative practices under bills of rights. These practices take place over a background understanding of bills of rights as possessing rich moral content and the highest rank in the legal hierarchy, and of courts as tasked with enforcing and promoting the rights contained in them to their fullest potential through judicial review of the decisions of other authorities. This background understanding of bills of rights and judicial review has become the global orthodoxy in legal academia and practice. There are many different arguments, narratives, and aspirations involved in justifying this trend in legal thinking. These different elements have typically come together, reinforcing each other, and providing support at the level of ideas to this background understanding. At the level of theory, there are different accounts that articulate the elements that compose this view. Thus, for example, Grégoire Webber and Kai Möller aptly explain one important aspect of this background understanding: its view of rights, their structure and force.[6] Others, such as Ran Hirschl, have addressed the phenomenon from the perspective of judicialisation.[7] This chapter is concerned with the way this background understanding of bills of rights and judicial review conceives the role of authority in legal adjudication. Implicit in it is a negative account of authoritative directives, which are viewed suspiciously as obstacles to the realisation of justice and rights. Such a view of authority obscures and diminishes the role of the legislature in defining, protecting, and promoting human rights. This negative view of authority in human rights adjudication is most explicitly articulated in the writings of recent proponents of the ideal of a 'culture of justification' in human rights law. We now turn our attention to them.

6.3 THE CULTURE OF JUSTIFICATION

The idea of a culture of justification was first introduced by Etienne Mureinik as a way to break with the 'culture of authority' that had governed the South African

[6] See Grégoire Webber, *The Negotiable Constitution: On the Limitation of Rights* (Cambridge, Cambridge University Press 2009), Ch. 2; Grégoire Webber, 'On the Loss of Rights' in Grant Huscroft, Bradley W. Miller, and Grégoire Webber (eds.), *Proportionality and the Rule of Law: Rights, Justification, Reasoning* (Cambridge, Cambridge University Press 2014) 123; and Kai Möller, *The Global Model of Constitutional Rights* (Oxford, Oxford University Press 2012). Though both authors provide similar descriptions of the phenomenon, they have different evaluations of it.

[7] See Ran Hirschl, *Towards Juristocracy: The Origins and Consequences of the New Constitutionalism* (Cambridge, MA, Harvard University Press 2004). Some works in this vein adopt a comparative perspective, exploring the legal trend mentioned above as it appears in different jurisdictions. Other works explore the same phenomenon but focusing on one jurisdiction. Thus, for example, Yoav Dotan provides an in-depth account of the Israeli situation in Yoav Dotan, *Lawyering for the Rule of Law: Government Lawyers and the Rise of Judicial Power in Israel* (Cambridge, Cambridge University Press 2014).

apartheid order.[8] On his account, the culture of authority had been distinguished by parliamentary sovereignty, the absence of justification, and an unquestioning 'ethic of obedience'.[9] The new South African constitution was to be a 'bridge' from this culture of authority to a culture of justification, i.e., 'a culture in which every exercise of power is expected to be justified' and 'in which the leadership given by government rests on the cogency of the case offered in defence of its decisions, not the fear inspired by the force at its command'.[10] Human rights adjudication under the new bill of rights was to be conceptualised as 'a compendium of values empowering citizens affected by laws or decisions to demand justification'.[11]

Recent writings have developed the idea of a culture of justification into a general account of human rights adjudication. The idea of a culture of justification that downplays the place and role of authoritative directives is said to have introduced a 'profound shift in constitutional law on a global level'.[12] In contrast to a culture of authority's 'need for finality', a culture of justification is said to emphasise the rationality of decisions.[13] Positive legal sources must yield to calls for justification, including to direct appeals to the requirements of justice. Under human rights adjudication, 'the judiciary's role is to demand that the government justify its actions', a conception of the judicial role that 'downplays the importance of the text'.[14] The text does have a role to play, however. It is said to allow 'for "outward" legitimacy' and so to secure 'the public status of the court', but that is not to confuse the importance of the text as 'essential to the court's authority to review governmental action and demand justification'.[15] Rather, the court's authority 'is derived directly from the court's function, and from the idea that government action is not legitimate unless it is justified'.[16]

This appeal to justification for government action is said to be invited by a conception of rights as values. In contrast to the conception of rights defended in this book,[17] rights are said not to designate a particular legal relation between persons. Instead, 'rights are viewed as values ... as positive values to be promoted and respected

[8] Etienne Mureinik, 'A Bridge to Where: Introducing the Interim Bill of Rights' (1994) 10 S *Afr J HR* 31.

[9] Ibid. 32.

[10] Ibid.

[11] Ibid.

[12] Moshe Cohen-Eliya and Iddo Porat, 'Proportionality and the Culture of Justification' (2011) 59 2 *American Journal of Comparative Law* 463 [hereinafter *PCJ*], 466.

[13] Ibid. 479. See also Moshe Cohen and Iddo Porat, *Proportionality and Constitutional Culture* (Cambridge, Cambridge University Press 2013) [hereinafter *Constitutional Culture*] 112.

[14] *PCJ* 479; see also 490: 'While it is true that the texts of new constitutions direct judges to assess whether the limitations are "justified in a democratic society", this amounts to an authorization by the text to downplay the text, i.e., to engage in the assessment of justification, rather than textual interpretation'.

[15] Ibid. 479.

[16] Ibid. 479. See also *Constitutional Culture* 120.

[17] See especially Chapters 2 and 5.

as much as possible by governmental action'.[18] A human right, on this view, does not specify what one is to do for another in a given set of circumstances, with the task of the court being to evaluate how someone legally stands in relation to another. A human right is thus not part of the system of positive legal relations, but rather is a superior value according to which the court evaluates positive legal relations.

To determine when the right-as-value is engaged and whether this engagement is justified, moral and political reasoning largely unconstrained by law is required. The exercise is unconstrained by law because adjudication is not directed to answer the question 'Which are the legal relations that govern the present case?', but rather 'Can those very legal relations be justified against the higher values embodied by this understanding of human rights?' Answering this question requires assessment of higher values, their reach, and their force, including when they compete with other values. It is a task that is said to require engaging 'in the assessment of justification, rather than textual interpretation'.[19] To this end, highly flexible judicial methods, such as the proportionality test,[20] now applied all over the world,[21] are deployed.[22]

[18] *PCJ* 478. See also *Constitutional Culture* 118. Courts often talk of human rights as values. See, for example: *Campbell* v. *MGN Ltd.* [2004] UKHL 22, [2004] 2 AC 457 [16]–[17] (where the court refers to the 'values encapsulated' or 'enshrined' in Articles 8 and 10 of the European Convention on Human Rights); *Re S* [2004] UKHL 47, [2005] 1 AC 593 [17] (where the court talks of 'the values under the two articles [the same Articles 8 and 10] [as being] in conflict'; *MGN* v. *United Kingdom* (App. No. 39401/04) (2011) 53 EHRR 5 [142] (where the court speaks of its duty to verify whether the authorities 'struck a fair balance between two protected values guaranteed by the Convention which may come into conflict with each other in this type of case, freedom of expression protected by art 10 and the right to respect for private life enshrined in art 8').

[19] *PCJ* 490.

[20] The test is formulated as a set of standards that a measure must pass so as to be considered 'proportionate'. Judicial articulations of those vary between jurisdictions and cases; Julian Rivers provides a helpful rendering:

1. Legitimacy: does the act (decision, rule, policy, etc.) under review pursue a legitimate general aim in the context of the right in question?
2. Suitability: is the act capable of achieving that aim?
3. Necessity: is the act the least intrusive means of achieving the desired level of realisation of the aim?
4. Fair balance, or proportionality in the narrow sense: does the act represent a net gain, when the reduction in enjoyment of rights is weighed against the level of realisation of the aim?

Julian Rivers, 'Proportionality and Variable Intensity of Review' (2006) 65 *Cambridge Law Journal* 174, 181.

[21] See Barak's comprehensive study in *Proportionality: Constitutional Rights and Their Limitations* (Cambridge, Cambridge University Press 2012), Ch. 7 B)–L).

[22] 'Proportionality is the central legal device to ensure the flourishing of this legal culture [a culture of justification]'. *PCJ* 482. See also *Constitutional Culture* 126. For a more thorough and critical analysis of this understanding of the proportionality test, see Francisco J Urbina, 'Is it Really That Easy? A Critique of Proportionality and "Balancing as Reasoning"' (2014) 27 *Canadian Journal of Law & Jurisprudence* 167. As a descriptive matter, some view the proportionality test as manifesting a trend for increased flexibility in rights adjudication, which relates proportionality to certain relatively unrestrained modes of legal interpretation, such as the idea of a 'living constitution' or a 'living

This flexibility of judicial methods is captured in a related way by attempting to frame the adjudicative function as one of 'Socratic contestation'.[23] On this understanding, the 'infringement of the scope of a right merely serves as a trigger to initiate an assessment of whether the infringement is justified',[24] such that 'the focus of rights adjudication is generally on the reasons that justify the infringement'.[25] The assessment of those reasons proceeds by putting questions to the government authority that adopts the particular measure that infringes rights, and evaluating the cogency of the reasons offered in justification. The task is unbounded by positive law, for it is said that '[a]ssessing the justification of rights infringements is ... largely an exercise of general practical reasoning, without many of the constraining features that otherwise characterise legal reasoning'.[26] On this account, the practice of following precedent or any positive legal source hampers the task of demanding and assessing reasons from defenders of the measure in question[27] – this account substitutes *discretion* for *authority*. Socratic contestation is, after all, a 'turn from legal interpretation to public reason oriented justification'.[28] This approach, it is said, brings greater rationality to the exercise of authority.[29]

---

instrument'. See Gonzalo Candia, 'Ponderación y constitución viviente como expresión del mismo fenómeno constitucional: la experiencia norteamericana' (2016) 107 *Revista Española de Derecho Constitucional* 41.

23 See generally Mattias Kumm, 'The Idea of Socratic Contestation and the Right to Justification: The Point of Rights-Based Proportionality Review' (2010) 4 2 *Law & Ethics of Human Rights* 142 [hereinafter *Socratic*].

24 Mattias Kumm, 'Political Liberalism and the Structure of Rights: On the Place and Limits of the Proportionality Requirement' in G Pavlakos (ed.), *Law, Rights and Discourse: The Legal Philosophy of Robert Alexy* (Oxford, Hart 2007) 131, 139 [Hereinafter *PL*]. The same formulation in *Socratic* 150 and in Mattias Kumm, 'Constitutional Rights as Principles: On the Structure and Domain of Constitutional Justice' (2004) 2 *International Journal of Constitutional Law* 574, 582 [Hereinafter *CR*].

25 *PL* 140. See also *Socratic* 150 and *CR* 582.

26 Ibid.

27 Thus, Kumm mentions precedent only to contrast legalistic reasoning – described as 'strongly focused on text, history and precedent' – with the proportionality analysis that allows for Socratic contestation. He remarks on passing that 'the conceptual structure of legal doctrine more often than not distorts public reasoning while it professionalizes legal discourse'. *Socratic* 157–8.

28 Ibid. 142. For a critique of this position and a corresponding rehabilitation of legal interpretation in bill of rights adjudication, see Grant Huscroft, 'Proportionality and the Relevance of Interpretation' in Grant Huscroft, Bradley W. Miller, and Grégoire Webber (eds.), *Proportionality and the Rule of Law: Rights, Justification, Reasoning* (Cambridge, Cambridge University Press 2014) 186–202.

29 The advantages of this new adjudicative practice are said to include remedies for four pathologies of political decision-making: (1) the inclusion in the decision-making process of reasons that are not legitimate and thus cannot ground a legitimate authoritative decision (e.g. reasons based on prejudice or on 'convention, tradition, preference'); (2) the inclusion of reasons 'relating to what it means to live a good, authentic life' (such as reasons based on 'comprehensive conceptions of the good'), which 'may not qualify as the kind of reasons that can be invoked in a liberal democracy to justify rights infringements'; (3) a '[l]ack of serious engagement with the realities to which the law applies' as a result, for example, of 'government hyperbole' or 'ideological radicalization'; and (4) 'the capture of the democratic process by rent seeking interest groups'. See *Socratic* 159–63. Elsewhere I have argued that the ability of legal adjudication to contribute to remedying these pathologies depends on the practice of legal direction that I explain below, and thus there is no reason to think that the

Let us recapitulate. On the view explained here, human rights adjudication realises an ideal of justification. Human rights are understood as embodying important values the scope of which is very wide and thus likely to conflict with other values, including values pursued by an authority's decision. The question whether a decision that engages a human right is justified is answered by courts, which are entrusted with the crucial task of assessing the reasons that justify (or not) the decisions of other authorities. This requires open-ended moral reasoning on behalf of courts, reasoning effectively unconstrained by technical legal categories.

This view of human rights adjudication gains additional support from well-known jurisprudential accounts of the legislature and the judiciary, reviewed in Chapters 4 and 5. On these accounts, legislative deliberation and choice aim for a utilitarian maximisation of interests or the electoral success of legislators. Courts, on the other hand, are the forum of principle, assessing rights and the substantive values at stake. The view of human or constitutional rights adjudication based on the ideal of a culture of justification appeals as well to the idea of judges cutting through the technical red tape of legal categories and directly assessing the values at stake. And, of course, it appeals to a particular understanding of authority, which it associates with a culture of authority, obedience, and formal Rule of Law values such as certainty and predictability. Legislation and positive law are thus associated with authority, and this form of authority is associated with particular interests, the preferences of the majority, political power struggles, and formal Rule of Law values. This understanding of authority is also associated with blindly following directives even if these directives violate rights. By contrast, human rights are associated with substantive moral values and with the possibility of judging authority from the perspective of reason and morality, unconstrained by legal categories. As one prominent theorist of the received approach has put it, 'the enactment of human or constitutional rights binding all state powers entails the opening of the legal system to the system of morality'.[30]

This account of legislation and adjudication misses an important aspect of legal practice. It is an account blind to the possibility that legislation, precedent, and other authoritative directives come to the aid of adjudication, including human rights adjudication. Adjudication that is unconstrained and unguided by the law confronts important obstacles that will likely frustrate its ability to realise human rights, and to realise the promise that proponents of a 'culture of justification' expect adjudication to serve. Legally directed adjudication, constrained by legal authorities, has a much better chance at succeeding in the highly difficult task of doing justice in the concrete case.

sort of unconstrained legal adjudication proposed by Kumm has this ability. See Francisco J Urbina, *A Critique of Proportionality and Balancing* (Cambridge, Cambridge University Press 2017) 207–10.

30 Robert Alexy, *A Theory of Constitutional Rights* (Julian Rivers tr., Oxford, Oxford University Press 2002) 4.

6.4 LEGALLY DIRECTED ADJUDICATION

Law provides many benefits to a community. By virtue of its ability to settle matters authoritatively, it can allow for complex and extensive schemes of social coordination.[31] It can provide guidance to those subject to it as to what should be done in a given situation. It can unburden its subjects from deliberating and choosing about certain matters when it would be costly for them to do so, as well as allow for other increases in efficiency.[32] Furthermore, law can also limit the discretion of those wielding some form of power, which in some contexts is desirable in and of itself. The law provides these benefits to legal adjudication as well. And in the context of adjudication, these benefits are not trivial. Adjudication typically faces obstacles such that, in the absence of the benefits that law confers on adjudication, it would most likely fail to realise justice and other relevant values commonly at stake in legal cases.

This applies to all areas of legal practice, including human rights. Legally unconstrained adjudication of the kind explained in the previous section confronts important problems. If the law is taken to invite open-ended moral reasoning in an area of legal practice, then the law is not performing an important service for judges in that area. That service includes the provision of guidance for the resolution of disputes through relatively precise technical legal categories. Such guidance helps remedy deficiencies that one would otherwise expect to find in the adjudication of disputes. For adjudication to benefit from such guidance, it needs to be legally directed. By legally directed adjudication, I refer to reasoning effectively informed, guided, and constrained by legal categories, that is, categories that determine authoritatively the legal significance of facts and their legal consequences – a broad class that encompasses legal definitions, requirements, prescriptions of different kinds (such as rules, principles, or standards), and so on. Legislation, precedent, government regulations, and certain epistemic authorities[33] constitute authoritative sources of law and as such they are sources of legal categories as well.

The benefits of legally directed adjudication are to be understood by reviewing the problems that arise in the absence of such direction. Legal adjudication presents many challenges. These challenges do not arise only in this or that case, or with respect to this or that party or judge, but rather arise from the circumstances in which adjudication commonly takes place (for example, the parties typically care

[31] See Chapter 3.

[32] See Larry Alexander and Emily Sherwin, *The Rule of Rules: Morality, Rules, and the Dilemmas of Law* (Durham, NC, Duke University Press 2001), Ch. 1. On law as allowing for social coordination, see Finnis, *Natural Law and Natural Rights* 276, and John Finnis 'Law as Coordination', Ch. 3 in *Philosophy of Law: Collected Essays of John Finnis Vol. IV* (Oxford, Oxford University Press 2011) 66.

[33] I am thinking of texts not issued by any political or judicial authority, but which are treated as authoritative by the legal community. For a careful study of such texts, focusing on non-legislative codifications, see Nils Jansen, *The Making of Legal Authority: Non-legislative Codifications in Historical and Comparative Perspective* (Oxford, Oxford University Press 2010).

deeply about the outcome of the case; the issue typically involves some exercise of authority that is unwelcome to one of the parties, etc.) and from the nature of adjudication (deciding about the fate of persons and property, entailing an adversarial context, etc.). The challenges are such that, were not for specific institutional advantages that courts usually possess, it would be unlikely that courts would succeed in realising justice and other relevant values at stake in adjudication. In what follows, I provide a survey of these challenges and of the way in which legal direction substantially aids courts in overcoming them.[34] My aim is to convey the potential of this technique and its importance for legal adjudication, which will serve as a basis for the case that we offer in the last sections of this chapter for a specific form of institutional interaction between legislatures and courts.

6.5 OUTCOME RELATED PROBLEMS

In this and the next section, I explore the obstacles that adjudication must confront and the way in which legal direction can assist a judge to overcome them. Positive legal sources, I argue, are a powerful aid for legal adjudication.[35]

There are two broad kinds of obstacles or problems that confront the good judge. The first, examined here, are outcome-related problems. They make it less likely that the conscientious judge will arrive at a reasonable or correct solution absent the assistance of law. The second kind, examined in the next section, are intrinsic problems, problems that are not outcome related but rather related to deficiencies generated by the way in which a case is decided. The benefits of legally directed adjudication are grasped by understanding the ability of legal direction to remedy these problems.

The problem of complexity. Cases presented for legal adjudication can be and commonly are morally complex. Making sense of the problem and understanding the moral and prudential considerations that bear on the case, and how they relate to each other, is a complex undertaking. An important way in which the practice of law provides a remedy for the possible asymmetry between the complexity of the problem before the court and the time and resources available to a judge, not to mention the judge's intellectual energy, is legal direction. The good judge has knowledge of the law and this knowledge comes to the aid of the resolution of complex moral problems by clarifying the relevant considerations.

Technical legal categories assist the judge to identify questions in need of answers so as to arrive at a just outcome. The technical categories of the law will normally allow the judge to break down a complex problem into more discrete and

[34] I provide a more detailed account of legally directed adjudication in Urbina, *A Critique of Proportionality and Balancing*, Ch. VII.

[35] There can be others. For example, rules that guard against partiality on behalf of the judges, prohibiting them to decide a case where they or someone close to them has an interest. Or the institutions that express the ideal that the office is to be distinguished from the person that holds it.

manageable problems and questions, thus making it more probable that the judge will address the relevant issues raised by the facts and decide the dispute in a way that is responsive to the demands of practical reason. Legal learning turns many morally difficult cases into legally easy cases. And even in the hard cases, it helps frame the issues and reduce the range of possible directions for reasoning.[36] Because legal knowledge performs these functions, legal systems do not need to search out a Hercules for judicial appointment. They can settle for a requirement much easier to meet: that the judge knows the law. Where there is sufficient legal direction, the judge does not need to be Hercules.

The problem of undue influence. The parties of a case will care deeply about its outcome, and so will a number of third parties. Any one or more of them could be powerful or otherwise influential members of the community, or people that have some proximity to the judge. Sometimes even the whole community is alert to the court's forthcoming decision and members of the public have strong preferences as to what the decision should be. All of this can place pressure on judges. Because the amount and direction of this pressure does not constitute a sound reason for deciding the case in one way or another, we expect judges to disregard it. Yet overcoming social pressure is not an easy task, especially when the pressure exerted is considerable. Without the legal direction that allows the judge to impute the decision to the law rather than herself, the judge would be called upon to bear the whole responsibility for the decision. This could create incentives – more or less strong depending on the circumstances of the case and of the institutional setting in which the court operates – for judges to change the standards of adjudication, shifting away from judging the dispute to trying to accommodate the parties and other stakeholders in a bargained compromise.

One way in which judges can deflect social pressure is by attributing the decision not to their own judgment, but to an impartial public standard that is independent of the judge: the law. Legally directed adjudication redirects the pressure applied by individuals or groups to the law, steeling the judge in her role and reassuring the whole community with regard to the legal system's impartiality.

The problem of the passionate judge. In confronting human misery and injustice, even good and virtuous judges will find that the pressures that influence and risk deflecting them away from responsible decision-making arise not only from external sources, but also from within, so to speak. A normal human being will feel empathy, anger, fear, disgust, sadness, compassion, and the like when confronting the facts of certain cases. Criminal law provides all too many examples where the alleged deeds of the accused can infuriate or scare any right-minded person. It is a known fact of

36 '"[E]asy legal reasoning" is a very important element in the structure of almost all hard cases: the "hard" issue in such cases is usually quite distinguishable from many other, more or less easy issues which are present in the case'. John Finnis, 'Practical Reasoning in Law: Some Clarifications', Ch. 17 in *Philosophy of Law: Collected Essays of John Finnis Vol. IV* (Oxford, Oxford University Press 2011) 353, 372.

human nature that these passions can affect judgment. Although there is no moral fault in these feelings as such, we expect judicial decision-making to depend on reason and not on the judge's passions and feelings. Adjudicating based on previously settled rules helps remedy the pull of these passions, by providing an external and extant standard for deciding the case. In criminal cases, for example, the judge is not invited to decide how to punish the guilty, all things considered, but rather is invited to apply the punishment established by or within parameters set by law. Absent this direction, a judge's passions – perhaps especially a judge's honourable passions – may have undue influence in decision-making.

6.6 INTRINSIC PROBLEMS

The problem of the subordinated party. Timothy Endicott refers to the 'best feature of a concern for the rule of law' as 'the determination not to subject the parties and the community to the arbitrary will of an official'.[37] As a legal subject, one is not to depend on the whims of others or even on their best reasons, if those reasons are not in some way embodied in the impartial standards of legal norms.[38] This requires both that the law provides 'public standards for the resolution of disputes',[39] and that adjudication be shaped and constrained by them, that is, that adjudication be legally directed. By reducing judicial discretion, legal direction increases the area of human affairs where the parties can trust that they will be subject to a decision substantially based on a previously settled public standard.

There is a moral deficiency in subjecting a person to the unbounded will of an official. This deficiency has not only an individual dimension, but a collective one. There is, of course, a deficiency in one person being subjected to the unbounded will of the one official in the community. But if the number of officials addressing the same issue is more than one, then the problem has an additional dimension. Imagine a community with no substantive law and no legal traditions, say a society of shipwreck survivors where none of them is legally trained.[40] In an attempt to bring order to this society, its members appoint three adjudicators who are sent to different parts of the island to resolve controversies. There is no substantive law that the judges can apply to decide the cases brought before them, and so they decide based on their best judgment. In such a situation, it would be desirable that the

[37] Timothy Endicott, 'Legal Interpretation' in Andrei Marmor (ed.), *The Routledge Companion to Philosophy of Law* (Abingdon, Routledge 2012) 110.

[38] This is why discoveries of statistical relations between judges' decisions and their political views, for example, cannot fail to have a controversial tone, as suggesting a scandal, or at least a deficiency. Of course, these findings are not a complete surprise. But we are right in thinking of this reality as a deficiency that we want to reduce.

[39] Lawrence Solum, 'The Supreme Court in Bondage: Constitutional Stare Decisis, Legal Formalism, and the Future of Unenumerated Rights' (2006) 9 *University of Pennsylvania Journal of Constitutional Law* 155, 181–2.

[40] This example is developed in Urbina, *A Critique of Proportionality and Balancing* 154ff.

three judges coordinate and identify a common approach to similar cases. This is so for three reasons. First, it is unfair for the parties that their case receives different treatment as compared to other similar cases only on account of their case being decided by this rather than that judge. Thus, if judge A is very lenient with people that accidentally drop a coconut on a fellow islander's head, and judge B instead is very severe, it is unfair for similarly situated coconut droppers to receive substantially different treatment on account only of the fact that their dispute has come before one judge rather than another. Second, there is something arbitrary when 'the best explanation of an individual's suffering a certain adverse legal outcome is that a particular standard happened randomly to be applied to his case'.[41] Third, it is wrong to subject human affairs to the avoidable uncertainty and unpredictability that would be produced by the lack of coordination between the judges.[42]

Yet, as desirable as the coordination of the judges would be, spontaneous coordination is extremely unlikely. Different judges have different values, which, absent any common legal standard, they would be expected to bring fully and without constraint to bear on the cases before them. Furthermore, the outcome related problems mentioned above also conspire against spontaneous coordination. Thus, the problem of complexity entails that in most cases there will be no obvious, salient answer that presents itself clearly to most people. The force and direction of the passions of judges and the pressure exerted on them by the parties and other people will not be uniform for different judges and will not correlate with the morally relevant similarities in the cases. Rather, the strength and type of passions will be different for different judges and cases, as will the pressure exerted on the judge in the contingent circumstances of the case (correlating, with the power of the parties, the notoriety of the case, etc.).

Legal direction is a technique that, among other things, increases the likelihood of coordination across different courts addressing similar matters. The law provides a common standard for all courts. When such a standard exists, and courts discipline their decisions so that this common standard actually guides and constrains their decisions, then the desired coordination becomes possible. Of course, legal direction is a matter of degree, and thus the coordination achieved through it will also be a matter of degree. Total legal direction is impossible and undesirable,[43] and so is complete coordination among courts. Yet a substantial amount of coordination can be achieved through legal direction.[44]

41 Jeremy Waldron, 'Lucky in Your Judge' (2008) 9 *Theoretical Inquiries in Law* 185, 191.

42 I take the three moral deficiencies from ibid. 190–1.

43 For discussion and qualifications, see the text in note 1, above.

44 This fact is often overlooked because in developed legal system much is made of the differences of approach between different judges, particularly in hard cases. These differences are not denied, yet they often take place in a legal context where several otherwise plausible alternatives are ruled out and over a background of a shared language and concepts to address the issue. Criminal sentencing provides perhaps the easiest example, in that different judges may be more or less severe, but all need

More generally, legal direction in adjudication makes an important contribution to the governance of human conduct through law, and, in that sense, to the Rule of Law. As Lon Fuller explained, in order for human conduct to be ordered by law it is necessary that the law satisfy certain requirements: laws must be *general* (there must be rules rather than individual prescriptions), *promulgated* (made known to subjects), *prospective* (ruling for the future), *clear* (possible to be understood, at least by legal experts that provide advice to the laws' subjects), *coherent* (they must not be contradictory), *not impossible to comply with* (requiring only actions that subjects are capable of performing), *stable over time* (not static, but stable enough for providing reliable guidance), and *there must be congruence between rules and the action of officials that apply them*.[45] There is a tight relation between some of these *desiderata* and legal direction. The last *desideratum*, when applied to courts, calls for the applicable rules to guide and constrain the reasoning and decision of the court, that is, it calls for *legally directed adjudication*. This, in turn, secures the achievement of the other *desiderata*. For example, stable laws are pointless if their judicial application changes constantly; general laws are pointless if judges decide on an *ad hoc* basis without respecting generally binding rules applicable to the case; and so forth. There is a special link between legal direction and the desideratum of prospectivity: because adjudication necessarily occurs after the facts of the case, there is a tension between adjudication and prospectivity. Legal direction reconciles adjudication with prospectivity: adjudication consists primarily in the application of legal categories that are prior to the facts of the case. Legally directed adjudication is crucial for realising Fuller's desiderata and, as such, it makes an indispensable contribution to the governance of human action by law.

The problem of legitimacy. A decision is normatively legitimate when it is a morally appropriate use of power. It is positively legitimate when it is perceived as such. There is a legitimacy of both kinds – normative and positive – in law, and legally directed adjudication benefits from these sources of legitimacy. Adjudication that is not legally directed is not necessarily illegitimate, but it lacks an important source of legitimacy. Because adjudication involves an often unwelcome exercise of authority (for at least one of the parties), and because the enforcement of a court's decisions ultimately depends (at least in most developed legal systems) on public bodies that are different from the court, legitimacy is crucial. As suggested below, when legal direction is provided by a democratic body (such as an elected legislature), then legal adjudication partakes of perhaps the most important form of legitimacy in our societies: democratic legitimacy.

The problem of uncertainty. Legal direction provides certainty in adjudication. This allows for planning and predictability in human affairs. Legal subjects are able

---

to choose a concrete punishment from a rigid set of alternatives determined by law, while the quantity of the punishment is also constrained by law.

45 Lon L Fuller, *The Morality of Law* (revd edn, New Haven, CT, Yale University Press 1969) 46–90.

to order their lives and engage in the necessary planning required to fulfil projects. In the context of adjudication without legal direction, this certainty is replaced by guesswork. This is connected to what was said above on the Rule of Law in relation to the problem of the subordinated party. A legal order that satisfies the *desiderata* of the Rule of Law is one that allows for the necessary certainty and predictability in human affairs. Included in these *desiderata* is the conformity of judicial deliberation and action with the legal norms that courts are tasked with applying. As seen above, this requires legal direction in adjudication.

6.7 THE ABSENCE OF LEGAL DIRECTION IN THE CULTURE OF JUSTIFICATION

Legal direction is needed in legal adjudication. As said above, the problems of legally unaided adjudication are not specific to one area of law. They emanate from the circumstances of adjudication and from the nature of adjudication. Legal direction is pervasive in legal adjudication, because the problems of legally unaided adjudication are pervasive. There is a need for legal direction in all areas of law.

Human rights adjudication is no exception, since the problems of legally unaided adjudication make no exception for it. Cases are no less complex: realising human rights requires specifying numerous relations of justice and in some cases establishing complex schemes of social coordination and specific convergence, as the previous chapters have argued (see Chapters 2, 3, and 5; on 'specific convergence' see Section 3.3). There is no less pressure from the parties or others and often there is considerable pressure arising from public opinion.[46] The personal views and passions of the judge are also present and retain their distorting potential. The Rule of Law applies to human rights cases no less than to other cases and coordination between courts is also both required and unlikely to arise spontaneously. Judicial decisions need to be legitimate and seen to be so, and because many human rights cases coincide with politically contested issues, this need for legitimacy is perhaps more pronounced in human rights adjudication than in many other areas of law. Certainty and predictability are as important in human rights cases as they are in many other areas of law.[47]

[46] As in the examples mentioned in Chapter 5, which relate to intense political disagreements relating to racial segregation.

[47] This is why the problem would still remain, even if one conceded that human rights adjudication does not pretend to be 'legal' adjudication, but just a form of moral or political decision-making for the common good. However we choose to call this form of judicial decision making concerned with human rights, the problems of legally unaided adjudication will remain – and so will remain the need for a remedy to these problems, and therefore the advantages of legally directed adjudication. For a survey of deficiencies related to relatively open-ended human rights adjudication (many of which coincide with problems of adjudication that is not legally directed), see Lord Sumption, 'The Limits of Law', in NW Barber, Richard Ekins, Paul Yowell (eds.), *Lord Sumption and the Limits of the Law* (Oxford, Hart Publishing, 2016), Ch. 2. Some problems associated with polycentricity in

The 'culture of justification' approach to adjudication trades on the strengths and virtues of judicial authority, all the while undermining the practices that sustain them. If legal adjudication had the unconstrained character attributed to it by proponents of this approach, it would undermine the merits of adjudication. This is a high price to pay, since legally directed adjudication is a solution for what would otherwise be severe limitations of courts. Without legal direction, adjudication loses an important institutional advantage, and thus sacrifices its ability to bring more rationality to the decisions of authorities through human rights adjudication and of realising rights and other relevant values at stake in human rights cases.

Prevailing notions of human rights adjudication tend to neglect the possibility and severity of intrinsic problems, even when good outcomes are reached. These include: the problems of the subordinated party, legitimacy, and uncertainty. To the extent that some forms of human rights adjudication are largely unconstrained by legal categories, they will be affected by the intrinsic problems just mentioned. But, as explained above, these problems point to important deficiencies in human rights adjudication as much as in adjudication concerning other areas of law. Outcome-oriented problems will be perhaps more visible. To the extent that human rights adjudication is in important respects unguided and unconstrained by law, we should expect judges to have difficulty reducing the complexity of some cases, leaving out important moral considerations, or including irrelevant ones in their reasoning of the case, and failing to provide a clear explanation of the reasoning that leads to the outcome, among other ways in which one can fail to engage with the moral complexity of a case. As evidence of these shortcomings in the practice of human rights adjudication, some commentators have noted that, while judgments can be 'long' and 'earnest', 'there often seems to be a gap between the statement of issues and the conclusion'.[48] Under the open-ended doctrine of proportionality, courts have appealed indiscriminately to the 'interests' at stake in a given case, without taking care to identify which interests are legitimate as public aims and which are protected as a right.[49] The result is a 'characteristically impressionistic assessment of the relative weights of competing considerations, which does not lend itself to a rational reconstruction'.[50] Others have objected that the 'attractive structure of the judicial

Lord Sumption's lecture would fall under the 'problem of complexity'. Polycentricity is a source of complexity. For a more developed analysis of polycentricity in legal adjudication, see Jeff King, *Judging Social Rights* (Cambridge, Cambridge University Press 2012), Ch. 7.

[48] JD Heydon, 'Are Bills of Rights Necessary in Common Law Systems' (2014) 130 *Law Quarterly Review* 392, 407.

[49] Stavros Tsakyrakis, 'Proportionality: An Assault on Human Rights?' (2009) 7 3 *International Journal of Constitutional Law* 468. Tsakyrakis is not alone in this claim. Finnis notes the European Court of Human Rights' notable lack of sophistication in dealing with the governmental aims in the *Hirst* (prisoner's right to vote) case. See John Finnis, 'Human Rights and Their Enforcement', Ch. 1 in *Human Rights and the Common Good: Collected Essays of John Finnis vol III* (Oxford, Oxford University Press 2011) 44–5.

[50] Tsakyrakis, 'Proportionality: An Assault on Human Rights?' 482.

role crumbles ... into an unstructured, opaque choice, when the task involves "balancing" the unbalanceable'.[51] In these circumstances, it is not surprising that a great disparity of results becomes possible and acceptable, given the ad hoc nature of the legal reasoning that justifies these results.[52] None of these observations impute bad faith or incompetence to judges; rather, they highlight how even the best judges are liable to struggle in the absence of legal direction.

Scholars working on the idea of a culture of justification at times concede some of these concerns, albeit without following the concession to its logical implications. Here we recall the claim made by proponents of justification through open-ended human rights adjudication who say that this culture 'downplays the importance of the text' and that the text 'is not essential to the court's authority'.[53] Nevertheless, it is said that notwithstanding this downplaying, the text fulfils an important role: it 'allows for "outward" legitimacy, and secures the public status of the court'.[54]

The argument here is surprising. The text, which provides some legal direction for adjudication, is said to be 'not essential to the court's authority', and a court need not settle cases by grounding its decisions in the law. And yet, the reference to how the text allows for 'outward legitimacy' concedes that, at least for members of the public, the legal grounding of decisions enhances the legitimacy of judicial authority; it also suggests that when decisions are not grounded in the law, the legitimacy of judicial authority is compromised. Another prominent proponent of justification through proportionality based human rights adjudication puts the idea in a more transparent way:

> Perhaps the secret of proportionality based judicial review is that it succeeds primarily because its true nature as a form of public reason based Socratic contestation remains publicly unacknowledged. Instead the institutions, rituals and the way that opinions are structured and provisions are cited emphasize institutionally and symbolically the connection to the ordinary 'legalistic' practice of law.[55]

This amounts to conceding the problem of legitimacy associated with unconstrained moral reasoning and the potential for legal direction to overcome this challenge. Grounding legal decisions in the law enhances their legitimacy. But it would not be a morally acceptable response to these truths about legal adjudication to represent

[51] Timothy Endicott, 'Proportionality and Incommensurability' in G Huscroft, B Miller, and G Webber (eds.), *Proportionality and the Rule of Law: Rights, Justification, Reasoning* (Cambridge, Cambridge University Press 2014) 328.

[52] See Heydon, 'Are Bills of Rights Necessary in Common Law Systems', on the disparity of conclusions across different judges and panels in the ECtHR. An illustrative example in the context of the IACtHR is provided by the striking contrast between *Kimel* v. *Argentina* C No 177 (2008) (IACtHR) and *Mémoli* v. *Argentina* C No 265 (2013) (IACtHR).

[53] *PCJ* 479. See also ibid. 490.

[54] Ibid. 479.

[55] *Socratic* 174–5.

courts' decisions as being grounded in the law, when they are not. What is more, to do so would be contradictory with the very ideal of a culture of justification, in whose name is this proposal made. It frustrates the demands of honest reason-giving, which lie at the heart of a culture of justification, to represent as reasons (the law) what in reality played no part in justifying the exercise of judicial authority.[56] The correct response to the problem of legitimacy is to take proper advantage of legal direction, so that the judicial decision is grounded in (guided and constrained by) the law, and thus partakes in its legitimacy.

On this score, it is telling that the need for legal direction in adjudication was recognised in Mureinik's original treatment of the idea of a culture of justification. Mureinik criticises the South African bill of rights in the 1993 interim Constitution for not guaranteeing absolute rights.[57] He was particularly concerned with non-emergency detentions without trial, which he considered to be 'the polar opposite of a culture of justification',[58] and engaged in a relatively detailed analysis of the general moral illegitimacy of detention without trial and of the exceptions that could be morally justified. He insisted that *the law* should express these distinctions. After providing examples of cases in which detention without trial could be acceptable, he wrote: 'These kinds of cases are commonly catered for by specific exceptions, and a constitution which valued freedom of the person highly *would enact mechanisms for ensuring* that they could be invoked only when their application was justified'.[59] Because this 'has not been done explicitly, there can be no guarantee that the Bill of Rights will be given its proper construction'.[60] To give judges the opportunity to challenge and evaluate detentions through unconstrained moral reasoning is not enough, on this view. Instead, there is need for positive law to direct the reasoning of judges. Mureinik is not blind to the possibility that judges might well arrive at the right result in the absence of legal direction. But he was aware, too, that they might not. That is why he argued that it is desirable for the law to embody 'the proper construction' of rights. In other words, it is desirable for the law to provide legal direction in human rights adjudication. But note that it is only when adjudication is directed and constrained by positive law that Mureinik's remedy can secure its promise.

The idea of open-ended human rights adjudication is an appealing one. It promises judicial institutions that they can engage directly with the reasons at stake, unencumbered by legal authorities and doctrines. The assumption is that if courts have this freedom to engage with the relevant reasons, they will do so successfully or at least more successfully than if they are constrained by legal authorities. This assumption is unfounded. Legally directed adjudication plays an important role in creating the conditions for legal adjudication to arrive at just decisions, and thus to realise human rights. There is a need for legal direction in adjudication. Without

56 See the discussion corresponding to note 10, above.

57 Mureinik, 'A Bridge to Where?' 35 ff.

58 Ibid. 35.

59 Ibid. 36. Citation omitted. Emphasis added.

60 Ibid. 37.

it, adjudication is unlikely to succeed in realising the important values it sets out to achieve. Even the ideal of a culture of justification, if it were an ideal to be achieved through adjudication, would require the assistance of legal direction.

This brings us back to authority, since legally directed adjudication is adjudication that is largely guided and constrained by authoritative legal sources. The advantages of legally directed adjudication can only be achieved if the judge is bound to follow the prescriptions of the law.[61] Thus, there is need for sound legal authority. This is why even after acknowledging the real possibility of mistaken legal categories or even the real possibility of morally repulsive positive law (as was the case with legal categories designed to give expression to and perpetuate apartheid rule), the practice of crafting sound authoritative legal categories to guide adjudication cannot be abandoned in favour of unconstrained moral reasoning.[62] Without legal direction, adjudication loses many of the advantages that would make it an appropriate institution for demanding the justification of acts of political authority.

Who, then, is to craft these legal categories? Whose authority is to bind judicial decisions so as to bring about the benefits of legally directed adjudication? There is no need to single out only one institution. Many different institutions help shape the law to facilitate legally directed adjudication. In what follows, I highlight the potential for one important institution to craft the law in a way that significantly realises the benefits of legally directed adjudication in the field of human rights.

6.8 LEGISLATION AND LEGAL DIRECTION

Legislation is crucial for the protection and promotion of human rights. The previous chapters have reviewed the ways in which human rights require statutory law for their protection and realisation. Statutory law can serve this end in another important way, as I have here aimed to demonstrate: by guiding legal adjudication. Legal direction in adjudication grounds some important institutional strengths of courts for addressing human rights issues.

Legislation has great potential to aid human rights adjudication. It should be conceived as an asset for the protection and promotion of human rights *in courts*. Of course, assets can become liabilities, but it makes a difference whether one evaluates legislation that frustrates human rights as pathological or as the normal case. In arguing that legislation aids human rights adjudication by providing valuable

[61] Though it could be the case that the judge benefits from legal direction even if departing to some extent from the guidance of the law. This happens, for example, when the law is developed through judicial decisions. When such a development occurs, judges typically rely for the most part on established legal categories, changing only a discrete aspect of these legal categories. Thus, judges are largely benefiting from legal categories, even if in some particular respect they are not following them. I leave the details of the problem of legal development aside for now, since it is unnecessary to address it here.

[62] I address the issue of bad legal categories and their relation to legally directed adjudication in Urbina, *A Critique of Proportionality and Balancing* 178–80.

legal direction, I recall that the problems of legally unaided adjudication are also present in human rights adjudication. Human rights adjudication can be greatly served by legislation that provides legal guidance for the resolution of human rights disputes.

The practice of legislative direction in adjudication requires institutional interaction between two bodies. Each body is required to undertake a course of action for the interaction to be successful. Courts are required to allow their judicial reasoning and decision-making to be generally guided and constrained by legal categories affirmed in legislation. Legislatures, in turn, are required to enact positive law able to provide sound legal guidance. This requires not only that legislation be morally sound, but also that it be precise and detailed enough to provide this guidance.

Here I focus on making the case for such institutional interaction by exploring the benefits it has for human rights adjudication. In what follows I analyse the potential for legislation to realise the benefits of legally directed adjudication, with special reference to human rights adjudication.[63]

Outcome related problems. In relation to the problem of complexity, the question is whether legislation is able to produce an epistemic benefit: guidance on reasonable outcomes, on relevant and irrelevant considerations, and on how relevant considerations relate to each other to arrive at a reasonable solution. According to the 'dual forum' approach, which was criticised in previous chapters, the legislature suffers from important epistemic deficiencies. When conceived as an institution designed to maximise the interests or preferences of the electorate, the legislature seems by nature incapable of addressing important moral considerations as such, perhaps especially those relating to human rights and justice. But, as explained in Chapter 4, this is a distorted view of legislatures. There is no reason to proceed on the assumption that, by its very nature, the legislature is incapable of addressing relevant moral considerations. And thus, in principle there is no reason to think that the legislature cannot offer important guidance for adjudication in relation to rights. The question is how apt it is for gathering the relevant information and for expressing it in legislative form.

It is tempting to think that the epistemic benefit provided by legal learning is owed more to the common law traditions of thought and years of legal thinking and decision-making than to legislative activity. And yet, the legislature can be a receptacle of legal learning – of knowledge of legal categories and their application.[64] There is much legal expertise resident in the legislature, in the form of the expertise of its

[63] Nothing in my argument entails or relies on a pessimistic view of courts, or assuming the best of legislatures and not of courts. My analysis focuses on courts and legislatures that are 'as they should be' and 'in good shape', this is, central cases of courts and legislatures (for the idea of 'central case' and a defence of its use in this book, see Section 1.1). The point is that even courts that are as they should be have limitations, and can and often do benefit from the type of institutional interaction described below to overcome these limitations. This institutional interaction explains some of the typical institutional strengths of courts that are 'in good shape'.

[64] See Adrian Vermeule, *Law and the Limits of Reason* (Oxford, Oxford University Press 2008), Ch. 2.

members, staff, legal advisors, and other actors that support the work of law-making (for example, the Law Commission of England and Wales). Furthermore, the legislature is empowered to call on legal experts from different fields, including judges, lawyers, legal academics, and public officials, and to use their knowledge in crafting law. Codification in civil law jurisdictions illustrates how the legislature can draw on traditions of positive law. No civil code is drafted without regard for history. Even so extreme an example as the Chilean Civil Code (the work of the genius of essentially one man, Andrés Bello, in the nineteenth century) draws heavily on Roman law, German law, medieval Spanish law, colonial law, and French civil law, among other sources.[65] Codification was a matter of selection, emendation, and reformulation of an already existing body of legal categories gathered from existing legislation, case law, and doctrine.

As compared with the common law, which draws primarily on the information made available to the court by counsel, legislation takes a more abstract and general perspective. It does not address one conflict or the claims of one person, but rather attempts to assess the claims of all those involved, as well as to take into consideration larger schemes of social coordination that have been put in place to respect other worthy claims. It assumes a more architectonic point of view, legislating for the whole of a community and its members instead of deciding a particular case involving particular parties. Assessing the interests and claims of all those potentially affected by a measure is a difficult task, without doubt. Courts can try to assess all relevant claims and bear in mind the schemes of coordination and specific convergence that attempt to realise them, particularly in cases where the government is a party. In the human rights context, after all, the issue is often presented as involving a contest between the human right of one party and the 'public interest' defended by the government. The label 'public interest' is liable to obscure what often are the diverse claims of other persons, their interests and rights, as well as the requirement of creating the diverse conditions necessary for all the members of the community to flourish.[66] Addressing this complexity is difficult. It should come as no surprise that the judicial exercise often fails to capture all the relevant interests[67] or to assess all the different moral requirements at stake.[68] When it comes to addressing diverse interests and claims, the legislature has specific strengths. Its larger and more diverse composition, its more direct relationship with people affected by its decisions, its

65 Alejandro Guzmán Brito, *Andrés Bello Codificador. Historia De La Fijación Y Codificación Del Derecho Civil En Chile* (Santiago, Chile, Ediciones Universidad de Chile 1982) 407–27.

66 See John Finnis, *Natural Law and Natural Rights*, Ch. VI.8 on the common good (which is not opposed to rights, but rather includes their fulfilment), and 'Human Rights and Their Enforcement' 32–5, on the inadequacy of such terms as 'public interest' or 'general welfare'.

67 Alexander Aleinikoff notes that courts applying balancing tests often purport to be assessing all the relevant interests, but they seldom do, leaving out of their reasoning the interests of one or more persons. See Alexander Aleinikoff, 'Constitutional Law in the Age of Balancing' (1986) 96 *Yale Law Journal* 943, 977.

68 See Tsakyrakis, 'Proportionality: An Assault on Human Rights?'.

ability to gather information through hearings and written evidence, and its professional staff devoted to conducting research, all provide it with a capacity to perceive and process the different interests and claims involved and to understand complex schemes of social coordination.[69] Furthermore, there are countless cases in which resolving the issue requires assessment of possible or likely consequences of a given measure so as to evaluate the way in which that measure will affect interests, claims, and schemes of coordination. Here, legislatures also have an advantage, in that they have the required institutional capacity to assess empirical evidence and to understand likely consequences.[70] All this is as expected: legislatures are designed to adopt the general, architectonic, view of the whole community required for deliberating aptly about norms of the generality characteristic of legislation. Courts are designed to address concrete cases involving the claims of specific parties (typically two) appearing before the court.

This is particularly important for the protection of human rights. As outlined in Chapter 2, to speak properly of a right – or, less controversially, to speak of something being actually required of someone in virtue of another's right – one must determine the just relation between persons. But because relations between persons are generally not to be understood one at a time, no one set of relationships may be contemplated without holding in view the full range of other relationships contemplated by other rights. If this is so, establishing the relationships that give shape to rights will be a task most naturally charged to an institution designed to hold in view *all* the relevant interests and claims of a community's members. The legislature is designed to have this architectonic view. The judicial process, on the other hand, is designed to focus on the claims made by the parties in a given case or line of cases. These are distinct ways of addressing moral and political questions, and wise inter-institutional collaboration will benefit from the strengths of each.

Legislation is able to produce clear guidance by issuing prescriptions that are systematic, ordered, exhaustive, and harmonised with each other.[71] In this way, legislation has advantages over precedent. Precedent can be ambiguous, for its reach beyond the immediate parties is not always clear or disclosed, and one case's fit with the rest of the law can require the clarification of subsequent cases. Furthermore, it is not always clear how the precedent binds other courts or the deciding court – whether the court will be bound by its own precedents, or by the precedents of others, and to what degree. Legislation, by contrast, is promulgated. While legislation can also be obscure, it exists in the form of a public act that announces a new law and its specific content. Judge-made law, on the other hand, 'has no canonical linguistic

[69] See Vermeule, *Law and the Limits of Reason*. Ch. 3.

[70] See generally Paul Yowell, 'Empirical Research in Judicial Review' in Peter M Huber and Katja S Ziegler (eds.), *Current Problems in the Protection of Human Rights: Perspectives From Germany and the UK* (Oxford, Hart 2013) 155.

[71] See Yowell, 'Legislation, Common Law, and the Virtue of Clarity' 128.

form'[72] and 'what clarity there is in the common law owes much to the work of commentators and scholars who compile and synthesise many case reports'.[73] The ability of legislation to produce clear prescriptions is crucial, and is relevant for many of the benefits of legally directed adjudication, as will be explained below. And it is generally beyond question who is bound by the acts of the legislature and that legislation is binding for other decision makers. None of these claims seek to promote the superiority of legislation over the common law except in this respect: as a clear guide for legal adjudication.

All this illustrates the potential for legislation to serve as an epistemic guide to courts in overcoming the obstacles associated with the problem of complexity in human rights adjudication. It can assess the relevant information, and it can express it by enacting clear and systematic directives that can reflect the complex array of relevant considerations. When the legislature does this, it can greatly aid in solving the problem of complexity. Furthermore, if, as Adrian Vermeule and Paul Yowell each argue,[74] legislatures tend to have better epistemic capacities than courts for addressing matters concerning abstract human or constitutional rights, then legislative direction in adjudication allows courts to benefit from the superior epistemic capacities of legislatures.

In relation to the problems of undue influence and of the passionate judge, there are no general advantages for legislation over judge-made law. In any given jurisdiction or context, one institution may better resist undue influence or the unwelcome pressure of the passions. Both the judiciary and the legislature are liable to be affected and both have their own ways of dealing with these opportunities for sub-rational decision-making. For example, the legislature has rules on transparency, lobbying, and political finance to address undue pressure; and it acts through an extensive and formalised procedure of law-making whereby different actors participate through different legislative institutions (such as chambers and committees), which, by forcing reflection and exposure to different views, makes it less likely that the institution will act in a fit of passion. Likewise, the judiciary has rules on the opportunity and manner in which judges may be approached regarding the issues before their courts, regulations on the impartiality of judges, and other measures designed to address the problems of pressure. And courts also decide after a process that is highly formal and requires them to give reasons for their decisions, all of which are institutional means to address the problem of the passionate judge. What is relevant to point out for the purposes of legal direction is that where the legislature is able to produce reliable norms, these norms can benefit the judiciary, aiding it to address the problems of undue influence and of the passionate judge.

72 Ibid. 126.

73 Ibid.

74 See Vermeule, *Law and the Limits of Reason*, and Paul Yowell, *Constitutional Rights and Constitutional Design: Moral and Empirical Reasoning in Judicial Review* (Oxford, Hart Publishing 2018).

Again, it here needs to be emphasised that many of the virtues often associated with judicial authority greatly depend on the traditional ways in which this authority is discharged. The impartiality and emotional detachment often associated with courts owes much to the practice of doing justice *according to law*, that is, to the practice of deciding cases according to previously settled public standards. Thus, Mattias Kumm is right to identify as a possible deficiency of the political process the '[l]ack of careful engagement with the realities' that government measures address due to pathologies such as 'government hyperbole' or 'ideological radicalisation'.[75] In situations such as emergencies, it is expected that an authority's decision-making can be affected by the heat of the moment. In these situations, careful engagement with the facts and the relevant reasons that apply to the case becomes less likely as it requires a level of detachment from the immediate situation that few people can achieve.[76] Yet the law, by providing external standards for decision-making, allows for such detachment. Because courts decide based on such external standards, they can be expected to show enough detachment. And in this sense Kumm is right that courts have an important institutional advantage – however, it is an institutional advantage that dissipates when courts adopt substantially unconstrained forms of decision-making.

Intrinsic problems. The clearer the rule, and the more consistent its application, the less scope there is for the problem of subordination. Here, again, the capacity of the legislature for producing clear norms is an important asset for realising this benefit of legal direction. Clearer norms facilitate the necessary consistency across courts in relation to this benefit of legally directed adjudication. Furthermore, legislation can realise the Rule of Law *desideratum* of prospectivity.[77] Judge-made law can only provide this benefit of legal direction after a body of precedent has accumulated; it may fail to provide this benefit in many cases that come to constitute this body of precedent. Without the ability to refer to authoritative rules established prior to the subject matter of the dispute which can fairly said to resolve the legal question before the judge, an adverse legal outcome will turn on a standard articulated, identified, and applied *in the course of* and not prior to adjudication. The parties in those cases are not ruled, in this respect, by clear law that applies prospectively to their case.

Clarity affects predictability. Clearer laws make for more predictable outcomes. Here, the potential for legislation to produce clear norms is relevant again. But legislation also has other advantages in terms of predictability. True, both legislatures and judges, when they change the law, affect predictability. Every change is liable to make matters less predictable. But this problem is particularly pronounced for

[75] *Socratic* 160–1.

[76] As Weber notes in relation to the specific virtues of the politician. See Max Weber, 'Politics as a Vocation', in HH Gerth and C Wright Mills (eds.), *From Max Weber: Essays in Sociology* (Abingdon, Routledge 2009) 115.

[77] On the rule of law *desiderata* of prospectivity, see Fuller, *Morality of Law* 51–63.

courts. Judge-made law introduces legal change that is retroactive for the parties whose case is being decided. If the judge has to develop and craft good law, and at the same time apply existing law to the parties, then 'the judge's duty as an adjudicator and his duty as a law-maker pull in different directions'.[78] The legislature does not confront this dilemma.

But perhaps the greatest strength of legislatures relates to the problem of legitimacy. The decisions of legislatures possess what is one of the most important forms of legitimacy in democratic societies: *democratic legitimacy*. This legitimacy is of the two kinds identified above: normative and positive. The laws that democratic legislatures create have a claim to democratic legitimacy, and decisions made in accordance with these laws partake in this legitimacy as well. This is an important contribution that legislative direction makes to adjudication. Without it, judicial decisions, particularly those affecting sensitive political issues, possess not only less normative legitimacy, but also less positive legitimacy, and therefore are more likely to be challenged as illegitimate and to have their authority compromised.[79]

Because of their very nature, cases concerning human or constitutional rights relate to the fundamental political and legal structure of society, and, as such, many such cases touch on sensitive political matters, giving rise to issues of legitimacy. As Lord Sumption puts it: 'Lack of democratic legitimacy is a potential problem about all judge made law ... But it is a rather serious problem in the case of judicial decisions about supposedly fundamental rights'.[80] In a sense, human rights

> are claims against the claimant's own community. In a democracy, they depend for their legitimacy on a measure of recognition by that community. To be effective, they require a large measure of public acceptance through an active civil society. This is something that no purely judicial decision-making process can deliver.[81]

As seen above, some proponents of open-ended human rights adjudication seem keenly aware of this issue, and concede implicitly that it creates a substantial problem for judicial practice – to the extent that it requires leaving unacknowledged the lack of legal support for judicial decisions so as to achieve 'outward legitimacy'. This, as I argued, is not an acceptable alternative. One tool that can greatly aid courts in overcoming issues of legitimacy in many cases is the practice of allowing the

78 Yowell, 'Legislation, Common Law, and the Virtue of Clarity' 125.

79 Whether judicial decisions unaided by legislation have enough legitimacy is a different question I do not tackle here. I suppose that the answer to this question will depend on the subject matter being decided (whether it is a highly sensitive topic on which citizens have strongly felt preferences), on the political circumstances in which the decision takes place (if, for example, there is an important consensus on the topic and the judiciary respects it, or if there is a sense that other political bodies are unable to address this issue, then lack of democratic legitimacy will be less of a problem), and on some features of the legal and political culture. My point here is only that there is an important source of legitimacy that will not be available to judicial decisions that are not legally directed by legislation.

80 Sumption, 'The Limits of Law' 22.

81 Ibid. 25.

legal categories embodied in legislation to inform and constrain the reasoning and decision of the court. Legitimacy is a distinct contribution that legislation – when produced by a democratic legislature, in a democratic culture[82] – can make to the success of adjudication in democratic societies.

In complex and large societies, democratic legitimacy is achieved mainly through representation. Legislatures are designed to represent the different political views present in society by virtue of its composition. This is an important contribution to the legitimacy of legislatures. There are two important legislative activities that work together with representation to increase the legitimacy of legislation: open deliberation and legislative compromise. Congresses and parliaments are deliberative bodies designed to allow for open discussion on public affairs where relevant points of view can be heard. The highly regulated procedure for law-making aims to produce a deliberative forum where different positions present both in and beyond the legislature can be heard and assessed.

Legislative compromise, in turn, is crucial for realising the ideal of the law as responding to the will of the people, and not merely that of the majority. The minority is also part of the community, and its views need to be adequately expressed in the political decisions that shape the community. There is a deficiency in a legal order that responds only to the views of one sector of the community. The deficiency is both moral (in excluding other sectors from the self-rule of the community) and political, since relevant parts of the community will not feel represented by their legal order, which can become a cause of political distress, instability, and anomy. The intensity of political divisions and its destructive power should not be underestimated. Statesmanship requires building stable agreements between different political sectors. Political compromise is a crucial tool for achieving this and an important part of law-making.[83] Legislation is the product of a highly formal and regulated procedure, one which in many places attempts to secure both some modicum of reasoned deliberation and some consensus around legislation. As John Manning has noted in the context of the American system, there are important structural features of law-making institutions that enhance the power of interested minorities, thus forcing legislative compromise.[84] Beyond these institutional features, many times there

[82] Legislation – which in in its central case is the activity of prospective production of general norms for the common good – may or may not be undertaken by a democratic legislature. Many of the benefits of legislation can be achieved regardless of the specific attributes of the body that enacts it (though it is always necessary that that body has at least the authority to do so). But additional benefits are associated with the kind of body that is charged with producing legislation in well-functioning democracies: a democratic legislature.

[83] On the value of legislative compromise, see Chapter 4, section 4.5, and Sumption, 'The Limits of the Law' 24–5.

[84] He lists bicameralism and presentment as prominent among such structural features. See John Manning, 'The Absurdity Doctrine' (2003) 116 *Harvard International Law Journal* 2388, 2437–8; John Manning, 'Textualism and the Equity of the Statute' (2001) 101 *Columbia Law Review* 74–6, and John Manning, 'Textualism and Legislative Intent' (2005) 91 *Virginia Law Review LR* 419, 435 fn 53.

are important political incentives for a majority to compromise with a minority (for the sake of not fully owning a controversial decision, for achieving a more stable outcome, etc.). As Waldron notes, '[l]egislation is ... the product of a multimember assembly, comprising a large number of persons of quite radically differing aims, interests, and backgrounds. Under these conditions, the specific provisions of a particular statute are often the result of compromise and line-item voting'.[85]

Because of its composition, its size, and its mode of operation, the legislature is particularly well suited for open deliberation and to achieve compromise in the making of laws. Adjudication that follows the direction of legislation partakes of the legitimacy achieved by legislation and its associated activities of deliberation and compromise. As said above, adjudication that does not partake of the legitimacy of legislation is not necessarily illegitimate. Here I take no position on whether human rights judicial review of legislation has democratic legitimacy. It is an open question whether there is a tension between democracy and judicial review of legislation. Prominent theorists of rights, such as Ronald Dworkin and Robert Alexy, have claimed that there is no such tension. Judicial review of human or constitutional rights would actually instantiate some fuller version of democracy – a 'constitutional democracy', on Dworkin's account, or 'representative argumentation', on Alexy's.[86] Yet even if this were so, any good faith observer must acknowledge that human rights adjudication is open to challenges of legitimacy. The sophisticated attempts of these scholars to present accounts of adjudication that address such challenges attest to the existence and relevance of questions about the legitimacy of human or constitutional rights judicial review. Dworkin himself remarks of a 'striking mismatch' between how widely the moral reading of the constitution is used by judges, and how little it is acknowledged by those same judges and commentators.[87]

This is understandable. An important tool for overcoming the challenges to the legitimacy of judicial decisions is to impute the outcome of a case to the law. The more a decision is grounded on the personal morality of the judges that make it, the more open it is to challenges to its legitimacy. Thus, as Waldron observes, '[c]ourts are concerned about the legitimacy of their decision-making and so they focus their "reason-giving" on facts that tend to show that they are legally authorised – by constitution, statute, or precedent – to make the decision they are proposing to make'.[88] As seen above, authors proposing open-ended human rights adjudication to further the ideal of a culture of justification concede this much.

85 Jeremy Waldron, *Law and Disagreement* (Oxford, Oxford University Press 1999) 125.

86 See Ronald Dworkin, *Freedom's Law: The Moral Reading of the American Constitution* (Oxford, Oxford University Press 1996) 15–38, and Robert Alexy, 'Balancing, Constitutional Review, and Representation' (2005) 3 *International Journal of Constitutional Law* 572, 578–81. For a critique of Dworkin's view, see Waldron, *Law and Disagreement*, Ch. 13.

87 Dworkin, *Freedom's Law* 3–4.

88 Jeremy Waldron, 'The Core of the Case against Judicial Review' (2005) 115 *Yale Law Journal* 1346, 1383–4.

My point here is simply to highlight that there is much good sense in the strategy of courts and commentators of presenting legal decisions on human rights as grounded in previously posited legal categories, particularly those posited by legislation, rather than on the moral ideas or intuitions of judges. Entailed in this is an important truth about our political and legal institutions. This truth is that there is something of great value in law and legislation, something that enhances the legitimacy of all law-abiding acts of authorities, including judicial decisions. Courts can, and usually do, take advantage of this potential of legislation to enhance the legitimacy of their decisions. The practice of legal direction in adjudication is an honest, non-deceptive, way of doing so.

6.9 CONCLUSION

Both courts and legislatures can make an important contribution to the realisation of human rights through adjudication. Both have different potentialities. Here, I have stressed the potentialities of legislatures. The legislature can make an important and specific contribution that greatly increases the likelihood that adjudication (*including* human rights adjudication) will realise rights, justice, and other important values. This contribution needs to be taken into account in discussing specific institutional designs regarding judicial review, and in shaping the legal practice of human rights adjudication. Much thinking about adjudication under bills of rights envisions courts as being in opposition to legislatures. In deliberating about the capacities of each for realising human rights, it is easy to miss that many of courts' capacities depend on a form of institutional interaction consisting in courts deciding *according to* law, and specifically, legislation. True, the realisation of human rights can pit courts against legislatures. But awareness of this possibility cannot blind us to the fact that the legislature plays a fundamental role in promoting and protecting human rights – inside the courtroom as much as out of it.

7

Majoritarianism and Pathologies of Judicial Review

Bradley W. Miller

7.1 INTRODUCTION

This chapter examines a question left open in the preceding chapters: is the practice of judicial review under a bill of rights inconsistent with the theory of legislated rights here defended? Not all legislative activity conforms to the central case of legislation that is given explanatory priority throughout the book, and this raises the question whether judicial review of legislation under a bill of rights is a proper means to address the risk of legislative pathologies and further a community's commitment to human rights. One reason to consider adopting judicial review of legislation is democracy's potential for what de Tocqueville called 'the tyranny of the majority'. This chapter critically interrogates this reason, partially with a view to the dockets of contemporary constitutional courts. The evidence, I argue, suggests that human rights litigation is increasingly a second forum for law-making (or law-unmaking) proposals that have failed a legislative vote, and failed for reasons other than the majority's contempt or disregard for any person or group.

This chapter further examines whether judicial review itself introduces risks for a community's commitment to human rights. I will argue that judicial review is not a predominantly technical exercise – like proofreading – and it does not offer a risk-free opportunity to correct the mistakes of the legislature. Among the costs of judicial review in its prevailing manifestations are a risk of (1) relying on flawed or uncertain empirical judgments regarding the evidence presented for or against legislation; and (2) dramatising the plight of the individual rights claimants through concrete examples while failing to bring into view the individuals that the challenged legislation aims to benefit. More broadly, judicial review is an activity that, through its structure, influences the course of legal reasoning, privileging some political commitments while marginalising others.[1] To decide whether judicial review is a good

[1] Cf. Matthias Jestaedt, 'The Doctrine of Balancing – Its Strengths and Weaknesses' in Mathias Klatt (ed.), *Institutionalized Reason: The Jurisprudence of Robert Alexy* (Oxford, Oxford University Press 2012).

idea for any particular community, one must attend not only to the problems that judicial review is expected to solve, but also to the problems that it is liable to create.

In drawing attention both to some of the reasons often tendered to justify judicial review, and to some concerns with possible pathologies in the exercise of judicial review, this chapter advances a simple proposition: judicial review is not *necessarily* a sound response to the risk of non-central cases of legislating. I do not claim that there is an overall balance sheet of competing risks that can be drawn up so as conclusively to make the case for or against judicial review of legislation. The aim is more modest: to highlight how an account of legislated rights provides additional resources for evaluating whether to introduce judicial review where it is absent, and for assessing practices of judicial review where it is present.

7.2 A CASE FOR JUDICIAL REVIEW: REMEDY FOR MAJORITARIANISM

To be in a position to assess a practice of judicial review, one must begin with a conception of legislative decision-making, attending to its achievements and shortcomings, as well as to its underlying rationale. On Ronald Dworkin's influential account, the rationale for legislative decision-making is built on 'the majoritarian premise': 'that political procedures should be designed so that, at least on important matters, the decision that is reached is the decision that a majority or plurality of citizens favors'.[2] Dworkin's reasons for this understanding are chiefly the equality of persons (such that each person shall have a single vote) and the good of participation in self-government (particularly over matters that will have an impact on the citizen). Dworkin's description needs some careful qualification, in that it risks implying (and indeed Dworkin sometimes makes the point explicitly)[3] that majoritarian decision-making is about voting for one's *preferences* for no reason other than that one happens to hold them. But as reviewed in Chapters 4 and 5, this is a parasitic account of legislating, and one that does not account for the reasons that political communities have to create legislative bodies.

As defended in this book, a more plausible account of legislating would hold that legislators paradigmatically vote for *reasons* about what legislators genuinely accept to be sound plans of action for their community. Legislatures exist to coordinate, to make laws for the common good. They typically use some form of majoritarian decision-making process, which can lead to a standing temptation for legislators to misuse their power instead. The fact that an institution (be it a legislature or a court)

[2] Ronald Dworkin, *Freedom's Law: The Moral Reading of the American Constitution* (Oxford, Oxford University Press 1996) 15–16. Majoritarian decision-making, it seems to me, is threatened most acutely in the circumstances of strong-form judicial review and those forms of weak-form review that mimic strong-form review in practice. To what extent weak-form review can, in theory, escape these problems is not a question I take up here.

[3] For a comprehensive exposition and critique of Dworkin's theory of rights see, Paul Yowell, 'A Critical Examination of Dworkin's Theory of Rights' (2007) 52 *American Journal of Jurisprudence* 93.

has a responsibility to foster the common good and the individual rights that are an integral part of it does not mean that the institution will do so unfailingly in practice. Majority rule, like all forms of rule, has its risks. In assessing the value of legislative decision-making, one must consider the good it achieves, frankly acknowledge its risks of abuse, and compare it to the risks of alternatives like judicial review.

The goods to be achieved by legislative decision-making are set out in the preceding chapters. As to the risks posed by legislative decision-making, three common (and related) risks are often raised: (1) that legislatures are paradigmatically willing to subordinate human rights to the common good; (2) that legislators will act in their own interests or in the interests of some influential group rather than for the common good; and (3) that legislatures will perpetuate a 'tyranny of the majority', which refuses to engage with the concerns of relatively powerless minorities.[4] What can be said about these risks?

(1) The problem of human rights versus the common good. The first concern, in a common formulation, is that it is in the nature of legislatures to sacrifice individual rights for the sake of achieving some public good (say, public security), where the harm to those individuals is judged to be outweighed by the aggregated good of others. However, if we start from this characterisation of legislative action, the resulting analysis will immediately miscarry. The nature of reasonable legislative action is not some utilitarian calculus, not some aggregate of what it is that the majority of persons in a community happen to want, but a reasoned judgment about what would be good for the persons of this community, a judgment that is awarded the status of law only because more persons (a 'majority') have favoured it than opposed it. It is a conclusion about (a specification of) the set of rights at play in a community: the rights of all persons to receive, say, the protection of the state from terrorist activity, considered together with all of the other (sometimes competing) rights of persons to have their privacy respected, not to be arbitrarily detained, and to be permitted to face their accuser. Sound legislation is a conclusion about what rights we all have.[5]

What does it mean to say that the common good is not an aggregation of the greatest good of the greatest number? The common good that legislators must consider gives effect to promoting the conditions necessary for each person to achieve his or her wellbeing, without favouritism. This is not to say that the legislator is required to accept, let alone promote, every person's self-understanding or life-plan. Government can be justified in facilitating and even promoting some choices while

[4] See Richard Bellamy, *Political Constitutionalism: A Republican Defence of the Constitutionality of Democracy* (Cambridge, Cambridge University Press 2007) 28 and, more generally, 26–48.

[5] It is in this way consistent with the account of legislative reasoning in Gardbaum's 'New Commonwealth' model of judicial review, with its emphasis on political review of legislation for compliance with rights: 'the new model treats legislatures and courts as joint or supplementary rather than alternative exclusive protectors and promoters of rights': Stephen Gardbaum, *The New Commonwealth Model of Constitutionalism: Theory and Practice* (Cambridge, Cambridge University Press 2013) 2.

discouraging and in some instances even prohibiting worthless or harmful choices. To the extent that legislators approach decision-making using a utilitarian calculus about what the majority wants, without regard to principle, they act on an insupportable political philosophy. Legislatures in well functioning democracies do not, characteristically, reason in this way. They do not treat an individual's fully specified constitutional rights as something to be negated or sacrificed in order to promote the good of others. They may well conclude, as courts often do, that a person's claim of right does not extend as far as the claimant has argued it should, but this is far from concluding that the legislature is entitled to assume in its deliberations that it is entitled to violate a person's genuine rights where it is to the general advantage of others to do so.

Consider, for example, a legislative requirement that a person submit to being photographed in order to obtain a government issued driver's permit.[6] The rationale is that the photograph requirement will aid in more accurate identification of persons and reduce incidents of identity fraud and its consequences. The photographic requirement is undoubtedly problematic for those persons whose religious beliefs prohibit them from being photographed voluntarily. How should such a conflict be characterised? Is it a question of the protection of millions of people *outweighing* the religious rights of a few hundred people, such that it is justified to sacrifice the rights of the few for the sake of the many? Even setting aside the practical matter of commensurating the rights of some against the rights of others, it is difficult to imagine a legislative assembly advancing a legislative proposal on the grounds that violating the rights of hundreds of people is an acceptable means to achieving an end. It would make more sense to say that the legislature had, after considering the religious needs of, say, Hutterites and others, voted to accept a proposal intended to realise the needs for identification and the avoidance of identity fraud. In so doing, it specifies where the limits of freedom of religion fall. It may be a poor specification. It may reflect an inadequate understanding of the religious burden it imposes on some individuals. It may be in many other ways unjust, suboptimal, or reflective of other potential problems of majoritarian decision-making discussed below. But to depict the legislature as pursuing a policy goal through disregarding or infringing human rights rests on an unsupportable account of how responsible legislatures function.[7]

The misunderstanding is fuelled by Dworkin's influential distinction between legislatures as a forum of policy and courts as a forum of principle.[8] The legislature, Dworkin tells us, operates in the realm of policy, setting out 'a goal to be reached,

[6] See *Alberta* v. *Hutterian Brethren of Wilson Colony* [2009] 2 SCR 567 (Supreme Court of Canada).

[7] This is both a conceptual objection and an objection based on the actual practice of well-functioning legislatures, particularly those jurisdictions that standardly conduct pre-enactment political review of proposed legislation for compliance with bills of rights.

[8] Ronald Dworkin, *Taking Rights Seriously* (Cambridge, Harvard University Press 1977) 20, 92–4; Ronald Dworkin, *A Matter of Principle* (Cambridge, Harvard University Press 1985) 359, 387. For comment and criticism, see Chapters 1, 4, and 5.

generally an improvement in some economic, political, or social feature of the community'.[9] Courts, by contrast, are guardians of principle, of those standards to be observed 'because it is a requirement of justice or fairness or some other dimension of morality'.[10] Principles describe rights, policies describe goals.[11] Accordingly, the final say on rights should, on Dworkin's account, reside with courts. But Dworkin's distinction between principles and policies is too neat to be plausible. A legislature that votes to require photo identification does not do so simply to further a policy or to satisfy majority wants or desires. It does so because it concludes that the genuine interests of the members of the community are served by this law. These interests, which include (for example) the maintenance of a framework in which persons are able to live out their daily lives without serious risk of identity fraud or unlicensed persons on the road, can be fairly described as a matter of the right of all individuals in the political community, rights which are secured by legislative action. The difficult question whether a political community ought to require photo identification as a prerequisite to obtaining a driver's permit is better understood as a matter of accommodating competing *claims* of right.[12]

(2) *Self-interest and pandering to the electorate*. This second concern is that legislators, even where acting from a sound understanding of the common good, will be deflected from that goal and instead legislate to further their own interests. Self-interested action includes straightforward corruption (putting private interest ahead of the public interest) and pandering to secure re-election (advancing legislation not genuinely believed to be for the common good, but that, e.g., favours a particular group or promises benefits without considering the ability to pay for them through public finances). The possibility of good faith disagreement about what are and are not sound plans of action renders the diagnosis of pandering to the electorate sometimes difficult to make. Nonetheless, there will be such instances, and judicial review is sometimes defended on the grounds that it is necessary in order to prevent abuses of legislative power.[13]

But what sorts of abuses? It is no secret that legislators may face a standing temptation to move their eyes off of the common good and to legislate instead in ways that further their own interests. But is judicial review under a bill of rights well explained as providing a free-standing corrective to legislative vice? I do not think so. A bill of rights typically provides no grounds to invalidate self-interested legislation. Few, if any, of the human rights that are posited in bills of rights bear directly on corruption

[9] Dworkin, *Taking Rights Seriously* 22.

[10] Ibid.

[11] Ibid. 90.

[12] Competing *claims* of right should be distinguished from a conflict of *rights*. See Grégoire Webber, 'On the Loss of Rights' in Grant Huscroft, Bradley W Miller, and Grégoire Webber (eds.), *Proportionality and the Rule of Law: Rights, Justification, Reasoning* (New York, Cambridge University Press 2014) 123 at 142–9.

[13] See, for example, the argument presented in Wilfrid J Waluchow, *A Common Law Theory of Judicial Review: The Living Tree* (Cambridge, Cambridge University Press 2007) at 115–20.

or pandering. Judicial review can bear on pandering only to the extent that the legislature, as a means to curry favour with what it may perceive to be the electoral majority, violates the specific rights of persons or groups that are protected under the bill of rights. Pandering, in this sense, is parasitic on another, more powerful, reason to adopt judicial review: the need to protect against the tyranny of the majority.

(3) The tyranny of the majority. Consider the third risk: those few but justly renowned canonical instances like *Brown* v. *Board of Education*[14] in which a court strikes down legislation that perpetuates the advantage of a majority and overlooks, or totally disregards, the legitimate interests of some relatively powerless minority. This is the long-running argument that judicial review is needed as a check against the tyranny of the majority.

What is the tyranny of the majority? Tocqueville's celebrated account rests on a conception of a majority (legislative or otherwise) which functions as 'an individual with opinions, and usually with interests, contrary to those of another individual, called the minority'.[15] To Tocqueville, it is axiomatic that just as an individual with power can abuse it 'against his adversaries', so can a majority abuse its powers against its adversaries.[16] Similarly, John Hart Ely describes a situation where 'representatives beholden to an effective majority are systematically disadvantaging some minority out of simple hostility or a prejudiced refusal to recognize commonalities of interest, and thereby denying that minority the protection afforded other groups by a representative system'.[17]

The scene painted by Tocqueville, of a majority that views a minority as its adversary, does not describe politics in ordinary times in most contemporary pluralistic societies, where any given majority is made up of a shifting coalition of minorities. Such coalitions make for a dynamic environment in which groups vie for support from others. Such a dynamic requires groups to hear the other side, find a common denominator, and build winning coalitions, issue by issue.[18] The coalitions may be organised over clusters of issues rather than single issues, and they may be more or less stable, but they are not permanent. Richard Bellamy's conclusion seems correct: 'The result of combining public reasoning with the balance of power is that most legislation is not the product of a homogenous majority imposing its will upon a consistent minority, but of a series of compromises brokered by winning coalitions of different minorities'.[19]

[14] 347 US 483 (1954).

[15] Alexis de Tocqueville, *Democracy in America* (New York, HarperCollins 2000) 251.

[16] Ibid.

[17] John Hart Ely, *Democracy and Distrust: A Theory of Judicial Review* (Cambridge, Harvard University Press 1980) 103.

[18] Bellamy, *Political Constitutionalism* 199–200. This occurs most publicly in circumstances of a minority government, but is no less present where there is a majority government: there are shifting minority coalitions within political parties, as backbenchers regularly remind their frontbench leadership.

[19] Bellamy, *Political Constitutionalism* 241.

But as Bellamy rightly concedes, minorities can nevertheless face difficulties in circumstances where they lack a 'common political identity with their fellow citizens within the cultural majority', such that it 'undercuts the minority's ability to form alliances with them on particular policy areas'.[20] The problem arises where the minority is both insular and perpetual. This holds not only for the religious, ethnic, and other minorities envisioned by Bellamy,[21] but by analogy for those who are not members of communities but live at the margins of society, such as prisoners and the homeless. Much of the force of the outcome-related, instrumentalist argument in favour of judicial review is that judicial review is a necessary corrective, not for cases where a stable majority necessarily despises a minority or stands to benefit at the expense of the minority, but rather where a minority is simply invisible or its interests and self-constituting practices are incomprehensible to outsiders and thus easily defeated by competing considerations.[22]

Where a stable majority disregards or deliberately adopts legislative proposals contrary to the wellbeing of individuals or groups who lack the ability to form coalitions, they can try to convince the stable majority of the justice of their cause. If the majority stands to benefit from its decision, the only prospect for relief is for the majority to be persuaded to act against what it understands to be its own interests, which may be difficult but is certainly not unprecedented. It is not always the case that the legislators who constitute a majority are *necessarily* deflected by self-interest or group bias, such that legislators will never respond to reason, never vote in a principled manner. Legislation extending universal suffrage and prohibiting racial discrimination are testaments to the contrary.[23] That is to say, even though the existence of self-interest presents a standing incentive for unprincipled behaviour, it is a risk and not a certainty. If a legislature is so dysfunctional that self-interest and tribalism govern instead of reason, then principled lobbying is almost pointless. But well short of this, minorities may still have a difficult time persuading those in power to make their issues a legislative priority. Judicial review, on this model, is attractive precisely because it promises to be responsive to the reasons that are inaudible to a majority.

To what extent is the phenomenon of the tyrannical, self-interested majority characteristic of contemporary legislating?[24] Canadian Prime Minister Pierre Elliott

[20] Ibid. 233–4.

[21] Ibid. 225.

[22] Consider, for example, the position of minority religious communities in trying to convey to others the importance of protecting self-constituting practices that, to non-believers, may appear irrational, valueless, or harmful (e.g. the practice of Jehovah's Witnesses in refusing blood transfusions; the refusal of some sects of Hutterites to have their photographs taken).

[23] See the discussion by Paul Yowell in Chapter 5.

[24] I am not here concerned with the phenomenon – all too common – of legislators pandering to the electorate by enacting legislation that will be well-received, but that they have no reason to believe will be effective or wise. There is a distinction to be drawn here between legislation that is merely self-serving (in the sense that it is believed to contribute to future electoral success) and legislation that panders to a majority of voters *at the expense* of a topical minority.

Trudeau, in a tract written in 1982 to advance the case for a Canadian Charter of Rights and Freedoms, leaned heavily on the tyranny narrative but came up short on contemporary examples. To be sure, it would be an awkward thing for a sitting Prime Minister to offer up a contemporaneous example of unjust legislation that called for a justiciable bill of rights but that his government had failed to repeal. The archetype example that Trudeau used to make the case for a judicially enforced bill of rights – the World War II internment of Japanese Canadians – instead demonstrated its frailty: Japanese Americans, who had recourse to judicial review under a bill of rights at that same time, nevertheless ended up with the same result.[25]

What are the relevant characteristics of a minority group that can fit comfortably into the tyranny of the majority narrative? Historically, the relevant criteria have been immutable or relatively immutable characteristics. Centrally, the tyranny narrative applies to discrete and insular minorities defined by such characteristics: minorities that not only were defined by such characteristics, but in fact formed *communities* (racial, ethnic, religious) that could be the objects of disregard or worse. However, the reach of human rights instruments of the mid- to late twentieth century has not been restricted to such communities. Can an individual who is not defined by community membership be treated unfairly by the majority? Yes: an individual who is homeless, for example, can be treated unfairly by legislation and can lack any meaningful opportunity to form alliances or participate in the political process, but may not necessarily be part of a community or group in a relevant sense (that is, as a member of a group having a shared purpose, a reason for coming together *as a group*). The tyranny narrative resonates most strongly with respect to the treatment of groups rather than individuals, perhaps because legislation is not, paradigmatically, addressed to individuals.

To what extent is the tyranny narrative reflected in the practice of contemporary judicial review?

7.3 TYRANNY, IDENTITY, AND MORALS LAWS

A tension with the tyranny narrative is the extent to which the protection of human rights instruments extend beyond personal characteristics, characteristics that correspond to objective realities (of sex, religion, ethnicity, citizenship, nationality, disability, etc.) and protect *choices*. The mainstay of twenty-first century bills of rights adjudication in jurisdictions such as the United States, the United Kingdom, Germany, Canada, and New Zealand has not been the adjudication of claims brought by persons on the basis of personal characteristics, let alone of singular and insular minorities. More prevalent are challenges to legislation said to restrict autonomy on grounds that have little in common with one's personal characteristics apart

[25] Pierre Trudeau, 'Foreword' in *The Charter of Rights and Freedoms: A Guide for Canadians* (Ottawa, Minister of Supply and Services Canada, 1982) at 7–8. Notably absent from Trudeau's account is any reference to *Koramatsu* v. *United States*, 323 US 214 (1944).

from the disposition to choose the acts or pattern of conduct that are prohibited by the legislation. These challenges must be framed in the terms of the specific bill of rights under which they are brought, but share an underlying premise: that the state (acting through its government and law) is unjustified in prohibiting or otherwise frustrating persons in acting in ways that reflect their chosen means to pursue their self-understandings of the good.[26]

The relationship between one's choices and one's identity for the purposes of constitutional law is not always straightforward. One's morally significant choices are self-constituting, but the identity that one constitutes through one's choices does not necessarily align with the grounds of protection offered in bills of rights. Now, it is logically possible to claim for any morally significant pattern of conduct that it is not only self-constituting, but constitutes the basis of group membership. A strategic advantage of this claim is better to harness the tyranny rationale for judicial review. Where this is successfully deployed, the claimant seeks to strike down laws that prohibit the desired conduct, arguing that the prohibition is unjust because it manifests contempt for the claimant and others on the basis of their group membership, which is prohibited under a bill of rights.

Suppose someone's sense of identity was constituted by a pattern of recreational drug use and claimed membership in a community of similarly identified persons. This sort of choice, and this sense of identity, do not correspond to membership in any community, except in the strained sense of a community that is defined solely by the prohibited act. Dworkin initially stated his objection to so-called 'morals laws' on the basis that government 'must not constrain liberty on the grounds that one citizen's conception of the good life of one group is nobler or superior than another's'.[27] Dworkin's concern was that legislatures would enact so-called morals laws not because they genuinely believed there to be any direct or indirect harm to others caused by such practices, or that such practices were self-destructive of those who would choose them, but simply because these are practices of which the majority happens to disapprove. In this frame of thought, to prohibit someone's self-constituting choice as unworthy or wrong is not to show contempt for the prohibited act, but to show contempt for the *person* who finds value in it. The decision to prohibit or otherwise restrict such practices, on Dworkin's view, would likely be based on disgust or animus or contempt for those persons who see value in the proscribed practices.[28]

Dworkin's 'argument from contempt'[29] would seem to support the 'tyranny of the majority' justification for judicial review. A legislature that bans self-constituting

[26] Indeed, prominent defenders of contemporary human rights adjudication summarise the case law as defending a 'right to autonomy', being an individual right to *choose*: see Kai Möller, *The Global Model of Constitutional Rights* (Oxford, Oxford University Press 2012).

[27] Dworkin, *Taking Rights Seriously* 272–3.

[28] See the discussion in Yowell, 'A Critical Examination of Dworkin's Theory of Rights' 136.

[29] This expression is borrowed from John Finnis, 'Law, Universality, and Social Identity' in *Intention & Identity: Collected Essays, Volume II* (Oxford, Oxford University Press 2013).

practices for no better reason than it dislikes the practices and is contemptuous of those who chose to live otherwise would indeed be acting tyrannically. But a few objections must first be met. First, we must ask whether the argument from contempt rests on an account of legislating that explains the practice of legislating. Second, we must ask in any particular case whether the factual premise of the argument obtains (that is, whether a legislature is *actually* contemptuous of any group when passing morals laws).

Dworkin's attribution of rationally deficient moral reasoning to the legislature seems itself unreasonable. To be sure, we can expect that members of legislatures face pressure in some instances to subordinate their judgment to what the voters might want. But we have no reason to expect that those voters reason about morals laws in the rationally deficient way presupposed by the argument. When considering, for example, how best to address social problems attendant on prostitution, the legislator and the citizen alike must consider the benefits and burdens of different schemes of regulation, whether a direct prohibition would itself cause suffering to prostitutes or expose them to yet more risk, and whether indirect prohibitions (on communicating for the purposes of solicitation, for example) would achieve the desired ends of regulation. They may also be asked to consider whether prostitution is morally distinguishable from other forms of work and should be treated analogously as a regulated practice. Legislation that restricts acts of prostitution should not automatically be understood as a manifestation of conventional morality either 'for its own sake' (i.e., motivelessly), for the sake of mere social cohesion, or to express contempt for persons engaged in prostitution. Legislators addressing the question of what (if anything) to do about prostitution may more fairly be said to be motivated by the moral judgment that certain acts are seriously wrong, that some (perhaps a preponderance) of persons engaged in prostitution are vulnerable and would not be engaged in prostitution if offered a genuine choice, and that they and others are treated *unjustly* by the failure of government intervention to prohibit or actively discourage the practice. That is, the legislature can be taken to have believed it would be an *injustice* to all for whom they are responsible if it failed to act legislatively. This way of framing legislative reasoning does not assume the legislature to have acted out of animus to or to have contempt for anyone. Indeed, it invites the possibility that the legislature acts precisely out of concern for the persons involved. The resulting scheme may still be judged to be unreasonable, but its reasonableness is to be assessed on other grounds.

Legislative reasoning is sometimes dismissed by courts on the basis that legislation is purely a matter of the adoption of conventional morality. To label some moral norm as conventional, properly understood, is simply to make the sociological or anthropological claim that a given moral norm, as a matter of fact, has been accepted as a moral norm by a particular community or by a majority within that community. Such a claim says *nothing* about whether this morality is true or false or capable of being true or false; it is a descriptive rather than an evaluative claim.

Even where a court does not formally (and perhaps not even consciously) evaluate the truth or falsity of the moral norms that it labels 'conventional', the context will sometimes suggest that it is covertly declaring the norm to be a product of convention rather than of reason. Indeed, when labelling a moral norm conventional, a court will sometimes imply the norm to be false in one of three ways: (1) as a moral judgment which, though widely held, is straightforwardly incorrect and arrived at through a defective chain of reasoning which overlooks or gives inadequate weight (or exaggerated weight) to some relevant reason; (2) as a judgment that is incorrect because it is not the product of reason at all, but rather of sub-rational prejudice, animosity, and the like; or (3) as a judgment which, though falsely believed to be morally significant, is in fact not a matter of moral judgment at all but of taste, etc. – it is something 'so indifferent in itself'[30] that legislation is not justified.

When reflecting on moral norms that are widely accepted, it is important not to misidentify the reasons that legislators have for accepting those norms. A moral judgment that has been labelled as conventional (and tacitly dismissed as false in one of the three ways explored above) has been judged not to count in deliberation because it does not as such – as a mere convention – provide a reason for action. There is a temptation to jump from the conclusion that some moral norm is in fact conventional (that is, is accepted as a moral norm by some social group) to the conclusion that the norm is also *merely* conventional and, *for that reason*, false. Characterising disfavoured moral judgments as 'conventional' allows judges to avoid the difficult task of explaining *how* moral judgments that motivated the legislation are rationally deficient.[31] It is uncharitable to assume that the moral norms of a person or group are *merely* conventional. Those people whose moral beliefs taken together form a moral convention need not, and typically do not, hold these beliefs *as* conventions or *on the grounds of* the social fact, but rather because they judge some conduct good or bad, constitutive or destructive of character, as worthy or unworthy, etc. Their judgments may be wrong, but in each case these are moral judgments and a moral argument must be given to explain how they are wrong. It is unsatisfactory for a court to side-step this task by simply labelling a judgment as 'conventional' and thereby tacitly implying that it is somehow false or held for no reason having to do with the wellbeing of persons. There is no uncontroversial way

[30] For various ways in which the expression 'indifferent in themselves' can be put and was put by Blackstone, see the discussion in John Finnis, 'Blackstone: Theoretical Intentions' in *Philosophy of Law: Collected Essays, Volume IV* (Oxford, Oxford University Press 2013) 199.

[31] See *R.* v. *Labaye*, [2005] 3 S.C.R. 728, para. 14, where the court, in discarding a legal test for indecency, mischaracterised that test (which in reality had been a call for reasoned judgment about what government owes to persons) as an inherently subjective and arbitrary imposition of personal taste. See, more generally, Bradley W Miller, 'Proportionality's Blind Spot: "Neutrality" and Political Philosophy' in Grant Huscroft, Bradley W Miller, and Grégoire Webber (eds.), *Proportionality and the Rule of Law* (New York, Cambridge University Press 2014) 370 at 381–3.

to judge between sound and unsound claims about the basis of one's identity; moral evaluation of the conduct in question is required.[32]

7.4 TYRANNY AND AUTONOMY: A CONTEMPORARY EXAMPLE

A second set of examples is a step further removed from the tyranny narrative. These cases involve the frustration of one's autonomous choices in matters that are profoundly significant, but are not acts that can form the basis of a personal or community identity. A paradigmatic case would be the decision to end one's own life. Euthanasia is not typically desired for its own sake, but as a means to achieve some other end, such as the cessation of suffering. In most jurisdictions, euthanasia and physician-assisted suicide remain criminal offences despite long-running campaigns for legislative change.

Is the refusal to authorise euthanasia legislatively a manifestation of tyranny? The tyranny narrative needs more than a chronic failure to attract sufficient votes to a legislative proposal; it needs the legislature to have disregarded the genuine good of a minority that is unable to be heard. It is questionable whether a euthanasia-seeker can constitute the requisite type of minority. The minority in this example can be described as those persons who wish to have the option, at some point in their lives, of seeking euthanasia or assistance in committing suicide. But being a euthanasia-seeker is neither a personal characteristic, nor a proxy for a personal characteristic; it is a manifestation of belief about the scope of personal autonomy in a society. Even assuming that euthanasia-seekers can form the requisite conceptual minority, to determine whether a person or group has been treated tyrannically or unjustly, one must attend to the reasons for the legislation. What are the reasons that legislatures have for criminalising or refusing to permit euthanasia and assisted suicide? Among them, legislatures can be understood to have acted on the concern that vulnerable persons could be manipulated into committing suicide and that allowing euthanasia and assisted suicide could communicate a message that the severely disabled and the dependent lead lives less worthy of living, thereby further eroding their already precarious place in society.[33]

Proponents of euthanasia who fail to secure legislative reform and are confronted with justifications such as these may well disagree, but cannot reasonably understand themselves not to have been heard, let alone treated with contempt. The tyranny narrative is further undercut to the extent that legislative proposals brought by the euthanasia-seekers are debated and receive careful attention before being rejected or defeated.

[32] This argument is made at greater length in Bradley W Miller, 'Morals Laws in an Age of Rights: Hart and Devlin a the Supreme Court of Canada' (2010) 55 *American Journal of Jurisprudence* 79 at 84–8.

[33] This concern is reviewed by courts examining legislative prohibitions on assisted suicide. See, e.g., *R. (on the application of Nicklinson)* v. *Ministry of Justice*, [2014] UKSC 38 and *Carter* v. *Canada (Attorney General)*, [2015] 1 SCR 331.

7.5 TYRANNY AND FAILURE OF LEGISLATIVE REFORM

Morals laws are not a comfortable fit with the tyranny narrative, and neither are claims about personal autonomy. A further step removed are social rights cases, such as claims for improved access to health care. Consider legislation that prohibits individuals from contracting for private, non-government healthcare insurance, effectively creating a public healthcare monopoly. The rationale for the legislation is to prevent defections from the government healthcare system,[34] which the government reasons would imperil the financial and political viability of the system and thus jeopardise the universality of healthcare to the detriment of the most economically disadvantaged. The constitutionality of this legislation is brought before the courts on the basis that it makes all persons wholly reliant on a government medical system whose backlogs prevent some from accessing health care in a timely fashion, thus jeopardising their health and perhaps their lives.

Such legislation was struck down by a plurality of the Supreme Court of Canada on the grounds that the prohibition, coupled with the backlogs, imperilled the health (and therefore the life and security) of the complainants.[35] The relevant minority in this example would be those persons whose health and lives are threatened by the unavailability of timely government medical services *and* who would be in a position to purchase private healthcare insurance so as to pay for alternative health care. Note that those who can afford to purchase their own private medical insurance are a comparatively privileged group, financially. And note, too, that the reason that the legislature enacted a scheme that frustrated the complainants' plan to purchase private healthcare insurance was because the legislature believed that such a scheme was necessary to ensure the financial and political viability of universal health care. Is this minority the type of group that can be accurately characterised as subject to the oppression of the majority? Its membership is constituted solely by a shared desire and financial ability to purchase private health-care insurance. Its membership is neither closed nor defined by an immutable, personal characteristic. Its membership is relatively affluent, and suffers no historical disadvantage.

Although the Supreme Court of Canada concluded that the legislative scheme was a violation of rights because it jeopardised the health and lives of persons who were bound to the shortage characteristic of the public healthcare system and prohibited them from making private arrangements to safeguard their own health, the injustice (if it is an injustice) cannot be characterised as tyrannical. There is no minority community or group to suffer persecution, because the health-insurance-seekers

[34] See Commission on the Future of Health Care in Canada, *Building on Values: The Future of Health Care in Canada* (Ottawa, The Commission 2002); Standing Senate Committee on Social Affairs, Science and Technology, *The Health of Canadians – The Federal Role, Final Report, Volume Six: Recommendations for Reform* (Ottawa, The Senate 2002).

[35] *Chaoulli* v. *Quebec (Attorney General)* [2005] 1 SCR 791.

do not have the requisite shared identity; and indeed the complainants did not claim minority status. There is no contempt for anyone. There is good faith disagreement about how best to secure the common good of a political community in matters of health care. The human rights challenge before the Supreme Court looks like the losers of a public policy debate taking a second run before a different forum. It does not fit into the tyranny narrative. If judicial review is justified in this case, it must be on the basis of some other ground.

For the avoidance of doubt, I am not denying that there have been historical injustices that are well described as manifestations of tyranny of the majority. Nor am I denying that some groups within some contemporary political communities face such a risk today. Where there is an identifiable minority group that is unable to form alliances, there may be a genuine risk. How much of a risk depends on the health of the particular political community, including the functioning of its legislature and its commitment to human rights. What I am highlighting is how the conditions for the tyranny of the majority argument are present only in a small class of cases: those cases where there is a marginalised group identified by a personal characteristic. Contemporary rights litigation, by contrast, is increasingly a matter of providing a second forum for arguments that have failed legislatively, and have failed for reasons that have nothing to do with contempt or disregard for any person or group.

7.6 PATHOLOGIES OF JUDICIAL REVIEW

Judicial review is one response to the risk of unjust decision-making in a political community. A political community facing the question of whether to adopt, continue, or modify a practice of judicial review must assess whether judicial review as practiced raises the risk of introducing other sorts of injustice and how, in the context of the particular challenges facing that community, the risk of these injustices are to be evaluated against the risks judicial review can remedy. After all, judicial review is not a purely technical process that gives judges the opportunity to correct mistakes, such that the only risk associated with judicial review is a failure of judicial intervention against rights-violating legislation. I wish to highlight how the questions that judicial review resolves are inevitably value-laden and cannot be answered from any 'neutral' standpoint.

Legislative decision-making and judicial decision-making are different in kind. This is not because of the supposed division between matters of policy (said to belong to the legislature) and matters of principle (said to belong to the judiciary), canvassed earlier. It is not only because of the well-known institutional limits of courts compared to legislatures: that courts lack the information-gathering resources of legislatures; must constrain themselves to the questions that are brought before them; must often function on accelerated and compressed timelines; can only rely on the evidence brought to them by the parties; and do not have jurisdiction over matters that are outside of the instant dispute.[36] The more salient point is that judicial reasoning, in its central case, is different in kind from legislative reasoning. Judicial reasoning proceeds according to the artificial reason of the law: an analytical structure that formally and pre-emptively rules out some lines of inquiry.[37] The nature of the differences between the reasoning proper to judicial review and the reasoning proper to legislating is well-travelled ground. It is sufficient to note, for present purposes, that the decision to adopt a legislative proposal more closely resembles open-ended, free-ranging moral reasoning. By contrast – and notwithstanding the appeals made by proponents of a culture of justification reviewed in the previous chapter – judicial reasoning is well-described as moral reasoning that is more or less artificially constrained.[38] Although moral reasoning can emerge close to the surface of judicial reasoning (particularly in interpreting concepts such as 'equality', 'reasonableness', 'liberty', and 'fundamental justice'), judicial reasoning, as practiced, is almost never coterminous with moral reasoning. Prior commitments posited through legislation and acts of adjudication, as well as common law doctrines including precedent and the more or less technical rules of statutory interpretation, all serve to constrain and direct the reasoning of judges.

That said, judges can overstate the nature of the difference between moral and legal reasoning by claiming that resolving a constitutional challenge to legislation is a matter of settling a *purely* legal question, implying that it is entirely a matter of value-free *technical* reasoning, with no room for moral reasoning or making evaluative judgments about what arrangements best meet the needs of the community. There is, of course, an incentive for judges to downplay the degree to which they are engaging in non-legal reasoning. Judges, trained in the techniques of reasoning with the law, can be expected to have comparative expertise in resolving the technical questions of law. But in circumstances where questions of law draw close to unbounded moral reasoning or evaluations of competing policy options, that comparative expertise disappears. Where the moral evaluation in question will be particularly controversial, courts risk push-back from dissatisfied legislators and members of the community who understand themselves to have been second-guessed on matters not solidly within the expertise of judges or lawyers.

36 On the competences of courts and legislatures with respect to institutional fact finding, see Paul Yowell, 'Empirical Research in Rights-based Judicial Review of Legislation' in Katja S Ziegler and Peter M Huber (eds.), *Current Problems in the Protection of Human Rights: Perspectives from Germany and the UK* (Oxford, Hart Publishing 2013) 166–72. See, more generally, Paul Yowell, *Constitutional Rights and Constitutional Design: Moral and Empirical Reasoning in Judicial Review* (Oxford, Hart Publishing 2018).

37 See Jeremy Waldron, 'Do Judges Reason Morally?' in Grant Huscroft (ed.), *Expounding the Constitution: Essays in Constitutional Theory* (New York, Cambridge University Press 2008).

38 See Neil MacCormick, *Legal Reasoning and Legal Theory* (Oxford, Oxford University Press 1994) and John Finnis, 'Legal Reasoning as Practical Reason' in *Reason in Action: Collected Essays, Volume I* (Oxford, Oxford University Press 2013).

In addition to the institutional limitations and the necessity of engaging in non-legal evaluations, a judge's reasoning can be distorted by other incidents of reasoning in judicial review. I explore three such pathologies, understood as 'structured tendencies towards misconceived decision'.[39]

(1) The pathology of concreteness. The rationale for legislating is to change the law in a way that will benefit the community; paradigmatically, legislation is enacted for the common good. But legislation will often have results prejudicial to the interests of some persons, whether as a side effect or, on occasion, intentionally. Those persons may be frustrated from carrying out plans or otherwise acting as they would like (for example, through the operation of noise by-laws) or their wellbeing may be negatively impacted through other kinds of setbacks (for example, where neighbouring land is zoned for use as an airport). Judicial review can serve as a corrective, not only for those relatively rare cases where a legislative assembly intends to act contrary to the interests of some group, but also where the legislature's ignorance causes it to overlook or undervalue some of the social costs of its legislation.

There is a standing risk of legislatures overlooking or inappropriately discounting the genuine interests of some persons and groups. But there is also a standing risk that courts, in conducting judicial review, will overlook or discount the genuine interests of some persons or groups. Where a court discounts those genuine interests or fails to understand the significance of legislation for the common good, it is more likely to strike down the legislation or restrict its application. The result is that while some persons will no longer be blocked in pursuing their chosen plan or in pursuing their wellbeing, others will be deprived of the protection and benefit that the legislation was enacted to provide. To the extent that some human goods (goods that are properly the object of legislative concern) tend to be overlooked by judges, courts that reverse legislative decisions using rights-based judicial review not only create new winners, they also create new losers. If judicial review creates a structured tendency against the legislative protection of some interests (as during the *Lochner* era in the US), this is a relevant cost to consider for a political community assessing the merits of judicial review.

Part of the challenge that judges face when conducting judicial review is that while the putative rights infringements placed before them are actual and concrete, attaching to persons represented before the court with specific names, histories, and aspirations, the persons who are intended to benefit from the law and its protection are present only as an abstraction. It will seldom be the case that the human goods protected by these prohibitions can be similarly personified, especially in the context of litigation that opposes an individual claimant to the Attorney General. To return to the example examined above, it is no straightforward task, as a starting

[39] See Timothy Endicott, 'Proportionality and incommensurability' in Grant Huscroft, Bradley W Miller, and Grégoire Webber (eds.), *Proportionality and the Rule of Law* (New York, Cambridge University Press 2014) 336–8.

matter, to explain how decriminalising euthanasia may change a medico-legal culture in evaluating the merits of preserving some lives; how these changes may result in the devaluation of the lives of the disabled and may increase pressure on some of them to submit to euthanasia; and how attitudes may shift towards accepting the proposition that an increasing set of lives are not worth the expenditures and attentions that are required to maintain them. What is much more difficult is to produce in court the individuals to make these concerns concrete: the vulnerable elderly, for example, who may face internal pressures due to physical pain (that palliative care could address, though at financial cost) or a sense of being a 'burden', or external pressure (however subtle) from family members motivated by a potential inheritance. In defending legislation, the government will often be disadvantaged by the absence of a singular defendant who embodies and vividly illustrates the concerns animating legislative intervention.

(2) The pathology of uncertainty. The way in which an impugned law benefits persons in the community (or even whether it benefits persons at all) is rarely free from controversy. Causality will not be beyond doubt. A party defending legislation will often be unable to present uncontroversial, evaluation-free empirical evidence establishing a causal relationship between the law and the expected benefit. Proof to a scientific standard is often unavailable for many reasons, including (i) the sheer complexity of the causality of human behaviour is beyond the current competencies of the behavioural sciences; (ii) even where the social science methodology is up to the task of answering the relevant questions, the data set that would need to be assembled will not be available now or into the foreseeable future; and (iii) even where satisfactory methodology and data are available, the relevant studies might not have been undertaken.

What is a court to do when confronted with complex social science evidence? Some courts have at times stressed caution on the basis that '[c]omplex human behaviour may not lend itself to precise scientific demonstration, and the courts cannot hold Parliament to a higher standard of proof than the subject matter admits of'.[40] At other times, however, courts have counselled that 'if a court is satisfied that all the evidence has been presented, there is nothing that would justify it in refusing to perform its role on the ground that it should merely defer to the government's position'.[41] Some have expressed concern that even in those instances where courts express confidence in their command of statistics and other social science evidence, their confidence is often misplaced.[42] Others have proposed, as an alternative to

[40] *R* v. *Sharpe* [2001] SCR 45, para. 89, echoing Aristotle, *Nicomachean Ethics*, Book I.3: 'it is the mark of an educated man to look for precision in each class of things just so far as the nature of the subject admits'. Note also Lon Fuller's admonition against 'a strong preference for those facts which can be statistically or graphically presented; a specious objectivity has been bought at the cost of significant, if intangible, realities': Lon Fuller, *The Law in Quest of Itself* (Chicago, IL, Foundation Press 1940) 65.

[41] *Chaoulli*, para. 87.

[42] See Yowell, 'Empirical Research'.

deference, that courts should refuse to entertain constitutional arguments that rely on empirical claims 'that cannot be verified, or are unduly controversial'.[43] For some, the worry is that empirical claims about causation made by the government in defending legislation will sometimes be made in bad faith so as to conceal 'moral beliefs that underlie a particular partisan position'.[44] Without doubt, there will be instances when 'empirical justifications ... mask what are really controversial moral judgments that negatively affect the lives of some of its citizens'.[45] But this should not lead us to conclude that legislation should be based only on non-controversial social science evidence. Such a requirement would result in a libertarian presumption, defeasible only by consensus on empirical questions of causality, and thus a readiness to strike down laws no matter the risk of harm to others.

(3) The pathology of the two-stage adjudicative model: the loss of the common good. As reviewed in Chapter 2, most jurisdictions that permit judicial review of legislation follow a two-stage adjudicative model, one that differentiates between the determination whether a right has been limited and whether that limitation is justified under the principle of proportionality.[46] In practice, the two-stage division between limitation and justification has proven to be unstable. Increasingly, the two-stage model has more or less collapsed into the justification analysis, with almost no analytical work done at the definition stage. That stage, however, frames the question for resolution and it is telling that, in evaluating rights, there is rarely any consideration of the needs of other persons living in community with the rights-holder. The requirements of justice are to be considered only from one point of view.[47] All other points of view and considerations are to be postponed to the justification stage. When the court confronts that stage and evaluates the needs of the community, the rationale of the legislation, and the common good, it proceeds on the troubling assumption that those general needs – if they are weighty enough – justify infringing the rights of persons.

The legislation's justification is determined according to a doctrine of proportionality, a structured set of inquiries that asks, characteristically: (i) whether legislation that limits a right is sufficiently important, (ii) whether the means chosen to carry out the legislative purpose are rationally connected to its purpose, (iii) whether it is minimally impairing of the right in question, and (iv) whether there is overall proportionality between the beneficial purpose (or effects) of the legislation and its negative impact on the claimant or others. A standing concern with reasoning under a proportionality doctrine is that the rationale for the impugned legislation – the

[43] Ronald C Den Otter, *Judicial Review in an Age of Moral Pluralism* (New York, Cambridge University Press 2009) 143.

[44] Ibid. 145.

[45] Ibid.

[46] See further Grégoire Webber, *The Negotiable Constitution: On the Limitation of Rights* (Cambridge, Cambridge University Press 2009), Ch. 2 and Bradley W Miller, 'Justification and Rights Limitations' in Grant Huscroft (ed.), *Expounding the Constitution: Essays in Constitutional Theory* (New York, Cambridge University Press 2008).

[47] See Webber, Chapter 2, in this book.

human goods and persons that it was meant to serve, the principles of a *society* that is free and democratic – will not make it into any of the four steps of the proportionality analysis.

The proportionality test sometimes excludes from consideration relevant interests promoted or protected by legislation. In many jurisdictions (and among several prominent constitutional theorists), proportionality has been assumed to require that legislation be agnostic as to what constitutes better or worse life choices; that is, proportionality has been understood as presupposing the commitments of anti-perfectionist liberalism.[48] The anti-perfectionist principle is well articulated by Joseph Raz: it is the claim 'that implementation and promotion of ideals of the good life, though worthy in themselves, are not a legitimate matter for governmental action'.[49] That is, government must be neutral on what constitutes the good life. On this model, government can base its action on judgments about what is right and wrong (understood as a matter of interpersonal justice, usually relying on a thin version of the harm principle), but not on the basis that some action is conducive to achieving what is morally good and others are not.[50] Regarding what is a morally good way of life and what is not, government is to take no position whatsoever.[51] The anti-perfectionist principle is central to the accounts of political liberalism that feature prominently in the proportionality theory advanced by constitutional theorists such as Mattias Kumm,[52] Aharon Barak,[53] and Robert Alexy.[54]

But the commitments of anti-perfectionist liberalism are in no way entailed by the commitment of a political community to enact legislation that is consistent with the 'principles of a free and democratic society'. There are many schools of political philosophy consistent with liberal democracy and, within liberal political theory itself, there is a vibrant range of competing schools beyond the anti-perfectionist strains associated with Ronald Dworkin[55] and John Rawls,[56] such as the perfectionist variants articulated by Joseph Raz[57] and William Galston.[58] There is reason to

[48] These questions are explored in Miller, 'Proportionality's Blind Spot: "Neutrality" and Political Philosophy'.

[49] Joseph Raz, *The Morality of Freedom* (Oxford, Clarendon Press 1986) 110.

[50] Ibid. 136.

[51] Note that 'morally good' is used here in the sense of the full range of the objects of practical reasoning.

[52] See Mattias Kumm, 'Political Liberalism and the Structure of Rights: On the Place and Limits of the Proportionality Requirement' in George Pavlakos (ed.), *Law, Rights and Discourse: The Legal Philosophy of Robert Alexy* (Oxford, Hart Publishing 2007).

[53] See Aharon Barak, *Proportionality: Constitutional Rights and their Limitations* (Cambridge, Cambridge University Press 2012) 468–72.

[54] See Robert Alexy, '13 Replies' in George Pavlakos (ed.), *Law, Rights and Discourse: The Legal Philosophy of Robert Alexy* (Oxford, Hart Publishing 2007) 340.

[55] See Dworkin, *Taking Rights Seriously* and Dworkin, *A Matter of Principle*.

[56] See John Rawls, *Political Liberalism* (New York, Columbia University Press 1993).

[57] See Raz, *Morality of Freedom*.

[58] See William A Galston, *Liberal Purposes: Goods, Virtues, and Diversity in the Liberal State* (Cambridge, Cambridge University Press 1991).

question whether the justification analysis should rightly and always proceed on one or another of these political philosophies.

* * *

Are these pathologies of judicial review worse than the risks of governing a political community without the protections offered by judicial review? That is not a question that can be answered in the abstract, and nothing in what precedes suggests that the answer ought to be one or another. However, in making this evaluation, I have aimed to highlight that judicial review should not be understood to be an unqualified good. Even for those communities that judge there to be strong reasons to attempt to secure human rights by introducing a check on the legislature by way of judicial review, those reasons will not be without some counter-balance, some reasons that invite the choice to be made in appreciation of the risks associated with judicial review.

An argument in favour of judicial review must be situated in the context of an actual community. Judicial review can be, and historically has been, an effective tool for addressing some forms of injustice. But it is not a general panacea suitable to all communities at all times. Any community deliberating about whether to adopt a practice of judicial review or whether to adopt a weaker or stronger form of judicial review than what is already practiced, should attend to the real risks within that community that judicial review is meant to correct. A sound study of the merits of proceeding or not should also attend to the possible risks of injustice that judicial review may inject into decision-making.

7.7 CONCLUSION

So: is the practice of judicial review under a bill of rights inconsistent with the theory of legislated rights defended in this book, including the account of legislation as reasoned activity and the claim that legislatures have primary responsibility for the specification of human rights? No. Does it follow, then, that judicial review ought to be introduced as part of a community's commitment to secure and protect human rights? The answer here depends on the community. Judicial review is not *necessarily* a sound response to the risk of non-central cases of legislating. The assumption that the practice of judicial review introduces only one risk – the failure to intervene – is false. The aim of this chapter has been to explore how judicial review itself creates risks that unjust and otherwise suboptimal decisions will be made in a political community, and to highlight how an account of legislated rights provides additional resources for evaluating whether to introduce judicial review where it is absent, and for assessing the scope of the practice of judicial review where it is present. These assessments themselves can only be carried out within particular political communities, by those with a deep knowledge of those communities, their people, and their institutions.

Index

For EU product safety concerns, contact us at Calle de José Abascal, 56–1°,
28003 Madrid, Spain or eugpsr@cambridge.org.

www.ingramcontent.com/pod-product-compliance
Lightning Source LLC
LaVergne TN
LVHW101502200926
848483LV00001B/196
* 9 7 8 1 1 0 8 4 2 6 5 7 2 *